SAN FRANCISCO'S CHINATOWN

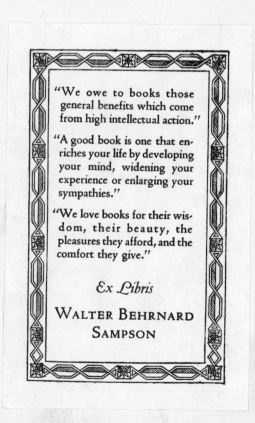

OLD CHINATOWN — BRENHAM PLACE

SAN FRANCISCO'S CHINATOWN

by

CHARLES CALDWELL DOBIE

Illustrated by

E. H. SUYDAM

D. APPLETON-CENTURY COMPANY
INCORPORATED

NEW YORK   LONDON

1936

FOR MY BROTHER

FOREWORD

THIS volume was evolved out of an idea to present a series
of word pictures of San Francisco's Chinatown in conjunc-
tion with Mr. Suydam's charming sketches of a steadily
vanishing section. It was our hope to catch a measure of the
quarter's quality and charm and put it in more or less
permanent form before it completely disintegrated.

As the work progressed, it seemed less and less possible
to confine the attempt strictly to mere pictorial adventures.
One found paths leading off in the direction of history, of
interpretation, of criticism. There were times when even the
scenes shifted and other backgrounds intruded. But, always,
it seemed with a certain pertinency to an understanding
picture of the Chinese quarter in San Francisco.

There have been Chinatowns in other cities of America.
There are Chinatowns in other American cities still. But it
must be conceded that San Francisco's Chinatown always
has been the most significant expression of this alien people

Foreword

dwelling in our midst. It ranks first in numbers and in wealth of transplanted traditions. To know the Chinatown in San Francisco is to know every other Chinatown in the United States.

Deciding to broaden the original purpose, I was amazed to find so much written material concerning the subject—newspaper articles, travel books, records of legislative investigations. My greatest sources of information were the Templeton Crocker collection of books on the Chinese in California at the California Historical Society in San Francisco, and the efficiently catalogued newspaper records at the State Library at Sacramento, California.

My thanks for invaluable assistance go to Miss Dorothy Huggins of the California Historical Society and Miss Mabel Gillis and Miss Caroline Wenzel at the State Library. I am likewise indebted to Little, Brown and Company for permission to quote from the work of Nora Waln and to the John Day Company for permission to quote from the work of Lin Yutang. Mr. Will Irwin also gave gracious permission to quote from the text of *Old Chinatown*.

I am grateful to executives of missionary organizations working in Chinatown for information, particularly to Miss Donaldina Cameron of the Presbyterian Mission and Father Johnson of the Paulist Fathers for granting time for interviews out of their crowded schedule.

The Chinese Chamber of Commerce was helpful, as well as Mr. S. H. Shum who guided me in some of the modern phases and problems of present-day Chinese-American life.

The articles of the Reverend Mr. Frederic J. Masters in current magazines of the nineties proved most valuable. Mr. Masters, before taking up missionary work in San Francisco, had spent years as a missionary in China. He was a clear and forceful writer and refreshingly free from bias—not always the case in enthusiasts for a cause. Most of his

Foreword

statements were too well put to paraphrase and the reader will find numerous verbatim excerpts from his works in the text of this book. Articles by Mr. Douglas S. Watson in the *California Historical Quarterly* were most helpful.

The illustrations of Mr. Suydam, who wishes to make special acknowledgment of the assistance he received from Miss Rose B. Chew, will provide a record of Chinatown in its visual aspects long after the quarter has become a tradition and a memory. For this rescue of Chinatown from ultimate pictorial oblivion, San Francisco cannot sufficiently thank him.

CHARLES CALDWELL DOBIE

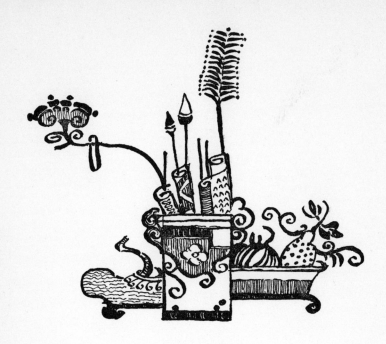

CONTENTS

Contents

ILLUSTRATIONS

Illustrations

SAN FRANCISCO'S CHINATOWN

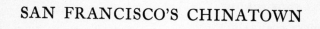

INTRODUCTORY

A GREAT deal has been written one way or another about Chinamen in America—for the most part with indifferent results. In the early fifties, men scribbled the most arrant nonsense about the Chinese, compounded of ignorance and patronage. A little later, ignorance survived but patronage gave way to hatred. And, at all times, the pious drew horrific pictures of the yellow man's vices supplemented by hopes for an anemic regeneration.

John Chinaman's advocates were equally destructive of any real appreciation of his quality. Their testimony was so tinged with the taint of a special interest that it lacked validity. A man who finds himself in need of sweat-shop labor can always scratch the surface and uncover virtues in people he wishes to exploit. If they are cheap and docile he asks for nothing more. If, added to these qualities, they are efficient, he is transported to a seventh heaven of advocacy.

I

San Francisco's Chinatown

It is often through the creative writers, the fictionists, that a public gets the most understanding interpretation of a people new to it. But, in the case of the Chinese, the creative writers of America only added to the confusion. For the most part, they chopped up a mess of exoticisms, stirred vigorously, added hot water and served a concoction as little fundamentally Chinese as a dish of chop-suey. They dealt in sensational surfaces and from even the best of them came a spawn that ended in melodramas of the *Queen-of-the-Opium-Ring* or *Chinatown-After-Dark* variety.

But these fictionists can be defended. It was not easy to know the Chinese. It is still difficult. When I was a young man, I read a book that in its opening chapters gave the reasons why the Chinese were a people apart. The author, whose name I have unhappily forgotten, described the unique geographical features of China which had kept it free from contacts with the outside world for centuries. Left to themselves, its people had built up a civilization peculiarly their own—how peculiarly, he proved by quoting for three or four pages the unique processes they employed in accomplishing the simplest tasks. As I remember, there was nothing, from planting a seed to its harvesting, that bore any relation to the methods used by any Western civilization or, indeed, any civilization at all engaged in the same pursuits. His point was that the Chinese were original and self-sufficient, that they had evolved their own formulas and by virtue of these solitary achievements, had developed a national egotism and contempt for foreign methods. His argument may have had exaggerations but the list he drew of unique procedures in Chinese accomplishment were imposing enough to warrant a belief in the main outline of his theory.

Whether or not the Chinese stood apart from the whole world in the details of life, they certainly stood apart from

2

Introductory

the world that they faced in California during the gold rush. Perhaps there has never been a time in history when two such utterly dissimilar people have met upon common ground. Even if difference in race had not been a barrier to understanding, there was the difference in outlook. The Americans were intent on building a new empire—the Chinese were intent on nourishing an old empire with sustenance from a virgin country. It was China that received the greater part of their gold gleanings; it was China that sheltered their hearthstones; it was China that would finally receive their bones. A people with faces turned ever toward the land of their origin do not take root.

Being self-sufficient and proud, the Chinese in California withdrew more and more within themselves. The people alien to them mistook this for ignorance or timidity, it never occurred to them to fancy that the Chinaman's attitude was an attitude of superiority. Old people are not given to explanations. They have learned that argument and self-revelation are futile. So they retire to a chimney corner and let the youngsters raise their voices.

American interpreters of the Chinese, baffled by this venerable reserve, this indifference to justification, had nothing to work on except invention and surfaces. They made the most of both. The inventions were puerile but at least the surfaces had gorgeous outlines.

Of these outlines in San Francisco's Old Chinatown, it is hard to determine which was the more impressive to the fiction monger—the squalidness or the color. At all events, the one intensified the other. There were no half-tones in the picture.

If, in some groping alley, one came upon a doorway smeared with yellow, or crimson, or blue that led upward into a humid blackness, it was human to expect something fabulous. It was human to be hopeful of an Arabian Nights'

3

tale at the end of the passageway. Anything could happen to a man who stepped from the gay daubings of the entrance into a thick gloom made all the more sinister by the gaspings of a pale lamp upon the first landing.

He might find himself in a bagnio filled with twittering slave-girls; or amid the sweetly sickish fumes of an opium den; or in a forbidden corridor leading to an illicit gambling club. He might find himself knocking upon a door that opened into the tomb of a creature still living but abandoned with Oriental fatalism to death; he might walk into a loathsome hole where a handful of lepers lay shivering; he might stumble upon the secret tribunal of a highbinder tong marking a man for destruction.

But this brightly daubed doorway, smothered so quickly in provocative gloom, might just as easily have led to a faithful wife stirring the rice-pot over a charcoal brazier; or an old philosopher reading the precepts of Confucius through his horn-rimmed spectacles; or a young musician drawing shrill notes out of a moon fiddle. But these last were not the stuff of which wonder tales are made and so there were few who recorded them. . . . An alien story-teller visiting Chicago in the sinister twenties would not have passed up gangsters for sweet girl graduates.

Vices are always too bright hued for oblivion but virtues have a way of coming to the surface, also. A Chinaman in your kitchen soon disproved the theory that all yellow men were essentially cut-throats having neither loyalty nor affection. When earthquake tumbled down your heavy cornices and unstable chimneys and set in motion flames that burned your home to the ground, who of your household was it who came with a gold-filled purse to tide over emergencies? Likely as not, it was faithful Sing. Your money was in a checking account and could not be reached until the smoke cleared. Sing had more primitive hoarding methods that suited such an occasion. You did not have to ask. Indeed, it would never have occurred to you that there was money to be had anywhere amid such havoc. Sing came and laid the bulging purse in your reluctant palm. "I no need," was his delicate explanation. "You take him."

Or if you had no such loyal servant, you at least had watched that exodus from the burning Chinese quarter on the first day of that April holocaust thirty years ago. You had watched the families fleeing, soberly, quietly, with their household gods and family chattels. If they were frightened they did not show it. They faced the inevitable with a heartening calm. . . . Later, still, if you were in the fire insurance business they came to you with a list of things saved. They were the only people who did. Everybody else worked on the theory that since nobody could prove anything, one might as well clean up.

One must admit that the flames licked up a pretty foul old quarter. There had been a bubonic plague scare within its fetid confines more than once and the day its residents had fled before the cleansing tongues of fire, an army of loathsome rats fled with them. When the city began to look ahead, one of the first questions that presented itself was what disposition to make of the Chinese. Everybody seemed agreed that they would never be allowed back on the old spot. A committee was formed that went about looking up desirable locations. I am not sure, but I think they picked one out—somewhere to the South, amid mud flats. The Chinese, with their accustomed serenity, had said nothing—had offered neither suggestions nor opposition. But once the site was mentioned they went on record in no uncertain terms: they would either be given back their old quarter, or they would move across the bay to Oakland. That settled it. The Committee on Securing a Site for Chinatown broke up and nothing was heard from it again.

San Francisco's Chinatown

This incident alone seems to me to very properly gainsay the belief that the Chinese have no sentiment. I am not sure but that a new location for the quarter could have been found that would have been more convenient. But the Chinaman was accustomed to the cobbled hills of Sacramento and Clay streets. He had been there since their very beginning. And what is sentiment, anyway, if it be not a sort of sublimated familiarity? We grow fond of what we have known intimately.

The new Chinatown began very unprepossessingly. It was slab-sided and utilitarian. But it is part of the Chinese genius to make the most of necessity and it was not long before unique touches began to manifest themselves. Window-ledges became fragmentary gardens and fire-escapes transformed themselves into balconies. But had we come all the way with the old quarter, we should have witnessed the same metamorphosis. The cocoon from which had emerged the murky brilliance called Chinatown had had the dullness of respectability as well as the dullness of unimaginative outline. The Chinese came upon a pretty piece of early Victorian stodginess, set just above the blare and license of a pioneer town, and overwhelmed it with an indescribably studied disorder. At first, they contented themselves with a shop or two along the Calle de Fundacion, later Dupont street, and later still, Grant avenue. Gradually, very gradually, they crept up the heights, taking over the two-story dwelling-places that thought themselves secure from waterfront bawdiness and Main street lewdness. They were—but not secure from the placid penetration of the Far East. Only the crest of Nob Hill halted the westward sweep of the victors.

But, by the time they reached this outpost, they were content to creep down the hill again and fill every crack and cranny that had escaped them. They had been trained in cen-

6

Introductory

turies of stifling gregariousness. They like crowds and clamor and elbow-jostling. Ten bunks in a room twelve by eight was their idea of social contact. . . . With a Chinese population today over fifty per cent American born, two blocks of Chinatown still remain the most densely populated in the whole of San Francisco.

Perhaps it is a familiarity with dense living that makes the Chinese such masters of arrangement. Give any Chinaman a half-dozen oranges, a couple of newly laid eggs and a green pepper and they will fall instinctively into a picture as he lays them on the kitchen table. If he empties a tub of salt fish and puts it out on the back landing, and throws a ravished rice sack of matting and two discarded ginger jars beside it, you will have a perfect study in still life. He has had to conserve space, he has had to conserve funds, he has had to conserve time. Ordinary people in such situations conserve, or more properly they stifle, beauty. But the Chinese are not ordinary people. They love beauty and if they cannot indulge their taste for art with Ming vases, they create art subconsciously out of ordinary materials of life—food, fragments, even refuse.

Once before the earthquake and fire, I boarded at a bachelor club. We had a very good Chinese cook and one night we decided to give a dinner party—to invite some of our women friends to taste his quality. At the last moment, somebody discovered that since it had been nobody's business to attend to flowers for the table, none were in evidence. We scolded Hong about it, although he was in nowise to blame. He merely grunted.

But when we came into the dining-room after cocktails, there were flowers—bouquets of ravishing beauty at either end of the table. On a sunless back terrace were a couple of stunted fuchsia bushes, a red geranium or two, a volunteer cineraria. Out of a clash of red and pink and violent

7

purple, Hong had evolved two formal masses of flowers springing conically out of as many mason fruit jars. They were not only triumphs of art—they were triumphs of art evolved from scraps of blossoms. They rivaled the dinner. Soon after, Hong was shot down in Chinatown by a rival gunman. It was alleged that he was a highbinder, himself. . . . How many white gangsters could be trusted to take a handful of fuchsia blossoms, mix them with some geranium petals and a cluster of cineraria bloom and evolve things of beauty for a formal dinner party?

It was not so much that the interpreters of San Francisco's Chinatown drew false pictures but that they drew pictures without real substance. They concocted posters, really, in flat tones, as if their real desire was to "sell" Chinatown. All the vengeance and clamor and color of the Orient were in the Chinese quarter unmistakably. But so were simplicity, and calm, and sanity. The authors gave us hatchetmen with fingers on the triggers of guns, never hatchetmen weaving flowers into table decorations. They must have had such incidents, but they either voted them incongruous or ineffective.

When the idea came to me to gather together fragments of Chinese incident into a more or less coherent account, in my zeal to be just to my yellow neighbor, I made a fleeting resolution to soft pedal violence and lust and cruelty. These points, concerning the Chinese, had been stressed too emphatically by my predecessors. But I had not progressed far before I realized that such notes had been struck not too loudly but too unintelligently. What was needed was not less emphasis but more understanding. One would miss half the point of gangster violence in America in the lush twenties, unless one had some appreciation of the events which brought gangsters into power during that period. So with the delinquencies of Chinatown. Highbinder wars, slave-girls,

Introductory

opium dens were facts too clamorous to be ignored. But there were explanations. If one understands, one is more tolerant.

A distinguished traveler in the sixties, returning from China, gave out an interview in which he professed himself mystified at the contradictions in Chinese character. He found them honest and thieving, pure and immoral, cleanly and filthy, tender and cruel, all in one breath. His confusion, of course, came from a Victorian conviction that things were either black or white. We, at a later date, I think, are willing to concede that all people are just as contradictory. "To know all is to forgive all," runs a French proverb.

I cannot pretend to tell *all* about the Chinese in California. They are too profound a people to stand revealed in a chronicle compiled from instances gleaned from newspaper accounts, from gossip of the market place, even from affectionate memories.

I can only hope to suggest their infinite variety. I merely give you the scent of their quality. Complete capture leads very far afield. Perhaps, we shall never quite run our quarry down. But if we get glimpses of them darting swiftly through the forests of intolerance and ignorance we shall at least know something of their form, their color and their capacities. We may even grow to believe that in all their essential attributes they resemble us strangely. At that moment our victory will be complete.

Chapter I

LEGEND

To state boldly who was the first Chinese to plant his feet upon California shores is to invite controversy. Does the honor belong to the cabin-boy on the brig *Bolivar,* which sailed into San Francisco Bay in 1838; the Cantonese merchant, Chum Ming, reputed to have come in 1847; or the two nameless men and a woman who were passengers on the good ship *Eagle* in 1848? Early-day chroniclers have made claims of priority in all three cases—one claim is as good as another—but to accept any one of these instances as authentic is to establish at least the fact that there were Chinese in California before the gold rush.

If we are historically venturesome we might go back even further and follow in the legendary footsteps of the Buddhist priest, Hui Shên. It was this gentleman, who, in the last years of the fifth century, disappeared from his usual

Legend

haunts to show up at the Chinese Court in A. D. 499, with a diverting tale of a fabulous country across the vast ocean.

In his company were several others, equally priests, and the stories of wonders which they encountered were convincing enough to be ordered incorporated into the official annals of the empire.

This land, according to Hui Shên, lay some nine thousand miles east of Japan, and had been named Fu Sang by reason of an extraordinary tree which grew there. In confirmation of which he presented an offering to the Emperor of "three hundred pounds of yellow silk, spun by the silk-worm of the Fu-Sang tree, and of extraordinary strength. The Emperor's massive gold incense urn, weighing seventy-five pounds could be suspended by six of these threads without breaking them."

But if the silk-worms raised upon the leaves of the Fu-Sang tree were marvelous the tree itself was not far behind. "The leaves of the Fu-Sang, when first produced," states Hui Shên, "resemble those of the bamboo. The inhabitants eat the fruit like pears, and weave its bulk into cloth for use as clothing and articles of embroidery. They have books which are written on the bark of the Fu-Sang."

Historians who profess to believe that Hui Shên's tale is something beyond sheer imagination find a corroborating resemblance between the Fu-Sang tree of Chinese legend and the *maguey* tree of Mexico which played such a part in Aztec civilization. The leaves of the *maguey* supplied an "impenetrable thatch for humble dwellings, thread of which coarse stuffs were made," and when bruised, a paste from which paper was manufactured. Pins and needles came from its thorns, from its juice an intoxicating beverage. Its root, "when properly cooked, was converted into a palatable and nutritious food."

Here was everything and more that Hui Shên had claimed

11

for the Fu-Sang tree, except the dexterous silk-worm that could weave threads capable of supporting the "Emperor's massive gold incense urn." But since Prescott, the historian, assures us that "strong cords were drawn from the tough and twisted fibres" of the *maguey* even this discrepancy is nullified. Certainly we cannot blame the worthy Hui Shên for rendering the virtues of the Fu-Sang tree in silken terms more understandable to the people of China.

But there are other confirmations of Hui Shên's story, if you are in a mood for belief. Chinese writers of the sixth and seventh centuries showed an amazingly accurate knowledge of the coast line of North America. They knew the exact distance from China to Kamchatka and they even mention a group of islands to the east of it which are unmistakably the Aleutian Islands. Was this the route that Hui Shên and his followers took to achieve the mainland, stopping at the Aleutian Islands long enough to be impressed by the painted bodies of the inhabitants and sailing on to the comparatively nearby peninsula of Alaska? If this be granted they must of necessity have passed through or touched at California in their long pilgrimage to Mexico where grew the Fu-Sang tree and the silk-worms that fed so fabulously upon its leaves.

But even so, they were not first in the field. The worthy Hui Shên might have thought it good artistic exaggeration to impute the strong threads of the Fu-Sang tree to a gigantic silk-worm but he scorned the honor of a discovery which he had not made. It seemed that he had been preceded, in A. D. 458, to be exact, by five mendicant priests, who had successfully introduced the religion of Buddha into the New World. It was these five priests, doubtless, that the Chevalier de Paravy, in 1847, writing to the French Academy, speaks of as "the shamans of Kabul, arriving from the southern point of Kamchatka, at the ex-

Legend

cellent port of San Francisco, in California." In the face of this statement how insignificant are the claims of the cabin-boy of the brig *Bolivar,* the honorable Cantonese merchant, Chum Ming, or the two nameless men and a woman who were passengers on the good ship *Eagle* in the early years of the nineteenth century! A. D. 1838, A. D. 1847, A. D. 1848! . . . A. D. 458!! It makes even the claims of Columbus look trivial to say nothing of the Northmen, who were reputed to have discovered America in the eleventh century.

In spite of the fact that these five shamans were reported as coming from Kabul, there seems to be a general opinion that they were of Chinese origin. Otherwise, how would one find so many parallels between ancient Chinese customs and the customs of the early Aztecs?

In the first years of the gold rush, there lived at Chinese Camp in California, a gentleman named James Hanley. Among other things he acted as interpreter for the Chinese living there. He was one of the staunchest pro-ponents of the theory that the Chinese had visited this continent and he assures us solemnly that if we look into the matter without bias we will discover that the arts, institu-tions and customs of the Aztecs were almost identical with those of the Chinese and that their religion touched Bud-dhism at many points. "Inquiring minds," he concludes, "will not doubt in the least, that the Chinese discovered this con-tinent a thousand years earlier than any other nation."

Mr. Hanley also found surprising parallels between the language of the Chinese and the language of the Digger Indians of the mining regions. He gives a long list of anal-ogies from which the following are gleaned. Ti-yam in In-dian means the moon. Ti-yam in Chinese means the god of the moon, or night. Hee-ma in Indian is the sun. Hee-ma in Chinese means the god of the sun, or day. Wallae is a word commonly used among the Indians to designate a friend; it

also means "man." Walla in the Hindustan means a man.
This last is without doubt the spirit of Kabul speaking. And
he goes further and claims that there is a great similarity of
features between these American aborigines and the Chinese, which would tend to prove that these five mendicant
priests who preceded Hui Shên did not confine their activities
to spiritual matters exclusively.

If you are still unpersuaded, there is record of the scrupulous Hui Shên's tale of life in the enchanting country of
Fu Sang. He tells of cattle with long horns able to pull heavy
loads; of chariots drawn by horse, cattle and deer; of deer
raised for milking; of red pears that do not rot all year; of
vines weighted down with lucious grapes; of homes made of
wood. He discourses on the fact that the country does not
produce iron but that copper is known; that silver and gold
are manufactured but not greatly esteemed; of the feast they
spread in the presence of a criminal condemned to die before
they leave him to be buried alive in quicklime.

He dwells particularly upon the fact that the citizens of
Fu Sang have no walled towns and that since they make
neither arms nor armor, war is unknown. Neither are there
taxes nor imposts upon trade as in other countries. Happy
Fu Sang! No wonder even the barest recital of its blessings
has kindled the imagination of the Far East for centuries!

What an honor to be King of such a land, marching out
in procession before the people, preceded by the blare of joy-
ful drums and trumpets—clothed in green raiment at the
first cycle of one's reign, then in garments of red, then yellow,
then white, then black, as the years roll on.

Hui Shên calls attention to the ceremonies of marriage—
how they are nearly the same as in China—how at the death
of parents a seven-day fast is observed; how they erect a
spirit image of the dead, before which they offer up libations
day and night; how they wear no mourning clothes. His re-

port is not only filled with many rites and customs that point to the influence of Chinese civilization, but which may be matched in the descriptions of the people of Mexico when Spain conquered them.

But if you are an incorrigible unbeliever you will find plenty of ammunition with which to defend your position. Fu Sang according to one of the doubters was "not a problematical country except for Europeans." On the venerable maps of the old empire it was one of a "long series of volcanic islands which protect the east coast of China against the waves of the Pacific." Formosa was among this group and the ancient and honorable kingdom of Japan.

The chief dissenter from the theory that Fu Sang and the western coast of North America was one and the same place, was a German professor named Schlegel, and he went about smashing this enchanting belief with systematic and irritating Teutonic thoroughness. He looked up an old Chinese encyclopædia and found a picture of a hairy gentleman of Fu Sang milking a reindeer. Herr Professor Schlegel decided that far from being a native of Aztec Mexico the milkman in question was a hairy Ainu from one of the northern Japanese islands. Under the picture was a note to the effect that the country of Fu Sang was to be found east of the country of Ta-han where the houses were built of planks and there were no walled towns. It mentioned how in the fifth century some men from Kabul visited the country.

Schlegel warns us that the Chinese are great exaggerators when it comes to figures and therefore Hui Shên's statement that the land of Fu Sang was nine thousand miles across the ocean is to be taken with many grains of salt. As all the writers about Fu Sang stress the tree which yielded a bark from which paper was made, the worthy professor states that "in the ancient province of Chou, paper was made from flax; the inhabitants of Fou-kien made it from bamboo; the men of the north used the bark of the mulberry." At one time Japan made paper from pine bark. As for the pears and grapes which Hui Shên mentions—the Island of Sakhalin is filled with them, to say nothing of black grapes at Yezo. Concerning cattle with big horns that carried huge loads, he is sure that Hui Shên meant reindeer esteemed of the inhabitants of Orotsko for transporting fishing material.

In short, the opposition place Fu Sang within a comparatively short distance of China. One thinks it the Island of Sakhalin, another the Island of Yezo, still others, Japan itself. And in this connection the Japanese on occasion refer to their native land as the Kingdom of Fu Sang while its original name is Nippon the "land of the rising sun." For the Chinese, the Kingdom of Fu Sang has ever been the "country where the sun rises." Which makes the claims of Japan doubly significant.

But perhaps the best guess is that Fu Sang has ever been a magical land which existed in the imagination of China very much as the lost continent of Atlantis existed in the mind of western civilization.

Certainly it was mentioned long before its alleged discovery, for as early as B. C. 219 we are told that an expedition of young men and maidens was organized to hunt for the magical land of Fu Sang. And, at one time, in the city of Canton, in a temple called the "Temple of Polo" the presiding deity was a man from Fu Sang. He used to stand with his eyes straining toward the East as if in longing for the land of his birth. An ancient poet sang a song of him which begins:

> Where the sun rises
> In the land of Fu Sang
> There is my home.
> Seeking Glory and riches, I came
> To the Kingdom of the Central Flower.

E H Suydam
The Pink Doorway

THE PINK DOORWAY

Legend

One critic says that the following lines are to console him for the loss of his Eastern home but it would seem that they are a comment on human inability to escape from reality.

> The cocks crow, the dogs bark,
> The same here as there,
> The almond tree blossoms
> The same everywhere.

In every clime, life goes on with much the same values—and even the magical Fu Sang is no exception to this rule.

In many of the fairy tales of the empire the name of Fu Sang recurs again and again. It lies, a place to be achieved either by daring or imagination, across a great sea. But what fabulous country in any clime or language does not? Its symbol is ever a tree—beautiful, magnificent, incredible—whose form varies. Sometimes it is a tree of stone, sometimes it is a tree of agate gems, sometimes it is a tree of pure jade. Again it turns into a tree of coral. But more often it is a "giant mulberry tree," towering to the sky, with leaves of incredible length and breadth upon which feed silk-worms three feet in length.

Earle Ross, writing many years ago in the Los Angeles *Times,* gives a charming translation of one of these wonder tales of Fu Sang:

In the extreme east is Fu Sang. A kind of silk-worm is raised there which is seven feet long and seven inches in circumference. Its color is golden. It requires one year to grow. On the eighth it spins a yellow silk, which is stretched across the branches of the Fu-Sang tree. This silk is very weak until it is boiled in lye made from the ashes of the Fu-Sang tree. Four strands of it will then hold up 100 pounds. The eggs of this worm are as large as swallows' eggs. The palace walls of the King of Fu Sang are of crystal. They begin to glow before sunrise, and during an eclipse become invisible.

San Francisco's Chinatown

About ten thousand miles north of this region is the Kingdom of Women. They have serpents for husbands. They are not venomous. They live in holes, while their spouses dwell in houses and palaces. No books are seen in this kingdom, nor have the people any writing. They believe much in the power of certain sorceries. The worship of their gods imposes obligations that no one dares to violate. In the middle of the kingdom is an island of fire with a burning mountain, whose inhabitants eat hairy snakes to preserve themselves from the heat. Rats live on the mountain, from whose fur an incombustible tissue is woven, which is cleansed by putting it into the fire instead of washing it.

North of the Kingdom of Women there is a dark valley. Still further north are mountains covered with snow, whose peaks reach to heaven. The sun never shines there, but the luminous dragon lives here.

West of it is an intoxicating fountain whose waters have the taste of wine. In this region is likewise found the sea of varnish whose waters dye plumes and furs black. There is another sea here, having the color of milk.

The land surrounded by these wonders is of great extent and exceeding fertile. One sees there dogs and horses of great stature, and even birds that produce human beings. The males born of them do not live. The females are carefully reared by their fathers, who carry them on their wings. They are remarkably beautiful, and exceedingly hospitable. They die before thirty.

Mr. Ross has other interesting fables to tell of this incredible country. He states that the first mention of Fu Sang goes back forty centuries. A description of Fu Sang is in the oldest geographical work known to man—*The Ancient Classic of Mountain and Sea*. This work was composed by a holy and intrepid potentate named Yao, who reigned B. C. 2357. But the account appears to have been ghost-written by a scholar named Mong-kien, who had it from another gentleman named Pe-y who had it from Yao, himself. Yao told the tale of his exploits; Mong-kien, who seemed to have a

Legend

knowledge of geography, named the places discovered, and Pe-y "consigned it to writing."

Under the intriguing heading of "Fu Sang, the Bathing Place of the Sun" appears the following description:

Above Warm Springs Ravine is Fu Sang, the place where the ten suns bathe. In the water there is a large tree, having nine suns in its lower branches, and one sun in its upper branches.

Formerly these ten suns all rose together, and the grass and trees were burned and withered. The Emperor Yao, then commanded Prince I to shoot nine of the ten suns, and the birds in the suns, until dead. The "Book of the Dissipation of Sorrows," says that I, the mighty archer, Prince of Kiung, brought the sun birds to an end, and that he took some of the feathers home and kept them.

No wonder, after reading such splendid and alluring accounts, that Mr. Ross, with becoming Californian modesty should close his narrative in such a burst of confident pride: "And this Fu Sang, the Oriental garden of the Hesperides, this Atlantis of the East, the home of fairies, is our own fair California."

But no controversy of this nature would be complete without its note of comedy. And in this case the comedy has been supplied by the Reverend Dr. Shaw who flashed a new theory of the discovery of the New World by Chinese through the columns of the New York *Tribune* in 1890. Dr. Shaw, it seems, while prowling around an interior Chinese city on the upper Hoang-Ho discovered an old Chinese manuscript written two hundred years before Christ. The good missionary was aided and abetted in this enterprise by a converted native from the mission station near Ta-Koo.

This priceless manuscript described the accidental discovery of America by a bold mariner named Hee-Li, B. C. 217.

According to this account, Hee-Li "was the owner and

19

commander of a small junk employed in the coast trade."
Upon a February morning, on the venerable date mentioned
above, a violent storm struck Hee-Li's vessel and blew it
out to sea. When things had quieted Hee-Li consulted his
compass and decided to steer west and home to the coast of
China again. For three and a half months Hee-Li sailed on
and on and still the coast of China seemed in nowise nearer
his vision. To be sure, on the twenty-fifth day out, a meddling
member of the crew named Hi-Thinc suggested respectfully
to the master that if they were sailing due west it was
strange that the sun rose constantly before them and set behind them. But Hee-Li, being a conservative soul, was inclined to trust the compass of his fathers rather than the
uncertain manifestation of nature, and Hi-Thinc came into
a just reward by being summarily thrown overboard.

As things turned out it was just as well to be rid of such a
literal individual as Hi-Thinc for no progress ever comes of
listening to routine observations. The result of Hee-Li's
faith in the compass of his fathers landed him on June 10th,
to be exact, on the shores of the present city of Monterey.
Two days later, while polishing up the compass, a member
of the crew discovered a dead yang-si bug lying belly up under the needle.

At once a great light dawned on Hee-Li. Apparently the
yang-si bug—in vulgar English parlance a cockroach—
crawled into the compass during the storm, became wedged
under the needle and in its death-struggles carried the
needle's point around until it faced directly south instead
of north.

Then in the language of the *Tribune* reporter:

Hee-Li and his crew of ten men remained in America about three
months, exploring the coast for fifty miles to the south and one hundred miles to the north. He speaks in high terms of the weather, thus

Legend

being the first to extol the glorious climate of California. He entered the Golden Gate, explored the Bay of San Francisco, giving it the name of Hong-Tsi, or Great Bay. He bartered with the natives, and finally started on his return to China in September, arriving there in the latter half of that year. . . . Hee-Li died in 197 B. C., twenty years after his discovery.

For a hundred years after, Chinese junks apparently visited San Francisco Bay every month or so, building up quite a trade. Then curiously their visits ceased. Doubtless the port charges were too great.

If one were of a very low comedy order one could say something about the names of Hee-Li and Hi-Thinc in an endeavor to discredit this most ancient of claims of the discovery of America. Douglas S. Watson in reprinting the *Tribune* article in the California Historical Quarterly says in an interpolation: "The Chinese made no use of the compass at sea until the sixth century A. D.; their compass points south and is known as the *South Pointing Chariot*."

But this may be mere quibbling. We have seen how James Hanley, the one-time Chinese interpreter of the Gold Rush, remarked upon the Mongolian features of California Indians and we are loath to believe that five holy men from Kabul could have been instrumental in stamping the faces of the original native sons of the Golden West with Chinese characteristics. How much more logical and pleasanter is it to ascribe the peculiar physical affinity of the two races as being the result of the philandering of Hee-Li's able-bodied seamen, aided and abetted by the monthly visits of the merchant marine of China for a hundred years thereafter.

But it is not the province of the author to argue any one of these claims. They are presented for what they are worth— or for such verdicts as they engender. Fact, fable or burlesque? It is for the reader to decide.

Chapter II

EARLY SETTLERS

WHATEVER one's decision concerning the appearance of Chinese on the American Continent before Columbus, there will still be the practical question to settle as to who was the first Chinese to land in San Francisco in the early years of the nineteenth century. What was the nucleus of that transplanted bit of China which was to become the most famous Chinatown the world over?

However authentic the visitation of the *Bolivar's* cabin-boy in 1838, he can scarcely rate as an early settler, since he stayed only long enough for the ship to fill its hold with hides and tallow and be off again. But, withal, there is something intriguing about this transient wayfarer. What was his name, his age, his previous condition of servitude? Was it necessity, or force, or an inquiring spirit that led him across the ocean? Had he been bought by the master of the brig

Early Settlers

Bolivar for so many pieces of silver to serve out a required number of years as cabin-boy? It was a common matter to sell the girls of China into slavery, but occasionally a family hard put to it, disposed of a youth in like fashion. It was like the early American fashion of a child "bound out," except, perhaps, that it was much more definite and hopeless. If he came as a slave he had no choice but if he came as a free agent, he rises in our estimation.

It was something, in the year 1838, for the product of a land of stay-at-homes, a land that had shut itself in with a Great Wall, to achieve such a wide horizon. In the year 1838 he could have been lured to the New World by no stories of fabulous wealth in the golden hills of California. He must have come, then, out of sheer curiosity, out of a desire to know what lay beyond the great ocean that Hui Shên had traveled, to see for himself whether the mulberry trees in the "land of the rising sun" were really eight hundred feet high and fed silk-worms three feet long, producing cocoons which yielded a pound of golden silk. Or, perhaps, his imaginings were of an even more poetical fancy, imbibed with the fairy stories of his youth. Perhaps he hoped to find trees of even greater beauty—of agate gems, or pure jade, or coral. Or to reach the kingdom where the women mated with serpents, and to climb the high mountains where the luminous dragon lived.

What he found was a trading post, called Yerba Buena, consisting of huddled shanties on the fringe of a muddy cove, a sleepy Mexican presidio with fortifications rusting to their doom; and an adobe mission house, named for St. Francis of Assisi but more often referred to as Mission Dolores, in the throes of temporary dissolution.

We shall never know what this Chinese cabin-boy's reactions to his first glimpse of the New World were. He kept no diary, he had no countryman to confide in. But we may be sure that he guarded whatever disappointment he felt with the mask of an immobility that was his heritage from sixty centuries of civilization and its repressions. He is a lonely figure, set against the background of an untamed country and an alien crew. He could have had no diversions that were native to him, except, doubtless, the solace of an occasional whiff of opium. When homesickness and longing and disappointment grew too hard to bear let us hope that an hour with his faithful pipe revived the wonders which the "land of the Fu-sang tree" had held out to him. And beautiful women born of birds flew by on the wings of their fathers, with a rushing sound that proved to be only the afternoon gales of the Pacific screaming in the rigging, as he stumbled out of his bunk to brew the captain a glass of grog.

We are equally in the dark about the enterprising merchant Chum Ming who is reputed to have arrived before the discovery of gold in 1847. Apparently like the bulk of Chinese who followed in his footsteps, he was from the province of Kwang Tung. But what could have tempted him to desert the market places of his venerable country?

True, the Chinese merchant was wont to establish himself in foreign seaports nearer home and nibble into any trade that offered. But there was no trade worth mentioning in California in 1847. It is possible that Chum Ming had heard of the port from some old New England sea-dog filling his ship's hold with blue-and-white Canton tea-sets for the matrons of Salem and way stations. The captain doubtless had told him about the Spanish señoritas and their love of rose-embroidered shawls, and gaudy fans to hide their ripe lips—or about the easy American conquest of the land the previous year, which made Chum Ming consider it good policy to be first in the field with subtle blends of tea for the initiated.

Early Settlers

It is even possible that he was compelled to flee his native land. The conquering Manchus had been on the throne of China for over two hundred years and though outwardly their rule seemed safely iron-clad there were always revolts against the invaders being promptly strangled behind the scenes. If this were so, Chum Ming proved to be the forerunner of a horde of revolutionists who escaped the headsman's sword by fleeing to California and setting up standards of blackmail and violence that were matched only by the Chicago gangsters of the prohibition era. Revolutionary plotting and escape to far climes seems ever to have been an old Chinese custom. Even the five sedate priests who preceded Hui Shên to the land of Fu Sang have been accused of being renegades from Imperial wrath, to say nothing of the amazing Hui Shên, himself.

But however vague Chum Ming's reasons for establishing himself in California, one thing seems reasonably certain, he was the only Chinese to be on the ground when gold was discovered in 1848. When the news came, he abandoned his chests of tea, his rose-embroidered shawls, his sandalwood fans or whatever his stock in trade and flew to the hills. He found gold; then, promptly securing a long sheet of rice paper, a slender brush, and a pot of thick ink, he wrote to his friend, Cheong Yum, concerning his good fortune. Cheong Yum immediately put his house in order, paid his debts, provided for his wife and took passage for the "golden hills." The news of his departure and the reasons therefore spread like wildfire through his native province, and, there followed the first thin stream of Chinese immigration toward California which was one day to reach the menacing proportions of a flood.

On the second of February, 1848, there sailed into San Francisco Bay, the American brig *Eagle*. On board were Mr. and Mrs. Charles V. Gillespie from Hong Kong as well as three Chinese—two men and a woman. Some chroniclers say that there were only two Chinese aboard—a man and a woman, but the weight of testimony seems to be in favor of *two* men and a woman. . . . Their names do not seem to have been recorded either officially or in the memories of those who have reported their arrival. The men, says one historian, "eventually went to the mines." But since the woman was a servant in the Gillespie household for over thirty years we must conclude that she came with them. It is even reasonable to suppose that the men worked, too, for the Gillespies, until news that gold had been discovered at Sutter Creek sent them scampering to the mountains.

Mr. Gillespie was a merchant and he brought a cargo of Chinese goods and established a business. He had gone from New York to Hong Kong in 1840, deciding to try his luck eight years later in the new land that had so recently come under the American flag. He had a knowledge of law and served as notary public and conveyancer. His first home was on a large tract of land in the vicinity of what is now Grant avenue and Washington street. The family kept a cow and three horses. Which establishes the fact that the first permanent Chinese resident of San Francisco, and a woman, at that, lived nearly a hundred years ago, on the very spot that is now the center of San Francisco's Chinatown.

In those days the Gillespie family rode far out to the Mission Dolores for their green vegetables. Riding two horses and driving before them a third horse rigged with panniers in which to bring home their purchases they were a familiar sight to the residents of early San Francisco. We cannot help wondering whether the Chinese woman ever rode over the sand dunes with them on any of these excursions. But, alas, the historians of these early days gossip for the most part about drab unessentials. Not only did her name fail to concern them, but the whys and wherefores of her coming. She, too, like the cabin-boy of the *Bolivar* is a lonely figure. For the first years of her servitude, she could have had little contact with others of her kind, and we doubt if even in later years, amongst a female population largely given over to prostitution, there were many opportunities to mix with her countrywomen. Even if her necessity had induced a compromise with the conventions and tempted her to seek out transient companionship with womankind of any class or condition, she would have had to reckon with the Gillespies' pious respectability: Mrs. Gillespie was an ardent church worker, having started the first Sabbath school in San Francisco.

For us to arrive at any approximation of this first Chinese woman's detachment and loneliness, we must try to imagine an American woman in a like situation—an American woman for thirty years in the service of a family in China, with practically no contacts with any of her people, uprooted from her native soil, standing alone amongst the alien corn. The idea is inconceivable. Such a woman would either have gone mad or worse. And therein perhaps lies a key to the eternal difference between the races—the older civilization accepting whatever comes in life with the resignation of age—the younger civilization, restive under adversity. The nerves of one calmed by centuries of bowing before the storm, the nerves of the other keyed to upstanding wrestlings with whirlwinds.

There used to be an old Chinaman in the employ of the Pacific Mail Steamship Company who made the claim that he came to San Francisco in the early months of 1848—but not directly from China. He in company with a gang of other Chinese had shipped to Callao, Peru, some months before under contract to build a road from the coast to the interior. All this contract labor with Callao and other southerly ports proved, not only in the forties but for many years later, to be virtual slavery from which there was little chance of escape. . . . A vessel bound for San Francisco, and short of hands, put into Callao. The master induced a number of the dissatisfied coolies to work for their passage north. They accepted and when the vessel put to sea, the master found not only the laborers he had bargained for but a score or more stowaways aboard. Arriving at San Francisco, the entire gang got jobs unloading vessels. Then gold was discovered and they all fled to the hills, except the one in question. He stayed on and made the shipping business a life job. In the seventies he was reputed to talk better English than most of the white men with whom he worked. He must have been of more intelligent mould than the companions who fled from slavery with him and it is safe to assume it was his brains that engineered the escape.

In 1899, there was released from the California State Prison at San Quentin, a venerable Chinaman named Lum Ah Hing. He was reputed to have spent forty years of his life in prison. He made the boastful claim that he had come to San Francisco as early as 1844, in the company of other Chinese in search of wealth. But his claim seems extremely dubious. He had been convicted six times of thievery and with true criminal unsportsmanship, he attributed his delinquency to the bad example that had been set him in the hell-raising fifties by white men.

Those who are ignorant or careless of the fact that a Chinese woman had come to San Francisco with the Gillespies in 1848, award the first place to the enigmatic Madame Ah Toy. The reports concerning this lady are conflicting. On the one hand we are given a picture of her entertaining "the ecclesiastical and political savants of the hour" at her tea parties and on the other, of exhibiting her person to curious miners at so much a head. The proponents of the first theory claim that she was of high caste, abundant wealth and keen intellect. They raise her afternoon tea parties to the dignity of a salon at which we see her presiding in apricot satin jacket and willow-green trousers with all the grace and fire of a Madame Récamier.

Just when she came and why is not made clear. Certainly it seems incredible that a Chinese woman of high caste with riches and charm should elect to set up a ménage in a bleak boom town where she could have no female companionship. All of which makes the other story they tell of her seem the more authentic. This account concedes that she was a woman of charm and action but there are dubious implications.

Madame Ah Toy, it seems, established herself in what was termed a "shanty" in a court or blind alley just off Clay street, above Kearny. That she lived in a shanty does not weaken her social position—in those days one was lucky in San Francisco to have even a shanty in which to lay one's head—it was her line of action which breeds scepticism as to her high level. Having settled herself as comfortably as circumstances permitted in the aforesaid alley, she wasted little time in making known the fact that the curious could come and gaze on her for a consideration.

A second Chinese woman may not have been a novelty to San Franciscans who had seen the Gillespie servant staking out the family cow amongst yellow spikes of wild lupin bloom in the vicinity of Washington street and Grant avenue, but she proved that and more to the miners who swarmed down from the mountains in search of recreation and thrills. Indeed, it is said that when the Sacramento boat would land in the evening that the miners would break into a run for Madame Ah Toy's residence. Sometimes there would be a queue a block long waiting for the chance, as one writer puts it with true Victorian gallantry and modesty, "to gaze upon the *countenance* of the charming Ah Toy." Each and every gentleman carried a gun and woe to the man who stepped out of line and tried to forge ahead.

It seems that the wealthy Ah Toy was not adverse to more riches, for each man was asked to deposit an ounce of gold dust before he could feast his eyes upon the aforesaid "countenance." More than that, the estimable lady had a pair of scales to see that she was in nowise cheated.

This story has authenticity, because it led to a difficulty, which became a matter of court record. Some of the miners began passing brass filings in lieu of gold dust upon the unsuspecting Ah Toy. She stood it until the custom grew so universal as to threaten to wreck her profits. Then she had two of the offenders arrested.

The day she was placed on the stand Judge Baker's court was crowded. Ah Toy not only gave direct testimony against the defendants but she took occasion to pick out several more delinquents from among the spectators. The judge then asked her to produce the evidence. She excused herself, went to her house and returned with a huge china basin filled with brass filings. A great shout of laughter came from the spectators and it is said that the "men she had picked out in the courtroom hung their heads in conscious guilt."

The prisoners acknowledged having given brass filings but declared that Ah Toy had accepted them knowingly. The judge was obliged to dismiss the case as she could produce no evidence to disprove their statements.

Those who still champion an irreproachable Madame Ah Toy, point out the fact that in the fifties women of any kind were such a novelty that miners used to file past them and throw nuggets at their feet, for the very joy of looking upon a woman's face. But most of these stories concern women in public places—in dance halls and gambling hells. Even if we allow Madame Ah Toy's complete respectability, we must discard the rest of the fable. A high-caste Chinese lady of wealth and refinement would scarcely have put herself on exhibition at a price. And we wonder, if the fee for just looking at her "countenance" was an ounce of gold dust, what she charged "the ecclesiastical and political savants of the hour" for admission to one of her "tea-parties."

In spite of all the goodwill and discretion in the world, we find that one of her historians admits that in this same court where Ah Toy lived were "several nice shanties occupied by respectable men, the majority of whom were obliged to move away on account of the nuisance." One of these gentlemen was the village carpenter named McAbee. He had his workshop around the corner from his home, facing the old Plaza, where scores of down-and-outers slept every night under the shavings.

On one point all of Madame Ah Toy's chroniclers agree. She was tall, well-built and fine looking. One suspects from her description that she may have come from one of the Northern provinces of China. After the trial she abandoned her pantaloons of willow-green silk and adopted American costume, from which we assume that her exhibition days were over. Doubtless the brass filings were a warning that she had ceased to be a novelty and men came more for the fun of cheating her than to satisfy their curiosity. The pathos of loneliness is not suggested by Madame Ah Toy's career. She appears to have been a self-sufficient woman who knew what she wanted and went after it. But, like all Chinese pioneers in San Francisco the mystery of her appearance upon the local scene is tantalizing. What a story must lie back of her excursion into the unknown!!

At the end of 1848, there were only seven Chinese officially registered in the State of California. This would account for the two men and a woman who came on the *Eagle,* the merchant, Chum Ming, and three more unnamed Asia-

San Francisco's Chinatown

tic soldiers of fortune, one of whom might have been the
old reprobate, Lum Ah Hing, who served forty years of his
life in jail. But this record can scarcely have taken in the
dozen or more who had run away from slavery at Callao.
On January 1, 1850, the check-up was seven hundred and
eighty-nine men and two women. By this time, doubtless
Cheong Yum and his party had responded to his friend's
glowing reports of the discovery of gold and Madame Ah
Toy had arrived to put her business talents and her genius for
publicity to the test.

But the seven hundred odd Chinese residents listed in 1849
were becoming race-conscious, and we find the first move
toward organization reported in the columns of the San
Francisco *Alta California* on December 10th of that year.
They held a meeting at the Canton Restaurant on Jackson
street, which was attended by about three hundred. The following resolutions which were adopted gives a complete outline of the object of their gathering:

WHEREAS, it becomes necessary for us, strangers as we are, in a
strange land, unacquainted with the language and customs of this,
our adopted country, to have some recognized counselor and adviser,
to whom we may all appeal, with confidence, for wholesome instruction and advice, in the event of any unforseen difficulties arising,
wherein we should be at loss as to what course of action it might
be necessary for us to pursue; therefore.

RESOLVED, that a committee of four be appointed to wait upon
Selim E. Woodworth, Esq., and request him, in behalf of the Chinese
residents of San Francisco, to act in the capacity of arbitrator and
adviser for them.

The next day a committee of four waited upon the afore-
said gentleman and obtained his consent to represent them.
Their names, according to the newspaper account were "Ahe,
Jon-Ling, Atung, and Attoon." To a present-day resident

SITE OF LEESE HOUSE, GRANT AVENUE

Early Settlers

of San Francisco, none of these names appear at all familiar, but the strangeness probably lies in the spelling rather than in the names, themselves. A few days later Mr. Woodworth was "entertained" by his new associates at a distinguished gathering which included Mr. Geary, the Alcalde of San Francisco, and a number of other officials. A good time must have been had by all for the newspaper reporter who was present assures us that "the whole affair passed off in the happiest manner, and many good things were said and sung by the numerous distinguished guests who were present." We fancy that it was the American guests who did most of the talking and all of the singing. The Chinese, undoubtedly, listened blandly with a note of respectful attention to what they must inwardly have considered a very tiresome exhibition of oratory and music. That the speeches were patronizing goes almost without saying.

The gentleman whom the Chinese picked for their first adviser had had a most romantic career, prior to 1849. To begin with, he was the son of Samuel Woodworth, the author of "The Old Oaken Bucket." He was born in New York City in November, 1815 . . . At the age of eighteen, having completed his schooling, he sailed from New York for a three-year cruise in the South Pacific Ocean. The ship was wrecked off the coast of Madagascar and all on board perished except Woodworth and a member of the crew. His historian, Bailey Maillard, says with tantalizing brevity that he "was protected by a native woman and thus escaped death." What kind of death? Was the native woman young and beautiful? . . . Or was her age sufficiently advanced to give her act merely the stamp of an eternal maternalism? Perhaps Mr. Woodworth never said. If not, his silence is illuminating.

But whatever the gentle rescuer's motive for shielding a young and handsome stranger, it was some time before he

33

was able to make his escape on a whaling vessel which touched at the point where he lay screened from the evil designs of the male population.

In 1838 he received an appointment as midshipman in the Navy. He continued in the service until 1846 when he asked for a leave of absence and took the Oregon trail for the Columbia River country. By the winter of that year he had worked his way down from the north to San Francisco in time to take charge of the rescue of the tragic Donner party. In 1849 he was elected to the California Senate. Later he became a Commodore in the Navy. Altogether, he seems to have been a very suitable choice for adviser to the Chinese residents.

Either the Commodore's absence from San Francisco on political matters or the press of business must soon have made it expedient to appoint an assistant for, as early as August, 1850, we find a semi-official mingling of Chinese and Americans with brother Frederick listed among those present as Vice Consul for the Chinese. It seems that in the interest of morality and religion a number of the leading citizens of the town conceived the idea that it would be a pleasantly pious gesture to acquaint the resident "China Boys" with the superior ethics of Christianity. Or, to put it in language of the fifties, they decided that "the dissemination of Scriptural truths among the members of a nation, *otherwise highly civilized,* was a great and good object." To this end, they ordered a number of pamphlets and tracts on divers scriptural matters printed in Chinese characters from Canton.

The arrival of this cargo of "Scriptural truths" was the occasion for quite a celebration. Invitations were sent out for the "China Boys" to be present on a certain afternoon in front of the old Mexican Custom House in Portsmouth Square to receive the aforesaid consignment of "Christian truths and useful knowledge." The "China Boys" responded with courteous gravity and at least three hundred formed in procession. They were dressed in their very best holiday attire, or to put it in the language of the daily press "with their pig-tails nicely braided, and presenting a perfectly neat and singularly picturesque appearance." Nearly all of them carried fans, not to shield their eyes from the sun but for a very characteristic San Francisco reason in those early days—to keep the wind and dust out of their eyes. All the élite of San Francisco were there, including Mr. Geary with his title changed from *Alcalde* to Mayor, Reverend Mr. Albert Williams, Reverend Mr. Augustus Fitch, Reverend Mr. T. D. Hunt, and a gentleman, referred to several times in the newspaper accounts of the project, as just plain Mr. Buell. In the ranks of the Chinese was at least one figure who merited attention—a tall, venerable gentleman, with tortoise-shell eye-glasses, a fur cape and an excessively large pig-tail. A modern reporter would have taken good care to discover the identity of such an imposing personality, but the man who wrote up the account next day was content to "presume he must be a Mandarin, at least." A Chinese named Ah Sing acted as interpreter.

There followed the usual exchange of flattery and platitudes, from the Mayor, the Reverend Mr. Williams, and the untitled *Mr.* Buell. All went decorously and with irreproachable gravity until the Reverend Hunt began to talk. He chose for his remarks a dissertation on the Christian hereafter. He admonished his hearers that in spite of the fact they were reputed to have come from a Celestial country that there "was another celestial country above, much better, much larger than their own." He told them that whereas in their own country "China Boys" sometimes were taken sick and suffered, that they died and were seen no more, and "that their fathers and mothers and sisters and brothers all died," in the other Celestial country, above, all good "China Boys" lived forever with all the aforementioned relations in a state of perfect contentment and bliss. The "China Boys" who had born up with such dignity under the remarks of the Mayor, the Reverend Mr. Williams and plain *Mr.* Buell had reached the limit of their endurance. It was all very well for them to pretend that they swallowed what the first three gentlemen had said concerning mutual admiration, friendship and brotherly love, but if the Reverend Mr. Hunt thought that they took seriously this Celestial Heaven, where "China Boys" or anybody else lived forever with kinfolk in perfect amity and accord he was very much mistaken. And so they broke into roars of laughter. Which is sufficient proof against the charge brought so often by the ignorant that the Chinese are stolid and have no sense of humor.

However, they recovered their gravity sufficiently to reply through their own Mr. Ah He to the effect that they were charmed with the books that had been ordered at such trouble and expense for them and to express their undying admiration for Americans in general and Californians in particular. Which moved one of the chroniclers of the event to forgive them their momentary lapse charging it to their "simple minds" and ending with the hope that "a few more such occasions and a few more years' further exertion" would "enable them to acquire a knowledge of divine truths." It happened that the next afternoon there was to form a mock funeral procession in memory of President Zachary Taylor, recently deceased. The "China Boys" were asked to join and accepted, rather inappropriately, if the expression of the recorder of the event is correct, "with great glee." This was said to have been the first time anywhere that "such a demonstration had been made" by Chinese outside their own realm. Be that as it may, they seem to have been the hit

CHINESE SHRIMPERS' HUTS AT
HUNTER'S POINT

of the parade, and their "glee" was further expressed in a following communication to Mayor Geary:

San Francisco, August 30, 1850

To Hon. John W. Geary, Mayor of the City of San Francisco—

SIR: The "China Boys" wish to thank you for the kind mark of attention you bestowed upon them in extending to them an invitation to join with the citizens of San Francisco in doing honor to the memory of the late President of the United States, Gen. Zachary Taylor. The China Boys feel proud of the distinction you have shown them, and will always endeavor to merit your good opinion and the good opinion of the citizens of their adopted country. The China Boys are fully sensible of the great loss this country has sustained in the death of its chieftain and ruler, and mourn with you in sorrow. Strangers as they are among you, they kindly appreciate the many kindnesses received at your hands, and again beg leave, with grateful hearts, to thank you.

Ah-Sing
A-He
In behalf of the China Boys.

After their initial appearance in the funeral procession of President Taylor, the "China Boys" became a feature of every parade which followed. At the first celebration of the admission of California into the Union, they are reported to have enlivened the proceeding with their "lavender trousers and plum-colored jackets of silk." Again, in celebration of Washington's Birthday, acclaimed as a "large delegation of our most orderly and industrious citizens" they took the palm for picturesqueness away from the "French, Spanish and Hebrew societies" passing in review. In this parade they had grown ambitious to show their musical quality. Seated in an express wagon were six musicians producing tunes that fell upon the ears of the spectators like the "sounds produced by a stick with a smooth surface rubbed across one with edges

notched." It was the Americans turn to laugh or, as our forefathers put it, "to have their risibilities stirred." Later that
same year the China Boys plaited their pig-tails afresh, put
on their straw hats and their pantaloons of "white, green,
red and yellow" and honored Independence day with their
presence.

With the smug satisfaction of youth the American of that
day and generation found any deviation from the human
pattern as he knew it either cause for patronizing indulgence,
or caustic abuse. The early San Franciscan attitude toward
its Chinese population, for the moment, leaned more toward
amused tolerance. The community was like a household welcoming a fantastic guest who for the time being was diverting
and unusual. This guest had faults, to be sure, but they were
all chargeable to improper upbringing. His taste in food was
bizarre, his clothes outlandish, his music excruciating, his
ethics unsound—but time would change that. It was inconceivable that he could remain long exposed to the superior
advantage of American culture, American religion, American
morals without being regenerated. That six thousand years
of a very definite civilization lay behind him mattered not
at all. Then besides, the proselyting urge was strong—it
would be such fun to reform him. But, above all, it was
being discovered that "the heathen Chinee" was making
himself very useful. While most of the arrivals from Canton
were bitten by the same gold bug that attacked their white
brethren, and fled soon after landing to the hills, there were
some with less imagination or more business sense who
decided to stay in San Francisco.

Presently, the first Chinese wash-house appeared on the
fringe of the old Plaza. Up to that time it had cost the
gentlemen of San Francisco eight dollars to have a dozen
shirts laundered. Now, under Asiatic competition the rate
was reduced to five dollars a dozen which caused the daily

press to issue the following warning: "There is now no excuse for our citizens to wear soiled or colored shirts. The effect of the reduction is already manifest; the tobacco-juice spattered bosoms are now no longer the fashion."

As competition increased the rate dropped further and the day came when the price of laundry sank as low as three dollars a dozen. But San Francisco was to learn that cheapness was by no means a guarantee of good service. A scribe writing in the columns of the *Herald* soon after this bedrock price was reached reported that "a garment, after undergoing a Chinaman's manipulation for three washings, will soon, no matter how snowy white it may have been originally, become of the color of the calfskin in which the statutes of California are bound, diversified more or less with streaks of darker hue." Further complaining that "a fine linen shirt is, by the power of their juggling, frequently converted into an inferior cotton fabric worn threadbare; and fine cambric handkerchiefs, not infrequently turned into bandanas."

But these shafts of sarcasm came mostly from journalistic individuals striving hard to be clever in the redundant style of the period. For the most part any and all reference to the Chinese was couched in laudatory terms tinged with the usual Nordic condescension. Publications vied with each other in welcoming the newcomers to our shores. One state publication said:

> Under our laws and with the treatment they will receive here they will be valuable citizens. And we shall be pleased to see large additions during the coming year to this class of our population. We congratulate our farmers on the prospect of obtaining that description of labor of which the country is so much in need.

And the San Francisco *Alta California* remarked in passing that "These celestials make excellent citizens and we are pleased to notice their daily arrival in large numbers."

San Francisco's Chinatown

At the close of a lecture on China the audience passed the following resolutions:

RESOLVED: That the present position of the Oriental nations is fraught with the most profound interest to the Christian world, and that we, as Citizens of California, placed by the wonderful leadings of Providence so immediately in contact with one of the most ancient, intelligent, and populous of these nations, hail with peculiar satisfaction the "Sign of the times"; And we feel an imperative obligation to employ our money, our influence, and utmost effort for the welfare of that vast portion of the human family—*our elder brethren*—the people of China.

One may be sure that whenever a body of men bring the "wonderful leadings of Providence" into the conversation that their admiration for the subject is tinged with a goodly measure of the reformer's zeal. This occasion was no exception to the rule for the resolutions finished thus:

RESOLVED: That we regard with pleasure the presence of great numbers of these people among us, as affording the best opportuniy of doing them good, and through them, of exerting our influence upon their native land.

Men in high places spoke of "the two civilizations which, parting upon the plains of Asia four thousand years ago, and traveling ever after in opposite directions around the world," were now meeting on the "coasts and islands of the Pacific."

It was a sort of love-feast—like a family reunion in its first stages. But like all family reunions the sour note was soon to creep in and the celebration was to end in a final and devastating burst of discord.

Chapter III

DISCORD

DURING 1850 the Chinese population in California increased from seven hundred and eighty-nine men and two women, to four thousand and eighteen men and seven women. In 1851 the population of males grew to approximately twelve thousand but there was no increase in females. A certain historian of that period laments the fact that with every wish in the world to give the devil his due he was bound to admit that the Chinese were lamentably given over to "gambling and prostitution." The singling out of any nationality or class for special condemnation on these two counts in San Francisco in the fifties must have made even our self-righteous forefathers smile. But granting the Chinese proclivities for gambling and prostitution, it would be hard to figure out with the ratio of twelve thousand males to seven females,

San Francisco's Chinatown

the opportunity for indulging too strenuously in this last named delinquency. Ladies of easy virtue of other breeds might conceivably have been hospitable to these males of another race but the Chinese themselves, except in rare instances, have never found the charms of white women even under extreme necessity, beguiling.

Exaggeration of vices or even customs of aliens is always a sure indication of irritation. The descriptive articles which now began to appear in the daily press had notes of intolerance. The indulgently critical shafts which had been shot at Chinese music in the Washington's Birthday parade were now tipped with scornful virulence. The orchestras in the gambling clubs were compared to "the wailings of a thousand lovelorn cats, the screams, gobblings, brayings, and barkings of as many peacocks, turkeys, donkeys and dogs." There was talk about "nasty-looking eatables" in the shops. And remarks were made concerning advertisements on the streets of the quarter "informing the public where the best rat-pies were to be had." Ending with the sarcasm that it was "generally believed that in this locality rats were not as numerous as elsewhere."

This story about the rat-eating proclivities of Chinese was circulated early and often and nothing seemed to down it. In a long article in the *Herald* entitled "Chinese Population," the charge was brought that the Chinese "live principally upon rice, and when they wish to indulge in animal food, all they have to do is to catch a few rats."

The baffling but always beautiful Chinese signs, surrounded by exquisite carvings colored and gilded, were described in a wise-cracking vein as being "a compound of phonographic and stenographic characters with a dash of low Dutch." The better class of Chinese were referred to sneeringly as "these upper-ten, or *codfish* Celestials." Even upon such a solemn occasion as the annual visit of the Chinese to the tombs of

Discord

their dead, the smart-alec scribes of the period took occasion, not to mention its beautiful aspects but to attempt to convulse their readers by describing the "ludicrous appearance" of the Chinese on horseback. A member of the present generation, smarting under the charge that manners have gone out of fashion, has only to read these accounts in the conservative newspapers of the fifties to realize that for cruelty, vulgarity and vanity our grandparents have not been matched by any generation succeeding them. Their chief fault was a smug ignorance. Anything they did not understand they ridiculed.

All this redundant sneering was a surface indication of mounting apprehension. In midsummer of 1852 within forty-eight hours over two thousand Chinese arrived in San Francisco. They came on ships bearing the romantic names of *Akbar, Viceroy, Duke of Northumberland, Gulnare,* and *Cornwall.* The *Alta California* which a year before had been so "pleased" at the arrival of Chinese "in large numbers" still pretended to be undisturbed. It was content with remarking that "this immigration during the last two days is quite unprecedented in our record of foreign passenger arrivals." Two months before, commenting on a forecast that the close of the year would see the Chinese population increased from twelve thousand to twenty thousand it announced itself as finding no "imperative necessity for the hue and cry which is attempted relative to this class of foreigners." It consoled itself with the fact that the "French and Spanish American population both exceed the Chinese very largely at the present moment, and no one fears danger or misfortune from their excessive numbers." To compare the problem of a French and Spanish American population with that presented by a like number of residents as foreign in race, religion and philosophy as the Chinese is plainly casting about for some sophistry to support a secret disquiet.

43

San Francisco's Chinatown

The "hue and cry" mentioned by the *Alta California* was already in full swing. The first shrill notes were coming from the mining districts and the politicians of the period were beginning to line up on the question, according to their sympathies and prejudices. These first mutterings did not emanate from a distinct laboring class. The hills of California were being ravished by aristocrat and commoner alike and California had not yet progressed industrially to a point where the shoe of competition had begun to pinch the feet of labor. It was an Anglo-Celtic movement more particularly —a movement begun by Americans and such old world groups as were related to them by blood and a common racial heritage. They wanted the gold of California for themselves and the further removed from kinship the other seekers were the greater became the irritation.

As early as 1850 the Legislature put through a bill taxing every alien miner twenty dollars a month. This was presumed to have been leveled at the Chinese more particularly but it resulted in so much injury to the mining camps and filled San Francisco with such a flood of penniless foreigners that it was soon repealed. Later, a milder tax was restored and all through the fifties taxes were levied and repealed, and levied again—taxes of every conceivable description in an effort to fleece the unwelcome and "heathen Chinee." The point was soon reached when no effort was made to conceal the fact that these laws were aimed at the Chinese rather than at foreigners in general. Presently a law was set in motion providing an entrance tax of fifty dollars for every Chinaman coming into the country, reinforced by a tax of six dollars a month for working in the mines. The entrance tax finally was declared unconstitutional but in the interim immigration from China all but ceased. But whenever the taxes proved prohibitive, the counties which shared in the

44

THE SHRIMP SHOP

Discord

loot, found their treasuries all but depleted and there was a resultant reduction in the levies put upon Chinese industry and thrift.

Governor Bigler was the first official in a high place to begin a move toward Chinese exclusion. In April of 1852 he addressed the Legislature to the effect that a restriction in Chinese immigration seemed desirable. He advocated, first, a stiff taxing program to discourage Chinese immigration and, second, the help of the Federal government in prohibiting coolies shipped to California under contract from laboring in the mines. There had been an increasing tendency for capitalists to import both Chinese and South American laborers to work the mines under contract conditions which the opposition declared was virtual slavery.

Prior to the Governor's message, a bill had been introduced into the Legislature, recognizing contracts made in China between coolies and mining interests "enslaving" them. It was lost; as was a bill introduced by the opposition to prevent "involuntary servitude and coolie labor in the mines." But an assembly committee reporting the situation viewed with the usual legislative alarm, "the importation by foreign capitalists of immense numbers of Asiatic serfs and Mexican and South American peons," predicting that no good would arise from such a condition. They recommended levying an entrance tax of one hundred dollars on every Asiatic who arrived in the country.

But apparently public opinion had not crystalized in any direction to the extent of forcing the law-makers of the State to decisive action. Except for the passage of a bill prohibiting any person not a citizen of the United States to take gold from the mines without a license costing three dollars a month, the "alarm" of the legislators ended in a mere flood of resolutions, of which the following is a sample:

45

San Francisco's Chinatown

We learn that myriads of tawny serfs are embarking for our shores from various ports in Asia, who will cover our land like the locusts of Egypt. They will meet our brothers and relatives in the rich mining regions—laying claim to mining locations to the exclusion of our own people. It needs no Solomon to predict the result. Disputes will take place, blood will flow, to be followed by the expulsion of that population, who will then be driven from the State by violence instead of law. This can now be prevented by the passage of salutary laws, prohibiting this class of foreigners from occupying the mines.

The new license fee was not exorbitant enough to discourage Asiatic immigration. Between January and August of 1852, eighteen thousand Chinese passed through the port of San Francisco. Women were again in a startling minority, only fourteen being registered. Since less than a hundred males returned to China in that period, the Chinese population was more than doubled in seven months.

But if the law-making bodies were indecisive, the "rough and ready" citizens of the mining districts were not. The first concerted move to rid the State of the "yellow peril" was made at Columbia in May, 1852. A mass meeting at that point covered reams of paper with resolutions filled with phrases, disparaging or self-laudatory as the tale ran, so usual to citizens in a high state of questionable moral indignation. These resolutions began with the plaint that is so well known in a democracy, to the effect that it was useless to "expect any efficient action" on the part of either Federal or State electors. It stated the old American principle that because of such delinquency in the law-giving bodies of the land it became the duty of the citizens "to take the matter in their own hands, and apply such remedies as the exigencies of the case seem to demand." In good old rabble-rousing diction it referred to the Chinese as "burlesques of humanity . . . long-tailed, horned and cloven-footed inhabitants of the infernal regions." Having thus politely linked the natives of Cathay with Mr. Satan himself, the miners proceeded to resolve in more temperate language that committees be formed to carry the gospel of exclusion to every mining community to the end that "no Asiatic or South Sea Islander shall be permitted to mine" either for himself or others, thus saving the pious and chaste miners, in their leisure moments given over to whiskey and lynchings, from the "influx of the degraded inhabitants of China and the Islands of the Pacific." The South Sea Islander, being no particular menace at all, seems to have been mentioned to give the effect of a laudable lack of narrow race discrimination.

As a matter of fact all this rumble-bumble about contract labor in the mines seems for the most part to have been an horrific mask donned for the purpose of frightening the white population into action. What it really represented was a racial repugnance pure and simple. Some of the leaders may have had a vague premonition of what ultimately Chinese competition would do to labor and the American standard of living but the majority of the movements against the Chinese were begun in a frenzy of prejudice too blind for distant vision. But instinct is sometimes a surer guide than intelligence or logic and many of the fictitious evils which the childish minds of the rabble-rousers conjured up to advance their cause later became realities.

During the immediate fifties the Chinese in the mines scarcely came in conflict with American industry or enterprise. They fled to the hills content to work over claims that white men had abandoned or found too unprofitable to develop. A news item in one of the San Francisco papers in the spring of 1852 gives an admirable picture of their aspirations and limitations:

San Francisco's Chinatown

The multitudes of Chinese recently arrived, who have for some days past been sojourning in our city, have nearly all left for the interior to try their fortunes at mining. Their outfit was the simplest and most meager possible—rarely consisting of more than a new pair of boots, in which the Chinese are as ill at ease as we should be in their wooden turned up slippers—and a pick and a pan. With this slight stock in trade, they have repaired to the spots most frequented by their countrymen, and they are very clannish, and most always congregate together on mining ground that has previously been worked by the Americans, and abandoned as no longer worth the labor of white men. These foreigners accustomed to receive the smallest pittance at home for their services, are more than repaid by the gleanings from the well worked fields left by their masters, the white race. They possess no enterprize—stick to one place without thought of exploring new and untried spots as long as a shining particle of the precious metal remains to reward them. In this way they rarely interfere with the Americans, and therefore pursue their eager search unmolested. Anything that escapes their keen vision and painfully laborious assiduity is hardly worth having. A place abandoned by them may indeed be pronounced exhausted.

Which indicates that a mere dog-in-the-manger attitude engendered by race hatred was responsible for the beat of war-drums by the opposition.

These aliens did not even rub elbows with their white brethren of the hill country. Their camps were always apart from town. They were mild, inoffensive and docile to a provocative point. They became the target of abuse, very much as a cringing dog sometimes does when he wags his tail in the face of brutality. A California tramp of the fifties records that he "heard an apparently fair man say that once when out of funds in the mining regions, he sat on the roadside waiting for a Chinaman to come along that he might rob him! He thought no more of it than knocking over a jackrabbit to satisfy his hunger." Which would mean little or nothing if the chronicler had not used the word "fair" in

LOOKING ACROSS PORTSMOUTH SQUARE

describing the thief. The man was not a criminal, he would never have thought of robbing his own kind, but a Chinaman to him was a biped only by virtue of a jest of nature which had provided him with two legs.

On another occasion a miner recorded in his diary that as Christmas was approaching and he lacked money, he robbed a Chinaman, so that he might properly observe the festival of peace on earth goodwill to men!

The tax collectors hunted Chinamen down, abused and fleeced them without compunction. If their victims could not put immediate hands upon a tax receipt they made them pay again. If any member of a group of Chinese was approached for taxes and lacked money to pay, the minions of the law demanded that his companions produce the money. If they refused, their pig-tails were tied together and they were beaten into submission.

This tying together of pig-tails to prevent the escape of Chinese was one of the pleasant outdoor sports of tax collectors and ruffians of early days. Without any particular check on these tax men it is fair to assume that a goodly proportion of gold dust collected was diverted into their own pockets. Indeed, many county treasurers commented sourly on the fact that comparatively so little money from this source found its way into public coffers. But, even then, the yield was astounding for those days, and, there came a time when, aside from capitalists and evangelical ministers, the Chinaman's only friends were the county treasurers.

But it must be admitted that the way of the tax collector, either upright or dishonest, was not easy. At the merest rustle of leaves kicked up by their approach the Chinamen fled like rabbits. They might have been American millionaires, so diligent were they in attempted tax evasions. It became the habit to go after them in the still watches of the night and drag them, stolidly protesting, from their bunks. This

San Francisco's Chinatown

method is admirably suggested by a note in a tax collector's diary of 1855:

> Mon. July 30th. Went up the River to Hesse's . . . bothered about there all day . . . hunted Chinamen in the night . . . done very well . . . collected about 80 licenses.

Hunted Chinamen in the night! That phrase presents the whole picture.

Sometimes the tax collector's game took on a note of violence as is evidenced by these entries in notebooks of other tax collectors:

> I was sorry to have to stab the poor fellow; but the law makes it necessary to collect the tax; and that's where I get my profit.

> He was running away, and I shot to stop him.

> I took all the dust the rascal had.

The Christmas spirit is again to the fore in this confession by a fake tax collector:

> I had no money to keep Christmas with so sold the Chinks nine dollars worth of bogus receipts.

When the tax collectors gave the hapless Chinamen a brief respite, the thieves and gangsters got busy. These adroit gentlemen were even better at tying queues together than their brethren of the law and they had subtle ways of making their yellow brethren disgorge gold dust. Chinamen were beaten, robbed, and outraged without recourse to law. That is, they could have had the culprits arrested but it always proved an empty gesture. In keeping with negroes and Indians they were not allowed to testify. The pretext for this was that Chinamen finding no significance in the Christian oath, lacked conscience in the matter of perjury. One

50

of the most profitable rackets of the period was to sell a mining claim to a group of Chinamen, let them work it for a few weeks and then descend and wrest it from them.

Even the despised digger Indians took a fling at John Chinaman. Seeing white men pose as tax collectors they learned to put over the same trick.

The Mexicans, too, were scornful of the Chinese and browbeat them at every opportunity. Joaquin Murietta, the most notorious Mexican bandit of the fifties, one day came upon six Chinamen. They had no money and were in nowise offending him. He cut the throats of all six in a spirit of clean, honest fun.

A few weeks after the initial mass meeting at Columbia, the miners of El Dorado County turned back all stages carrying Chinese passengers and freight while the white inhabitants of Weber Creek burned the tents, merchandise and mining equipment of many Chinese in the district.

One mining community after another not only passed general resolutions condemning the Chinese but in many cases posted notices ordering them out of the district. The following notice posted in Mariposa and other towns in the Agua Fria Creek district in 1856 is typical:

> Notice is hereby given to all Chinese on the Agua Fria and its tributaries, to leave within ten days, from this date, and any failing to comply shall be subjected to thirty-nine lashes, and moved by the force of arms.

The Mariposa *Gazette,* in commenting upon it, observed blandly that to carry weight the notice should have been signed so that "John" might be apprised just why and by whom he was to be whipped. But some of the Chinese did not take the order so lightly—they fled before the ten days were up. Those who remained, secure in the idea that an unsigned notice lacked authority, were promptly beaten after being forced into the open by the ever efficient device of setting fire to their cabins.

Some of the communities were a little more concerned with justice and ethics than those along Agua Fria Creek. At Vallecito, for instance, such Chinese as owned mining claims were exempted from the ten-day order and given ninety days in which to sell out and leave. But it was perhaps less of a nuisance to get legal possession of a claim at a forced sale which yielded its luckless owner a pittance, then to go to the physical annoyance of beating it out of him.

The first movements toward expulsion were directed against Chinese working mining claims, later on they spread to merchants and laborers in the towns themselves. Two years after the notice had been posted in Mariposa warning Chinese off claims in the Agua Fria Creek district, that town itself took steps to be rid of their presence. Under the pretext that the Chinese quarter was a fire hazard they forced property owners not to rent or renew leases to Chinamen. The contention was that Chinese used fires in open pans instead of stoves for their cooking, that they shot off firecrackers on their feast days, and that they were continually burning punk sticks before their gods.

Town meetings, miners' conventions, labor assemblies, legislative bodies tore the dictionary apart in an attempt to make the simplest statements about the Chinese menace impressive. The public were bombarded by alliterative and redundant resolutions whose real content was drowned in a heavy sea of words. A minority report by a committee on Mines and Mining interests exploded this turgid bomb in the face of a defenseless public:

RESOLVED: That their presence here is a great moral and social evil —a disgusting scab upon the fair face of society—a putrefying sore upon the body politic—in short, a nuisance.

Discord

By what formidable and circuitous routes did our fathers arrive at the most simple conclusions! . . . *In short—a nuisance.* Here is the gist of their argument all but smothered under the barrage of fireworks which preceded it.

Restive as the late fifties were in respect to the presence of Chinese in the mining regions, it remained for the Shasta region to stage the first really serious disturbance. Heretofore, the authorities had been for the most part passive. District conventions met, orders to vacate claims were posted, the Chinese left and that was an end of it. To be sure the county tax collectors grumbled but there were few clashes between vigilante committees and enforcers of the law.

Early in 1859 movements were begun to call a county convention of miners in Shasta county for the "purpose of devising the best means of ridding themselves of the presence of moon-eyed sons of the Orient." The best means proved to be the tried and true means of terrorism and force. In March a gang of a hundred or more miners in the vicinity of Horsetown rounded up all the Chinese and proceded to escort them beyond the borders of the district. The sheriff with a posse of men, awaited this wholesale kidnapping party at Townsend Flat. The rioters, hearing of the sheriff's move, changed their course. They headed for the town of Shasta, collecting all the Chinese in Oregon Gulch, Middletown and way stations. But the sheriff caught up with them and retrieved some seventy-five hapless Chinamen. The situation grew so serious that Governor Weller was obliged to act. He sent one hundred and seventeen guns and ammunition by river boat as far as Stockton, and enlisted the aid of the sheriff of that city to assist the Shasta authorities in restoring order. This outburst was serious enough to have been referred to as the War in Shasta County.

Evidence of these riotous days is marked by a location in the Shasta region that still bears the name of Igo. The invariable retort of Chinese miners ordered to quit the territory was, "I go!" Hence the designation.

But while disorder and violence were operating in the mining regions, what of conditions in San Francisco the gateway to the "golden mountains" where opportunity and strife went hand in hand? . . . If we can trust to the daily press of those days, conditions were extraordinarily peaceful. Here and there a minor disturbance took place which had little significance. For instance, when the city celebrated the completion of the Atlantic Telegraph with an inevitable parade the usual Chinese contingent was conspicuous by its absence. Inquiry revealed that on a previous fête-day dirty water thrown upon their embroidered robes had ruined them to the tune of several thousand dollars. This came as near being a public display of opposition as developed in the decade which followed the landing of the first Chinese.

But notes of apprehension were being sounded, editorially and otherwise, by newspapers that had once been distinctly cordial to the idea of Chinese immigration. The first mild note of opposition was struck by the *Alta California* at the end of this inconspicuous news item in its issue of February 16, 1854:

CHINESE.—We have recently received a fresh immigration of this singular people. Within the past week about eight hundred of them have arrived, and may be seen on the wharves or carting their "plunder" on drays to the different Chinese headquarters. If the city continues to fill up with these people, it will ere long become necessary to make them the subjects of special legislation.

This is mild enough in all conscience but it is the opening wedge in a change of policy. For do not forget that this is the same paper that only two years before had said: "These celestials make excellent citizens and we are pleased to notice their daily arrival in large numbers."

Discord

By the end of summer the change of policy is complete and the editorial columns are filled with such observations as, "More Chinese pour in. Steps should be taken to force them to regard sanitation." Or, "The domiciles of this singular race are filthy beyond description. . . . San Francisco will not be exempted from the scourge visiting Atlantic cities. Health inspectors should be appointed for Chinese." Again the editor refers to the situation as "appalling," following the arrival of twelve thousand Chinese in less than a week. He is fearful that soon the majority of citizens in the town will be Chinese—"a consummation not devoutly to be wished."

The fantastic guest was no longer diverting or amusing. He was beginning to be something of a nuisance. He was deserting the guest room more and more and spilling his person and his trappings over the whole house. In fact, the host and his family were in danger of being crowded out of their own bailiwick.

In the smaller communities, where the Chinese Quarter invariably was a huddle of huts on the fringe of the town, its presence was not particularly irritating. But in San Francisco the first arrivals had settled themselves in the heart of the city—around the old Plaza. A dozen, a hundred, even a thousand alien souls may merely serve to leaven the lump of provincialism which, after all, is merely the less flattering term for nationalism. But tens of thousands dropped into the mixture are on their way to become the lump itself.

When these editorial protests began to be circulated, the city of San Francisco consisted for the most part of unadorned two-story brick buildings and wooden shacks climbing from the water's edge to the top of the first outpost of hills to the west. It was not much of a city in terms of beauty or grace but it was all the city there was. It had a strange fascination and its citizens loved it. It had a pattern unusual, bizarre, fantastic, and, at first, the threads of the Orient weaving through it added another note of charm. On the flat ground at the foot of the hill were the marts of trade; close by but aloof, by reason of the sharp upward thrust, were the homes of the merchants.

From Stockton street, westward, these homes climbed the hill, up Clay, up Washington, up Jackson streets. There were resident districts to the north and south, to be sure, but these took on a more suburban air—the concentrated city still crowded itself more or less between the points mentioned above. It happened, also, that this eastern slope of what later became known as Nob Hill, was climatically one of the mildest in San Francisco. The brisk summer fogs and winds assaulting the hill's battlements arrived on the other side in more or less breathless condition, their vigor spent. This was the section which the Chinese finally took for their own and a commentator on the fact of their presence there once said:

The advance guard of the Mongolian army saw that the location was good, and they advanced upon and captured it. Its capture was but a work of form for civilization retreats instinctively from contact with the race [Chinese] with the same feeling of horror that the fair and innocent maiden would exhibit in shrinking from the proffered embrace of an unclean leper.

The first charge is, of course, sheer nonsense. The Chinese settled where they did at the beginning because it was the established center of the town and because their presence was tolerated where it was not cordially welcomed. Any concentrated effort to shift them to another location at the beginning would doubtless have been successful. Indeed they would have had no alternative in the face of public opinion. But the entire statement is interesting more as an attitude of mind than because of its fact or fancy. "Civilization" to the author spells America, or, at least, the Nordic fringe of culture. He is apparently ignorant or heedless of six thousand Chinese years of established order. He did not know or he had forgotten the trite comparison to the effect that his forebears were living in caves and covering their bodies with bear hides at the time when the Chinese were building pavilions of lacquer and gold and clothing themselves in garments of satin and silk. He might not have liked the brand of civilization which the Chinese had evolved, he might have considered it dying or decayed, but by inference to have denied its existence is an extraordinary feat of prejudice and ignorance.

He was right in saying that the younger civilization withdrew and left the field to the conqueror. Youth is notoriously intolerant and always conventional. As the Chinese settled down and began to establish their household gods the Caucasian took flight. The younger civilization did not like the smells from Chinese food shops, or the crashing cymbals from the newly established Chinese Theatre, or the squeaking fiddles which were being played in the gambling clubs. They found great fault with the Chinese Daughters of Joy weighted down with gauds and elaborate headdresses. The Chinese games of chance seemed puerile and ridiculous, their religion a thing of empty symbols, their immoralities too tinged with fatalism. For the most part, the quarrel was about differences on the surface of things. But it is always so. We may pretend to be shocked by deeper variations but a passionate believer can more readily suffer a blasphemer for a neighbor than one who uses his backyard for a garbage heap.

San Francisco of the fifties was all but submerged in Caucasian forms of gambling and prostitution and lewdness but while all these things were deprecated by the pious they were operated in terms which they understood.

San Francisco's Chinatown

If the opposition had said quite frankly: "We don't like your smells, we don't like your fiddling, we don't like the odor of your punk or the sound of your firecrackers," that would have been fine. But they covered the superficiality of their reactions under a cloak of high moral indignation and alleged racial superiority.

Just how superior our forefathers felt may be gleaned from their public expressions. Let us glance first at an editorial in the *Alta California* of June 4, 1853. This was printed as a comment on the action of the State of Illinois in barring free negroes from its boundaries. It began by stating that the Chinese had "most of the vices and few of the virtues of the negro," then went on to say that every reason urged against the blacks in Illinois could be urged equally against the Chinese in California. It declared the Chinese "more clannish therefore more dangerous than the negro, more cunning and deceitful, *and less fitted to become menials or servants.*" That they *"were not so provident as negroes,* were more offensive in their habits, and *were mentally inferior to whites."* All three of the charges set down in italics will bring a smile to any present-day Californian even if he be hopelessly biased.

The report of a Committee on Mines and Mining Interests in that same year yielded this flag-waving gem:

The superior energy of the Caucasian will always conquer the sullen industry of the Mongol, and the latter can never, either in the struggle of commerce or arms, compete successfully with the former. And of all the Caucasian tribes, the American, last in formation, but destined, undoubtedly, to be the most perfect in its development, fears least to meet other races.

And another newspaper commenting on the need for restrictive Chinese legislation quotes from the Honorable

58

Discord

Mr. Meade, of Virginia (God bless him), whose faith in the white race was admirably couched in the fine, tolerant spirit of "Ole Virginny":

The European white man will make slaves of, not only the African, but every other race with whom he comes in contact. He is by nature superior to all other races, and he will make all others serve him. There are various modes of doing this; legal enactments are only one. In one way or another the fact will be accomplished. Wherever the white man constitutes one tythe of the population, it will make hewers of wood and drawers of water of the rest. In other words they will be practically slaves, if not by law.

The following opening to an article on the Chinese, in another newspaper, gives a splendid picture of how a robust and godly generation of Anglo-Saxons look down upon an inferior race that even the dogs in their infinite discernment despise:

The Chinese districts of this city, redolent with dried fish, and all the various, and, to us, nameless articles of food and merchandise for traffic which are seen in their houses, are illy calculated to give to an "outside barbarian" any great degree of admiration for them or their mode of life. The Chinaman, too, rank and fishy as he smells, dressed in uncouth habiliments, with pendant que, and close fitting skull cap, is an object of ridicule on all hands, not only with Young America, but with the more dignified of mankind, who have attained the age of reflection and discretion. Intuitively the dogs seem eager to vent their dislike upon the Chinamen, by rushing out upon every occasion and seizing them by their loosely flowing bag breeches, the generous dimensions of which, fortunately in these instances, not unfrequently proving of great protection to John's legs, which, otherwise, would be mangled and torn by the fangs of these canine quadrupeds. Their mode of life, their clannish habits, strange customs, and heathenish religious ceremonies, all cause them to be looked upon by the Anglo-Saxon race as scarcely a degree removed from the brute.

59

San Francisco's Chinatown

Even that alleged towering mountain of intellect, Horace Greeley, although he is fair enough in many particulars, writing back to the Atlantic states insists that "John Chinaman . . . is thoroughly sensual, intent on the fullest gratification of his carnal appetite, and on nothing else," eating and drinking "as much as he can hold."

This sensual gratification seems for the most part according to Mr. Greeley to have been his capacity to "gorge rice" which surely is a very economical and rather chaste form of sensuality. But in one thing are Mr. Greeley's findings unique. He charges John with being an "habitual rum drinker," a vice that even the Chinaman's worst critics in a later and more inflamed day, never discovered.

Another gentleman, writing into the papers, declared that Americans were born masters, and, since masters must have servants it behooved the Legislature to pass a law designed to make all Chinese servants. This suggestion ended up with the gratifying observation that Americans "never served aught but God, and Him in their own way." Evidently a creature called Mammon was not known in the hell-raising fifties.

But occasionally, the charge against these alien brethren rose above trivialities. The American never understood, never can hope to understand, the indifference of the Oriental to sickness and death. When a vessel named the *Libertad* came into port with several of its Chinese passengers mortally ill, San Francisco was righteously shocked at the refusal of the dying men's countrymen to lift a hand in their behalf. The wretches stretched themselves out upon the landing dock and yielded up the ghost while their companions busied themselves with matters of evading customs and kindred details. Those who died were given the attention of proper burial against the day that their bones would be scraped clean and sent back to China but the ailing were abandoned to the care of white men. Several of them were taken to public hospitals where they died almost instantly.

And, later, the body of an Oriental Daughter of Joy was found dead under the floor of the bagnio where she had been held as a slave. Ah Yee, the madam of the house, admitted quite readily that she knew of the girl's death. She had whipped her for stealing some money from an American patron, whereupon the little minx had grown sick and died. Ah Yee could not understand what the fuss was all about. But she was held for accessory to the fact of murder, nevertheless, though there is no record that she was ever convicted. Life and death to these fatalists were mere matters of natural routine. One conceivably took steps to check a disease but when the victim was known to be marked for the grave, there was no sense in useless pother. There was an element of Spartan dignity in this attitude. Instead of senselessly trying to withold those whom the gods have called it was far better to busy oneself with a proper preparation for their long sleep, rather than waste time on expediencies and ministrations that had lost power to stay the inevitable.

There were even instances where not only was care denied the mortally sick but where they were turned out into the streets. This was said to have been the result of a superstition that it was bad luck to let a stranger die in one's house. But the other reason advanced seems to have been more practical and therefore more to the point: If a man died in another's house, his host was liable for the funeral expenses. If he failed in this obligation the spirit of the dead would haunt his house.

It will not be necessary to quote the expressions of self-righteous wrath which such instances called forth from a people who, if they did not turn strangers out to die, were never hesitant about stringing them up to the most convenient tree or lamp-post when the spirit moved them. Their

San Francisco's Chinatown

horror and indignation were genuine enough but unleavened by the slightest desire to get at the root of such racial practices. It was all very well for the citizens of an opulent land to sit in judgment on such apparent inhumanity. But a people inured to centuries of living on the verge of famine and starvation could not be too squeamish about the manner in which they conserved vital sparks of life at the expense of the doomed. The cry of "women and children first" which is rooted in western civilization has its sources not in chivalry but in an impulse toward race conservation.

The pioneers did not turn men out to die for fear of wasting upon a futility the substance belonging to their flesh and blood but they had their own forms of cruel expediencies. The annals of those who crossed plains and climbed mountains in pursuit of fortune were filled with instances of weaklings left to perish in their tracks lest they endanger the lives of the fit by this menace of halts and delays. Every condition of life—every civilization has had at one time or another, to make such decisions. It is the form and not the substance of these impulses toward the survival of the fittest which varies.

But however callous these aliens seemed to our fathers in the matters of the flesh, no one could gainsay their scrupulous attention to things of the spirit once the life-spark had fled. The concern of the Chinese for a fitting and adequate disposal of a dead body is proverbial. The living are often filled with a secret apprehension that they will not be provided with a suitable resting-place and nothing is more acceptable than the gift of a coffin. A son will soften the blow of impending death with the present to his ailing father of a coffin. To hardened Christians the funeral forms and symbols of the Chinese are empty tinklings—the funeral baked meats, the exploding firecrackers, the strips of red paper scattered before the hearse, signify nothing.

Discord

Without slighting the influence of Confucius or Lao-tze or Buddha upon the religious pattern of Chinese life the motivating force in conduct and the hope of a peaceful immortality lies in a belief in spirits—good spirits, evil spirits, the spirits of the dead. Charles Walcott Brooks, a distinguished scholar and traveler, summed up the matter simply and briefly when he wrote:

The Chinese religion, as I understand it, is very much like what might be called pure spiritualism. It is very much like modern spiritualism. I am not speaking of the Buddhists, but of the religion of the masses of China. Their religion is called Fung Shuy, to a great extent. Fung means wind and Shuy means water.

It is open to argument whether the masses of our own people are not similarly minded. It is not such a far cry to the weird sisters who shoved Macbeth forward to his doom, or to the ghost of Banquo at the feast, or to the pale wraiths of murdered chieftains and kings which passed in review before the one-time Thane of Cawdor. And, even now, through varying forms of Christian dogma run the fallen Lucifer and his devilish cohorts in conflict with guardian angels and patron saints, forces of good and evil to be routed and implored as necessity stands. All of which is neither here nor there, except to point out that it does not behoove a man to sneer too openly at the symbols of another unless he is sure that they are not his very own in strange guise.

But the pioneers were very sure that there was no vestige of any belief at all in the outlandish incantations of their yellow-skinned comrades, much less that they contained certain fundamentals that might easily be translated into Christian terms. The first deaths which occurred among the Chinese in San Francisco were deaths of obscure coolies and the funeral rites were simple, confined to the beating of gongs, the firing of a few strings of crackers, and the scattering of fluttering bits of red paper as the hearse and carriages dragged their way over the sand dunes to the dead man's temporary resting place. But, presently, there came a time when one of the wealthy merchants of the quarter died and the residents of the town were treated to a Chinese funeral in the grand manner.

They saw the corpse carried out of the house in the warm sunshine of noon and placed upon a platform covered with a barbaric canopy. They saw the freshly roasted pigs grouped at the foot of the bier, the cakes, the sweetmeats, the pots of tea, the jugs of wine. They saw candles of soft grease, dyed a deep vermilion carved with fantastic symbols, smoking and sending up pale flames in the glare of midday. They saw great paper chests of orange, appliqued with mincing human figures in faint pink and blue, with gold butterflies, with green dragons. They saw dolls of paper, paper clothing, representations in paper of the deceased's most treasured possessions, a huge brown paper purse filled with paper "money" purchased from the priests of the temple. They heard the crash of gongs, the strident voice of the piccolo, the wail of the fiddle.

Presently the coffin was lifted into the hearse; the orange-colored chests filled with the dolls, the paper clothing, the paper symbols of the dead man's most treasured possessions, the baked meats, the cakes, the pots of tea, the wine, into a huge wagon. A draped picture of the deceased was carried on the front seat of the hearse, twenty hired mourners, with white bands about their foreheads, followed making the air hideous with their cries and lamentations. The crash of cymbals continued.

The cortège moved forward. Clad in shabby clothes, their feet bare, their heads bowed down, walked the sons of the deceased supported by canes and two friends on either side.

INTERNATIONAL CAFÉ, MOW FONG COMPANY

Discord

From the huge brown-paper purse came innumerable flutterings of red paper as the procession made its way through the
narrow streets of the town and across the wind-swept sand
dunes.

At the grave a rude table was set up and piled with the
roast pigs and other delicacies; the wine and tea were poured
out on the ground, the paper dolls, the paper clothing, the
paper treasures were tossed into the flames of a stone furnace.
Incense was burned, more candles fluttered in the afternoon
breeze.

What was all this about? asked our grandfathers. The
incense, the candles they understood. But did they really?
Could one man in a thousand have told just what the burning of incense and candles meant in terms of Christian worship? But at all events, here were customs which were outwardly familiar, at least. But the scattering of red paper
squares from the brown purse, the crackling of fireworks,
the burning of paper effigies, the pouring of tea and wine
upon the ground, the roast pig, the sweetmeats—what of
these?

To the coolies they were very real devices evoked to
placate evil spirits and to enlist the help of spirits with more
amiable proclivities. To the educated Chinese they were
doubtless merely the empty forms of custom which hold the
high and low of every land in thrall. The high and low in
Christendom still burn the Yule log and decorate trees at
Christmas, or dye eggs at Easter, or peer into wishing wells
on Hallowe'en without troubling overmuch about the pagan
origins of these rites. The red strips from the brown paper
purse were known as "road money" and were thrown out
to placate bad spirits. The clash of gongs and the explosions
of fireworks were to frighten off the evil spirits who were
not beguiled by conciliating symbols. The paper dolls represented servants who were to accompany and minister to

the dead spirit in the hereafter, the paper clothing, the paper representation of the deceased's treasures were equally for the spirit's comfort and delight. They were cast into the furnace and burned that they might be translated by flame from material into spiritual possessions. The wine and tea were poured out upon the ground for thirsty spirits, the roast pig and sweetmeats for spirits that were hungry.

Marco Polo mentions on more than one occasion when he visited China in the thirteenth century this burning of symbols to provide the dead with comforts in the after life. In Mongolia, he came upon a funeral where they had painted upon paper the figures of men, women, horses, camels, pieces of money and even dresses. These were burned so that the dead man could enjoy servants, clothing and transportation in the spirit world. Again in the city of Kin-Sai he found the same custom.

When the great Khans who were then ruling China, died, this custom of providing them with servants took a more realistic and bloody turn. The tombs of these mighty lords were on top a certain high mountain. No matter where they died, they were conveyed thither for burial. An escort of warriors went before the funeral cortège to slay any and every person they met on the way. As they accomplished the deed they said: "Depart from this life and attend your dead Emperor in the next world." Many of the Khan's finest horses were likewise slain for his spiritual joy and comfort.

Here are ceremonies that go back to the very threshold of civilization. The wonder, of course, is that they have been preserved with so much fidelity. But the genius and the weakness of the Chinese is this capacity for holding fast, not only to that which is quick but to that which is dead.

That these ceremonies have no relation to the higher forms of Chinese religious life—to Confucianism, to Taoism, to Buddhism—goes without saying but they are survivals from a primitive past, grafted upon more profound revelations, as is the Yule log, the Christmas tree, the Easter egg and the wishing well. Doubtless every Chinese—except the simplest coolie—realizes that a spirit had no need of food and drink or servants or treasure or clothing. For above everything else the Chinese are a logical people. In the final analysis these things become merely symbols of the regard and solicitude the mourners feel for their dead, as our floral offerings express our love.

In those early San Francisco days the responsibility of the living to the dead was not ended with burial. In all contracts the Chinese signed with relation to their passage money or their labors were clauses touching the matter of eventualities in case of death. The great passion of every Chinaman, from the wealthiest merchant to the humblest coolie, was to have his bones returned to the tomb of his ancestors. This was something more than a sentimental or patriotic gesture and was actuated by a desire to prevent loosing a link in the spirit chain. The living were under the protection of the spirits of their dead ancestors but it was necessary to bury the bodies in long rows, father by the side of son, *ad infinitum,* to get the best results. An unbroken line of bodies in this sequence meant an unbroken line of spirit protection.

There was a Chinaman in San Francisco named Shoy Chew who was reputed to have had a hundred and eighty-seven ancestors buried in a line in the proper sequence. He was blessed among men for he received the protection of the entire hundred and eighty-seven spirits. With this belief it would be tragic to be lost at sea or allowed to rest in an alien tomb. For in addition, these lost spirits are restless spirits.

This belief must be a very ancient one, for the Old Testament is replete with instances of patriarchs from Abraham down the line having been buried with the bones of their fathers. But it has remained for China through all its centuries of civilization to bring the custom down almost unscathed to modern times.

When a Chinaman died in California it behooved the association to which the dead man belonged to see that his bones were shipped home. If he belonged to no association and died penniless the wealthy merchants subscribed to a fund to give his body the proper attention. The Five Companies, which was what its name implied, an alliance of five district benefit associations, had representatives who traveled over the entire State checking up deaths, making calculations for decomposition, gathering up the relics of their late members. It was said that the body of a Chinaman decomposed very quickly—after five months nothing remained but dust and bones.

The procedure in such instances was very meticulous. The first thing to be removed from the coffin was the longest bone. This was measured and a box was made of proper length, two feet wide. Each bone was then dipped in a bucket of brandy and water and polished with a stiff brush until it shone. The polishers were careful never to touch the bones but handled them with great dexterity with two sticks. Great care was taken to see that no bones were missing. At first, of course, the business of collecting the bones of dead Chinese was a small enterprise but as their ranks increased as many as twelve hundred a year were exhumed and shipped to the land of their fathers.

Toward the close of the fifties, it was estimated that at least ten thousand bodies had been shipped home. These were the bodies of adult males. No such care were taken of the bones of females. Ancestor worship meant father worship, therefore there was really no point in adding female bones in proper sequence for the family's spirit protection. The Jesuits found this reverence for the head of the household

精製脫味

茂

利

加

瓤

油

承

接

金

豬

SHOP WINDOW, COMMERCIAL STREET
AND GRANT AVENUE

so strong that they concluded it was best to permit ancestor worship among their converts to Christianity. But the quarrels with other Christian sects in China who objected to any such compromise caused the Jesuits to be expelled from their mission houses.

For the most part the bodies of women and children received scant ceremony when they were buried. But, occasionally, a woman of quality was made an exception to this general rule. In 1859 Wee Lan was given a very elaborate funeral. Doubtless she was the first Chinese woman to die in San Francisco. She was reputed to have been a member of one of the first families in the interior of China. The story runs that she went one day on a visit to some relatives in Canton, was kidnapped, shipped to San Francisco and sold into a life of prostitution. She was only twenty when she died.

But in these fabulous fifties it was not only the dead who returned by the thousands to their native land. Every boat that sailed bore an increasing number who returned to the land of their fathers to live in ease and luxury to the end of their days. On one day in January toward the close of the decade, three hundred were reported as sailing on the good ship *Atmosphere* for their homeland. Each man carried a fortune in gold and the tinsmiths of the town were swamped with work making boxes to hold the treasure.

The reports of this exodus in the papers with full details of the golden treasure which had been ravished from the hills of California, caused a renewed outburst of editorial wrath directed against these people who "added nothing to the wealth of California but, on the other hand, robbed her legitimate children of their heritage." That these "legitimate children" were Nordics with a strong dash of Celt goes without saying.

Chapter IV

RAILROAD BUILDING

THERE are several misconceptions concerning the source of the movement against Chinese immigration in the State of California. First and foremost is the idea firmly rooted in the minds of San Franciscans that the employment of Chinese in the building of the Central Pacific Railroad provided the spark for this opposition. It may have provided additional fuel but anyone with a knowledge of the riots and disorders of the fifties must be convinced that the antagonism began at a much earlier date and was primarily a result of racial antipathy. This was aided and abetted by an intuitive feeling that however expedient Chinese labor might be at the beginning, in the end, it would take its toll in lower standards of living.

The construction of the railroad was not begun until 1863 and it was a year and a half after that before the first Chinese were employed. Yet as early as January, 1862, Governor Le-

Railroad Building

land Stanford, in a message to the Legislature had this to say of the Chinese situation: "Asia with her numberless millions sends to our shores the dregs of her population. There can be no doubt that the presence of numbers of that degraded and distinct people will exercise a deleterious influence upon the superior race."

This is an instance of the way indiscreet statements by politicians rise up in later years to plague them: Governor Stanford was one of the Big Four who built the Central Pacific Railroad. He was therefore a party to adding materially to "the presence of numbers of that degraded and distinct people" which in 1862 he was so sure would "exercise a deleterious influence upon the superior race" to which he belonged. . . . It was said that when he was prodded unduly about this change of face he was inclined to place the blame for the hiring of Chinese upon the shoulders of his partner Charles Crocker. Mr. Crocker, never having made any public statements for or against Chinese prior to breaking ground for their enterprise, and never having been a candidate for office, was quite ready to take the blame.

As stated, construction of the Central Pacific began in 1863. Necessarily the first work was preliminary and there was an adequate supply of Irish and Mexican labor to carry it forward. These were the years when every boat from the British Isles landed in New York had a steerage filled with husky young Irishmen ready to put their hands to whatever came their way. Shoveling dirt at day wages was attaining the first rung on the ladder which led upward to the police force, to seats on boards of Aldermen, to mayorships and governorships and other high pinnacles which another decade was to achieve for them.

As the time passed the need for man power grew. On January 7, 1865, there appeared in the Sacramento *Union* the following notice:

San Francisco's Chinatown

WANTED, 5000 laborers for constant and permanent work, also experienced foremen. Apply to J. H. Strobridge, *Superintendent,* on work near Auburn.

Now five thousand white laborers, in a country sparsely settled was something that could not be conjured out of hand. It is doubtful if five thousand yellow laborers or half that many would have materialized at once had the notice named them for the jobs. It takes time for word to fly from California to China that a new enterprise is pressed for workers. And even after the word has flown, it takes time for vessels to load and plough through the water with human freight. But it would have taken no longer for such word to fly to Ireland. Which brings us to the point that in any case there would have been delays in mustering a full force. Mr. Crocker with an eye to getting as many workers as possible, hinted to his superintendent that it might be well to hire some Chinese. Mr. Strobridge was lukewarm to the suggestion. Then the inevitable happened.

Some of the Irish laborers were filled with that divine discontent of which orators prate and poets sing but which men of affairs find extremely irritating when exercised out of their own personal spheres. In short, the Irishmen began to grumble about their wages. They went even further—they sent a committee to the superintendent to ask for an increase. That settled it! Mr. Crocker's hint became a command. He ordered Strobridge, to quote his own words, "to go over to Auburn to get Chinese."

In spite of the Irishmen's protests which soon fell to the level of pleadings, a crew of fifty Chinese was hired. They did so well that fifty more were added. . . . In the end, between ten thousand and twelve thousand were employed before the railroad was finished.

Railroad Building

Meanwhile, the pother that was raised throughout the State, for the moment, clearly defined the battle as between the Chinese and the Irish. However steadily growing and effective opposition among other factions developed, it was the Irish element that translated rancour into action. There could have been no greater contrast in psychology and temper than the contrast between the Irish and the Chinese—the one fiery, impatient and rebellious under restraints and adversity—the other, calm, plodding, bending neck to yoke. Furthermore, they were fated to meet on common battleground—in pick and shovel gangs, in mines, as domestic servants.

Mr. Crocker's excuse, if his self-satisfied testimony could be rated so humbly, was to the effect, that, aside from any other consideration, enough whites could not be recruited to speed up construction. Certainly not enough whites could be obtained at the wages offered. In support of which the record of workers in the latter years of construction averaged a thousand whites to nine thousand Chinese. Whether the enterprise could have withstood what in these non-conformist labor days is called "a living wage" must be left to the economists. There were others who insisted that the work was too hard for white men—a singular confession to come from a frontier people who were continually seeking more wildernesses to subdue.

To those who pointed out to Mr. Crocker that he was sowing dragon teeth that one day would spring up and devour American civilization Mr. Crocker replied with irritating calmness: "I know when I was a boy I assisted in riots in the city of Troy, New York, when the Irish immigration was coming into the country. This same hue and cry was raised against them. It was said they were going to overrun the country and the people were mobbing them."

When faced with the charge that after railroad construction was over the country would have a serious unemployment situation to deal with, Mr. Crocker retorted in effect: "Not at all. Supply and demand will settle the question. Even now, the Chinese go home when work is scarce."

But, with all the undercurrent of opposition to Chinese labor on railroad construction, it is surprising that there is very little record of any riots or clashes between factions. Either the wilderness swallowed up the record of such disturbances or the railroad management was expert at concealing them. One riot, at least, became front page stuff but this had for its battle-ground the streets of a city. When Chinese were hired to do grading on railroad property in San Francisco, a band of Irishmen set upon them, gave them a beating and burned down their shacks. Ten white workmen were arrested, convicted, fined five hundred dollars and given ninety days in the county jail. This served to cool the ardor of the opposition and no further violence was reported.

All in all, the sixties while providing fuel for a smouldering blaze did not see a vast amount of open conflagration. The mining boom had dwindled, or, at least, entered a new phase. Most of the nuggets and grains of gold dust strewn carelessly in forest and stream had long been washed out and the field was for the most part left to capitalists with money enough to sink shafts and build stamp mills and otherwise exploit the hills of California on extensive and intensive scales. The personal clashes of the fifties between rival claim stakers had ceased. A Civil War was in progress and though California was thousands of miles from the scene of action the conflict still presented problems enough to absorb the attention of the politically minded. Work on the railroad was far enough removed from civilization and the direct eye of the public to be merely a tale that was told. True, Chinese by the thousands poured daily into San Francisco, were commented upon adversely by the press, and melted away again. Only the

Railroad Building

Irish workmen grumbled and formed societies for Mongolian exclusion, at the same time passing resolutions favoring an eight-hour day and other whimsical legislation. To a city, in spite of its cosmopolitan aspects, in which the ruling class was still predominately Anglo-Saxon the grievances of the Irish laboring men were not to be taken seriously. Nor the grievances of any labor group for that matter. It was a "rugged American individual" society that suspected any collective attempt to change conditions. It subscribed to the theory that "all men were *created* equal" but it was content to let equality stop right there. At heart it still believed in a ruling class and a serving class. Laborers were for hire at wages offered—not for meetings and protests.

Mr. Crocker's reception of the demands of his Irish workmen for more money was typical of the times. He did not call them in and talk the thing over, he did not trouble himself with the fantastic notion that they might have a legitimate grievance. He merely said to his superintendent: "Go over to Auburn and get some Chinese." In the language of the street, he knew his stuff. The Chinese never struck for more wages, the Chinese never questioned the length of the working day. They were grounded in conformance and obedience. Economic problems did not assail a people who could live on a bowl or two of rice a day.

All through the years that followed, a discussion involving the merits or demerits of Chinese labor always brought forth the triumphant statement from employers, "They never strike for higher wages!" A Congressional report refers to Chinese labor as "cheap and docile" in extenuation of alleged faults. And a gentleman named H. C. Bennett, who was Secretary of the Labor Exchange, tossed off this gem in meeting the charge that one should give some thought to the source of supply rather than to the supply itself: "Is it essential that we use only the purest water to generate steam

75

to give motion to machinery?" The inference is a veiled insult to the Chinese. It means in plain language: "Why not use dirty Chinese labor to turn the wheel?" But Mr. Bennett is nothing if not a philosopher. He dismisses the threat of a lower standard of living with: "The Chinese . . . will teach us how to be better off upon less wages by being more economical in our habits!" Of course Mr. Bennett's "us" is not inclusive. No one ever includes himself in extolling the bright and shining uses of economy. The opposition had its comeback. They pointed out that dirty water had a habit of clogging the boiler pipes and was apt to prove dangerous in the long run.

The Eastern press was also very philosophical about Chinese labor, and the St. Louis *Republican,* for one, unwittingly echoed Mr. Bennett's sentiments by declaring, "If it be an invasion of cheap labor, we should repel it by doing *cheaper* and better work." Which might have been a more practical suggestion on the economical side if the editor had led off with a personal demonstration of how to be cheerful and gay on rice flavored with dried fish sauce three times a day. But it had the same weakness that Mr. Bennett's formula betrayed—it was obviously designed for the other fellow.

But the Chinese it would appear could not only teach us economy, they could likewise teach us manners. Employers of labor were not concerned solely with the Oriental capacity for industry and thrift. After all, there were such things as the amenities of life. Said a fruit grower in a Congressional investigation:

"When I go out to the field the Chinamen bid me good morning in a very polite manner."

Which was met by his cross examiner with this sarcastic retort:

CHINESE PLAYGROUND, WAVERLY PLACE

Railroad Building

"Was that not true of slaves in the South while they were in slavery?"

Even the eminent Mrs. Frank Leslie writing back letters to her famous *Weekly* is constrained to say:

What makes Chinese labor cheap is its excellence and reliability, the absence of a disposition *to strike,* and a quiet and gentler acceptance of the disagreeabilities of labor and poverty which many of our native workmen seem disposed to treat as unwanted hardships, and injustice on the part of their employers.

Not only are the Chinese "cheaper" but they are cheerful about it. There is something well-bred in the acceptance of their hard lot. They may blame Fate, perhaps, even God, but *never* their *employers!*

Meanwhile, in an attempt to equalize matters all sorts of new taxes were devised in the halls of the law makers, directed against the pocket-book of the "cheap and docile" John Chinaman. There were entrance taxes, mining taxes, taxes for permission to fish in the streams, taxes to the right of them, taxes to the left of them. Passed, declared unconstitutional, repealed, passed and repealed again. Caucasian Societies were formed, an anti-Mongolian society called the Knights of St. Crispin began to flourish. The original St. Crispin was beheaded in early Christian days for his faith. He was a shoemaker and became the patron saint of the shoemakers' craft. One of the first trades which the Chinaman began to cut in upon was the shoemaking trade. The Knights of St. Crispin was a shoemaker's trade union.

But in the midst of all these sordid bickerings there was a brief interval of sweetness and light. In the early days of the year 1868 word was wafted across the broad expanse of the Pacific that the Emperor of China was organizing a goodwill Embassy to the Western world. These messengers of cordi-

77

ality and friendliness were to proceed to Europe via the U.S.A., and their first stop, naturally, would be San Francisco. Later there was added confirmation of this fact, and on February 25th the steamer *Costa Rica* left Canton for Yokohama, bearing on board the personnel of a mission that was to set political circles and high society aflutter from San Francisco to Boston. At Yokohama they were transferred to the steamer *China,* en route to America, and the Chinese Embassy became an accomplished fact.

At the head of the Embassy was an American, Anson Burlingame, a gentleman who had been associated with the Chinese Court for several years, having been appointed as Minister to China, by Lincoln, in 1861. In this new adventure he bore the grandiloquent title of "His Excellency the Honorable Anson Burlingame High Minister Plenipotentiary and Envoy Extraordinary from the Court of Pekin." With him was J. McLeary Brown, Esq., First Secretary of Legation; Monsieur De Champs, Second Secretary of Legation; their Excellencies Chi-Ta-jen and Sun-Ta-jen, Ministers of the second rank; six Chinese student interpreters, two of whom knew English, two who knew French and two who knew Russian; two writers; a native doctor and fifteen servants.

This was by far the most colorful and impressive set of visitors that San Francisco ever had had the good fortune to entertain. No wonder, then, that the colonels on the Governor's staff polished up their brass buttons; the Mayor and the city fathers sent their swallow-tails to the tailor to be overhauled and pressed; and the millionaires took their diamond shirt studs out of safe deposit boxes. Whether the females of the species were equally excited is a matter of conjecture. It soon developed that the main event was to be a banquet and for the most part in those benighted days, banquets were for males, with the ladies allowed to creep into the galleries to listen to the oratorical pearls of wisdom which dropped from the lips of their superiors.

The celebration took place in the banquet hall of the Lick Hotel, April 28, 1868. This banquet hall was unique because the owner, James Lick, had designed and executed the woodwork himself. Thrift plus luck had made him many times a millionaire, but he remembered and did honor to the wood-working craft of his youth in this final burst of self-expression. About two hundred and twenty-five guests were on hand, all males, with the galleries reserved for tip-toeing ladies in the most approved manner. Governor Haight was the Chairman. "Among those present" were all the consular representatives; General Halleck of the Army; R. B. Swain, Superintendent of the Mint; R. G. Sneath, president of the Chamber of Commerce; Thomas H. Selby, president of the Merchants' Exchange; judges and chief justices galore and such public-spirited citizens as Newton Booth and W. C. Ralston.

The general news gatherers of the local press, promoted for the moment to positions as society editors, outdid themselves in describing the event. They began by giving the impressive proportions of the banquet hall in precise measurements, even to the eight-foot depth of the gallery. This was followed up by an equally precise description of eleven panels of Pacific Coast scenery, seven feet wide and nine feet high, done in oils by Thomas Hill. They described the tiny flags and bouquets of flowers—"one at each place"—upon the tables, the "delightful odor of roses" which pervaded a room "brilliant with the flashing lights of the chandelier reflected in the large mirrors." They assured their public that the "paintings and flower garlands gave an air of elegance to the walls" and that a quartette of French horns accompanied by a piano produced sounds alliteratively "soft and soothing" which "mingled with the hum of conversation without distracting from it." And in a final burst of proper masculine chivalry and condescension they commented upon the "amiable intrusion into the balconies of a few ladies as spectators in the latter part of the evening." All in all, it seems to have been an affair of perfect gentility and refinement, quite the most *recherché* gathering that the young and gangling city ever had attended.

The speeches were numerous and long, with allusions, veiled and otherwise on the American side, to the hope that China's face would one day be turned toward the true religion. Governor Haight commented in a fleeting phrase on China's "lack of knowledge of the religion of the Bible" as one of the incentives to opening the doors of China, naturally giving "trade" as one of the other stimuli. Even Mr. Burlingame opined that the "occasion" reflected an "enlarged spirit" which, among a score of other things, did not cease to hope with the Christian martyrs of China "that the day would arrive when that great nation would stretch forth its arms toward the shining banners of Christianity."

Mr. Chi-Ta-jen responded for the Emperor of China. He was brief and confined himself to thanks and amiable generalities, quite omitting any hope that Americans would be won to Confucianism. But he took the opportunity of speaking the following words of greeting and admonition to his countrymen:

In conclusion, I would, with permission, say a word to my own countrymen resident in California. Gentlemen, Directors of the Six Companies—I address you, and through you all our fellow countrymen in the State. It has given me great pleasure to meet you in this distant land, and to learn that you are prosperous in your several callings. On leaving Pekin, I was charged by his Majesty, our august Emperor, to assure you of his affectionate interest in your welfare. It is his Majesty's hope that, though living in a distant land, you will ever strive, by your conduct, to uphold the respectability and good name of your native country. To do so, let me urge you not to forget the precepts which have been handed down from age to age by the wise and good men of China. Do not fail to pay due regard to the requirements of the various social relations, and neglect not your moral duties as men. Be careful to obey the laws and regulations of the nation in which you reside. If you do so, and at the same time pursue your callings in accordance with the principles of right and propriety, success cannot fail to attend your labors; while a contrary course will infallibly bring on you failure and misfortune.

I feel confident that you will show yourselves, by your good conduct, worthy of his Majesty's affectionate interest in your welfare, and will not disappoint the good opinions I have been led to form of you.

This model of propriety and good taste in speech-making out of the way, the Americans again had their innings. A letter was read from Mr. Eugene Casserly who did not mention Christianity or the Bible but went refreshingly to the point in the matter of enlarged business opportunities which would flow to the port of San Francisco as a result of the mission.

Mr. Newton Booth of Sacramento, a political figure who some years later was elected Governor of the State on an anti-Chinese platform, had the last word. He responded in a lighter vein to the toast, "Tea: The cup that cheers but not inebriates." He began with a rather bad pun about the difference between tea-cups and hic-cups, gave a brief history of the introduction of tea into Europe, dragged in the Boston Tea Party by the hair of the head and quoted:

> Venus her myrtle has, Phoebus his bays:
> Tea both excels, which she vouchsafes to praise.
> The best of Queens, the best of herbs we owe,
> To that bold nation which the way did show
> To the fair regions where the sun doth rise,
> Whose rich productions we so justly prize.

San Francisco's Chinatown

Proving to his hearers "whatever was King of Commerce" tea was its Queen reigning "by the blessings dispensed to all her loving subjects everywhere."

However pleasant and novel Mr. Booth's discourse was to the Chinese members of the Embassy, they were fated to grow very weary of like dissertations before they quitted American shores. At whatever town, or village or hamlet they were entertained, somewhere on the program was sure to be a toast to "the cup that cheers but not inebriates," couched in identical phraseology.

At the Boston Dinner, no less a person than Ralph Waldo Emerson referred to tea as "the cordial of nations," after which the band rather inappropriately played "Champagne Charlie," and Dr. Oliver Wendell Holmes delivered an original poem, sounding suspiciously like doggerel, which began:

> Open wide, ye gates of gold—
> Till Nevada's breezes fan
> The snowy peaks of Ta Sieue Shan—
> Till Erie blends its waters blue
> With the waves of Tong-Tin-Hu—
> Till deep Missouri lends its flow
> To swell the rushing Hoang-Ho!

But perhaps the most diverting thing that happened to the Embassy was in New York when the redoubtable Susan B. Anthony called on them. She told them in no uncertain terms that the "one thing that the American woman wanted to make her supremely happy was a vote." Whereat one of the Chinese members replied with infuriating lightness, "I thought you were going to say a set of jewels." Which caused an English reporter to observe rather sarcastically, "Of course the ladies of America are above such vanities."

In fact, most of the London press were sarcastic over the

Embassy in general and Mr. Burlingame in particular. They seemed apprehensive that all this "feasting and carousal" in America would give the United States a slight edge in the matter of concessions and privileges. "We are afraid," said the *Pall Mall Gazette,* "that the Americans have already spoiled the Chinese Ambassadors." And it accused Mr. Burlingame of being "carried away by the great American notion that America is in the fore-front and the rest of the world nowhere." Mr. Burlingame said some things about the iniquities of the "dangerous concession doctrine" in treaty ports, which further riled the British newspapers. They granted that this sort of nonsense was "all very well for the American point of view" but they felt that every argument which Mr. Burlingame made for the acceptance of the Chinese proposals by the United States was "an argument for its rejection by Great Britain."

At one of the dinners, Mr. Burlingame was reported to have said that Americans might learn from the Chinese, among other things, "good manners and how to cultivate fish." "These," replied one of the London scribes, "are very useful accomplishments but it is to be hoped that Mr. Burlingame has something stronger to offer as inducements for England to accept the policy of which he is mainly the author."

The British press was not the only dissenting voice with regard to Mr. Burlingame. The workingmen of America were not altogether pleased with Mr. Burlingame's political record—especially those of foreign birth and Roman Catholic persuasions. Nor were those who sympathized with the lost Southern cause enthusiastic, although their influence was for the moment negligible. It was pointed out by the latter that Mr. Burlingame began his political career as a member of the Free Soil Party, which opposed the extension of Slavery into the Territories awaiting the seal of Statehood. It

was this Free Soil Party that elected him to the Massachusetts' Senate in 1853. From there in 1861 he was sent to
Congress under the banner of the "Know Nothing Party."
This was a political organization started in the forties, to
discourage Irish immigration. It soon broadened its field,
stung to action because of criticism of United States laws and
institutions by the adopted sons of the Republic, principally
of Irish and German origin. One of the hopes of this "Know
Nothing Party" was to restrict materially the rights of
citizens of foreign birth. It began as a "secret" organization
and its name was derived from the fact that if any of its
members were quizzed concerning its tenets they replied, "I
know nothing."

Added to the opposition of the foreign-born malcontents
were also the slurs that many Americans threw at Mr. Burlingame's alleged snobbery. It was charged that he had re-
signed from his diplomatic job in the service of his country
to become an attaché of the Foreign Office of China because
he found court life more to his aristocratic taste.

Prior to the coming of the Chinese Embassy under
Mr. Burlingame, the United States had ratified one treaty
with China. This was known as the Reed Treaty and was consummated in 1858. To this treaty was now added features
extending and clarifying it. Among other things it gave China
the right to appoint consuls at American ports who were to
have the same privileges as the consuls of Great Britain and
Russia, provided for religious liberty on both sides, but withheld naturalization.

The élite of the country had been impressed by Mr. Burlingame and his party but the man in the street was either
unconcerned or coldly hostile. Reading accounts of champagne quaffing and the airy persiflage of society leaders and
politicians over the festal board did not make the hearts of
the workers yearn any more mightily toward their yellow

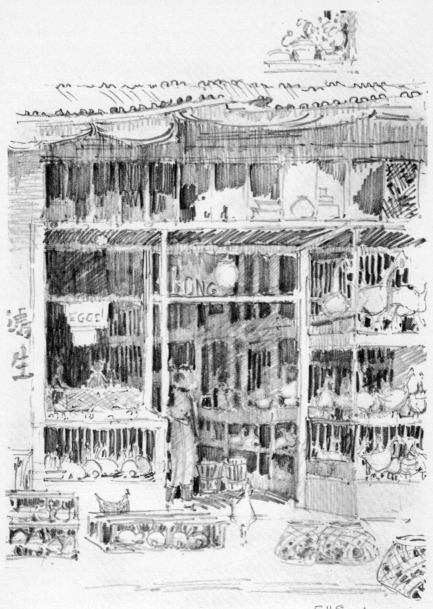

THE POULTRY SHOP

brethren. And, besides, there were portentous rumblings from other quarters. The work on the railroad was nearing completion. Already the people were wondering what was to be the effect of a release of ten thousand coolies into other labor channels. *Would* Mr. Crocker's prophesy come true— *would* the law of supply and demand settle the issue and send the frugal aliens back to their native shores?

The last railroad spike was driven at Promontory, Utah, in May 10, 1869, a subtle note of comedy giving point to the labor drama of the moment. On the Union Pacific side, thrusting westward, the last two rails were laid by Irishmen; on the Central Pacific side, thrusting eastward, the last two rails were laid by Chinese!

Mr. Crocker's prophesies did *not* come true. The record of home-going Chinamen did not rise above normal. Even with knowledge that railroad building was over, two thousand Chinese entered the port of San Francisco in May, 1869. In the ten years which followed, the Chinese population in California was increased by some thirty thousand.

Here and there, over the length and breadth of the United States, were sporadic records of Chinese settlers, but California, in spite of growing opposition, was the State that held most of them in thrall. We hear, for instance, of a band of a hundred being sent to North Adams, in Massachusetts, to break a strike in the shoe manufacturing industry. This was in 1870. . . . In that same year, the British ship *Niagara* sailed with over five hundred laborers for New Orleans. Again and again, there are references to Chinese in the State of Louisiana with allegations that they were marrying whites in some of the parishes.

In 1868, a Chinaman was naturalized in the city of Boston. How or why is hard to determine. But it is doubtful whether the proceedings "took." Perhaps the question was never raised and Massachusetts holds the record for having had a single alien of Mongolian blood as a voter. There are records of the massacre of Chinese in Washington and Wyoming, at that time both territories. Which is indication not only of attempted occupation but of fatal opposition.

But, taken by and large, in spite of riots against the Chinese in the mining districts and disorders in labor circles, their massacre was never a favorite American pastime. . . . One demonstration in Los Angeles in 1873, however, comes under that heading. The trouble started in a foul street called Negro alley which harbored the off-scourings of many mixed breeds.

A tong war started between the Ah Choy Company and the Yo Hing Company over the usual question—possession of a woman. One afternoon during a street fight, a white officer named Thompson was killed. A crowd gathered and the Chinese fled to their shops and houses and barricaded themselves against the enemy. The mob began storming these improvised citadels with the result that they finally smoked out one Chinaman who with an ax in his hand ran from a building. . . . That settled it. The crowd promptly bore down upon the hapless creature and hung him to the crossbeams of a gateway.

Having tasted blood the rabble went wild. They climbed upon the low adobe buildings and began to tear tiles off the roof. Then through the holes and crevices they had created they shot down men and helpless women and children.

For three hours they played at this game of potting their cowering victims, after which, they broke open the doors, dragged out all the males that were alive and strung them up. One victim was little more than a child and it was said that white children ten years old assisted in his execution. Having disposed of all the Chinamen they could find, the mob then went through the houses and looted everything they could lay their hands on. In extenuation of this dreadful circumstance, it can be said that the people who indulged in it were the very lowest types. What the authorities were doing during those three hours is a matter of conjecture. But at that time, Los Angeles was little more than a sleepy sun-baked village and doubtless lacked officers and facilities for putting down so violent a disorder. . . . Arrests were made and penalties enacted later but it is notable that only one of the Chinese cruelly murdered had any part in the killing of Thompson. All the others had managed to escape.

Again in 1877, six Chinese laborers were shot down in cold blood on a ranch just outside Chico. They were involved in nothing more reprehensible than earning their bread. The Order of Caucasians warned them to leave but since they paid no attention a delegation came upon them suddenly in the night, killing four and badly wounding two.

But, however terrible these instances, the toll of life was comparatively small. In the history of their immigrations to other lands, the Chinese have not always been so fortunate. In 1603 the city of Manila saw twenty-three thousand Chinese killed by Spaniards. Thirty-six years later, another massacre in the Philippine Islands netted several thousand. Again, in 1653, in resisting an order for all Chinese to leave Manila, there were twelve thousand slain.

Batavia, in the middle of the eighteenth century, had a drive against Chinese that yielded nearly thirteen thousand.

Nor have Occidentals been the only offenders. The seventies saw plenty of strong-armed opposition to whites in China. In 1870 at Tien Tsin, for example, the French consul, foreign merchants, their wives and children, and one hundred orphans in charge of Sisters of Mercy, were cruelly murdered. The rioters set fire to the Orphan Asylum, dragged the nuns into the street, stripped, and outraged them. Then they cut up their bodies and distributed them as souvenirs, much as mobs in the romantic and chivalrous South still do to their negro victims.

There were many other instances of outrages to white missionaries in China during that decade. But mob violence is the same the world over—fire, sword, pillage—with rape, torture and souvenir hunting on the side. The source of uprisings is usually ignorance, aided and abetted by wild stories concerning the dark and foul practices of the alien.

The Tien Tsin uprising, for instance, had to do with stories about how the Sisters of Mercy picked up children on the street, murdered them and ground their eyes to powder to obtain a cure for ills—or some such nonsense. The story of children slain and offered up for sacrifice is as old as the race. It has operated with striking success in Christendom whenever the faithful decided to clean out a ghetto.

The Chinese subscription to this age-old formula is mentioned here merely to absolve our forefathers of being unique in their prejudices. Racial antipathies remain racial antipathies, under whatever religious or economic guises they masquerade.

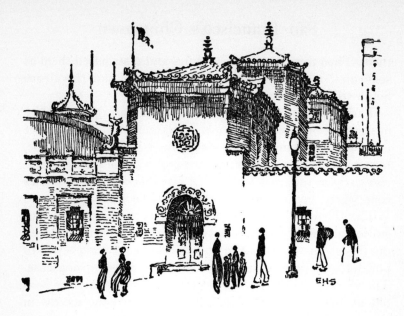

Chapter V

SANDLOT DAYS

THE ten years from 1870 to 1880, showing an increase of thirty thousand Chinese in the State of California, were years which decided the future of Asiatic influence on the Pacific Coast.

The railroad was finished, the Chinese employed in building it did not go home, and, more than that, every steamer from the Orient was crowded with new immigrants. Mr. Crocker had said that supply and demand would regulate the labor situation. He probably was right. There still seemed to be a demand for unskilled labor. At all events, the Chinese were absorbed by the stream of industry, whether to its detriment or advantage will never be determined.

In these ten years, California was finding herself, in spite of moments of flightiness. These were the years of abnormal fortune poured in a steady stream from the silver hills of Nevada; these were the years of boom and bunk and ballyhoo; these were the years of extravagant hope and speculation. But they were also the years of moves toward less spectacular and more solid performances.

California was still a sprawling, tawny giantess only half awake to her possibilities. Or, to put it more literally in the words of a writer of the period, California "was still under the domination of the idea that mining and cereal farming would remain its chief dependence." This was written more specifically of the city of San Francisco, but San Francisco in the seventies was the pulse of California.

The gold mining boom had settled down to a jog-trot performance and the frenzy of treasure hunting had been transported to an adjoining state, which was being ravished of its silver treasures by Californian capital for the benefit of Californians. For the moment, California was in the position of an extravagant young whelp, receiving a shockingly large allowance from an indulgent relation, many miles removed. This on the mining entry in the ledger.

In the realm of farming, grain held full sway. The land was in the hands of a few baronial owners, who had inherited, or married into families who had inherited colossal Spanish grants. Or the new owners had come by them through foreclosures and the ability to drive hard and often crooked bargains. Their realms stretched for uncounted miles. Much of this land was given over to grazing—for cattle and sheep and horses. But on the lowlands where soil was deep and blackly rich and rainfall adequate, golden fields of grain stretched out in long monotonous sweeps. Gold, silver, wheat, sheep, cattle—these were the sources of California's wealth at the beginning of the seventies— primitive sources held for ravishment. Conservation was a word that was unknown in the lexicon of California. If gold was in the hills, wash down the hills and destroy them. If sheep lack grazing ground burn down the forests to give them more open country. If the lowlands produced wheat, sow it year after year, without rotation of crop or enrichment of soil, until the soil was impoverished. As for the rainless lands, think nothing of them—they are valueless.

Thus argued the majority. But, somehow, feeble rays of imagination and intelligence began to filter through. If the wheat lands showed signs of debility, reclaim the marshes. Bring water to the desert. Vary crops. What about the orange, the grape, the plum? They all flourished in the sheltered gardens of the old Missions. Here was work for the Chinese. Let them reclaim the marshes, and dig irrigating ditches in dry country, and cultivate the vineyards and gather the fruit. They work for a dollar a day from sun-up to sun-down. And they board themselves. All you have to do is arrange with a Chinese boss for their services, give them a frame shack lined with bunks in a far corner of your ranch, and let nature take its course. Hold onto your vast domains and let the "gold dust twins" do the work. Once you fancied there might come a day when you would be compelled to cut your huge holdings up into small farms that a white man and his family could work. But no need of that, now. Here are willing workers eager to be exploited. Or as one defender of coolie labor puts it, here are laborers "who trot with the quiet humility of pack-loaded mules" working "from daylight to dark"; who are "rarely sick and use only salt and water" as a remedy.

Small farms might be well enough for a niggardly country like New England where one wheedled a harvest out of the rocky hillsides, but California is on a grand scale. It can be maintained in a sort of feudal splendor, with an aristocracy holding the whips and an infinitely lower class bending beneath the lashes—not only a lower class but an alien class, which makes it all the better, for, here, there never can arise any question of equality.

The beautiful thing about the whole arrangement is that beyond hiring him one does not have to give a Chinaman a second thought. The Southern slave-owners had to see that his slaves were fed and housed and doctored after a fashion —even the nobility of England sent their women with warm woolen petticoats and moral advice to their tenantry. But a Chinaman was his own concern. You gave him a dollar a day and there the matter ended. His morals, his health, his problems were not your affair. And, as one Christian gentleman said of the servant problem in these feudal seventies in California, "It is a great convenience to have servants who don't have to go to church."

These large landowners were the men whom Henry George in the late seventies called "the great lords of the soil—the men who by fraud, bribery, perjury and chicanery had obtained legal title to broad domains" and were perfectly willing to see the State submerged by a flood of cheap labor. "See these men," he goes on accusingly, "proclaiming to the East that railroads could not have been built but for the Chinese, when the truth is that but for them and such as they, this State would have had three miles of road instead of one."

Whether or not Mr. George's single-tax analyses of the railroad situation were true, with the railroads completed and transportation assured, many of the dreams of a more opulent California came to pass. The marshes were reclaimed by Chinese working in muck up to their waists, and irrigation ditches were dug through the arid country by lean coolie laborers sweating but not groaning under a temperature of 110° in the shade in the San Joaquin country. The vineyards were planted by them, the crop of grapes were gathered by them, the raisins were spread out on trays

TUCK FUNG CAFÉ

to dry, by their tawny fingers. Empires that had once been desert began to blossom, and fruit, and stagger under harvests. Grapes, figs, olives, nectarines—all the classical delicacies of antiquity began to flourish. No wonder the Chinese did not go home. Even with the railroad finished there was plenty of work for them.

Then, too, California began to think of manufacturing some of its products. It had inexhaustible supplies of leather from its cattle ranges. Why not begin with shoes? But white labor was scarce and expensive. With railroad transportation one could buy more cheaply in the Eastern market. How about the Chinese? They answered the question perfectly. And not only shoes but overalls. A Chinese could sit twelve hours before the sewing machines and not blink an eyelid. He could turn out cheap overalls within the purse of white laborers. And the white laborers bought them, as they did the shoes turned out by sweatshop labor. In fact, it was protesting white labor that was the market for cheap, Chinese-made goods. Millionaires, or even the moderately well-to-do were not interested in workingmen's boots and denim trousers.

In field and factory, Chinese labor underbid white labor, where white labor was at all available. But in the rôle of servant, a Chinese earned twice as much as any "cook-lady" or housemaid. Where Irish servant girls earned fifteen or twenty dollars a month and "found" the Chinese house-boy commanded double that amount. But he was cheap at twice the sum paid white women-kind. He was more efficient, less complaining, always on the job. He didn't have to have a day off except once a year at the Chinese New Year. He worked on Sundays, holidays—rain or shine. He was never ill, he told you none of his troubles, he was oblivious to anything that went on in the household. There was never a Chinese servant who ever testified in a divorce case, or an alienation of affection suit, or a suit for breach of promise. It would have been hopeless to have hailed him to the witness stand. "I no sabe," would have been his reply to any direct question concerning the delinquency of any of the members of the household where he served. Even the irrepressible Mrs. Frank Leslie admitted in her magazine that "Chinese servants were the best in the country, neat, orderly, apt at learning and reliable in an emergency." Although she gave them a left-handed swipe by declaring that in spite of all this they were "above all flesh deceitful, devoid of personal attachment and suspected of cultivating the most odious vices beneath a demure and dishonest exterior."

One can never reply to the charge of deceitfulness in others because it is too vague a term, but any Californian who has been served in his home by a Chinaman of the old school can refute the slur that he was devoid of personal attachment. There was no more loyal member of the household than the Chinaboy in the kitchen, provided he found you a fair employer. But woe to the family that incurred his wrath. His rancor extended beyond his own term of service. You dismissed him with a shrug, quite sure that there were plenty of better and more efficient Chinaboys to be hired. But you were in for disillusionment. Other servants of Oriental blood, came, stayed a few hours, and left. It turned out that the departing house-boy had left behind him mysterious signs to the effect that you were a "white devil" not to be trusted. His revenge was complete.

One could recite pages of testimony in support of their loyalty. There is the story about the family who went away on a trip leaving their house in charge of a Chinese house-boy during that fateful April in 1906 when San Francisco was shaken down and then burned up. They returned home a

Sandlot Days

week later. Sing was sitting on the front steps—all that was left of the old home—blandly awaiting their arrival.

Or there is the tale of the Chinese retainer who had been with the family for thirty years. He left his master and mistress for a year's leave to return to China. Three months after his departure his master died. Six weeks later the bell rang and his mistress found her old servant Tong at the door. "The boss—he dead," announced Tong. "I come back look after you." Without another word he brushed past her, flung his carpet bag into his old room and began preparations for dinner. Just that, nothing more. Giving up the first holiday he had had in years to come back and look after his old mistress. How he had heard the news no one ever knew. The Chinese seldom waste time on senseless explanations.

Sometimes, unless you understood, this loyalty took on a tinge of impudence. A certain university professor living in Berkeley sent for his mother to pay him a visit. She was a lovely old lady who had borne sons in the bargain, and Lee, the Chinese cook, adored her. The family had the good old Californian custom of drinking wine with dinner. On the first night of her arrival the mistress noted that there was no wine glass at her mother-in-law's place. She rang for Lee and indicated the deficiency. Lee, gave an ominous grunt, went to the sideboard, picked up a wine glass and banged it down before the old lady's plate. "Wine no good for old woman," was his blunt comment. . . .

The old lady stayed all summer and every night this same comedy was enacted. Every night for three months, Lee set the table with one wine glass short, every night for three months his mistress rebuked him, and every night for three months, irrespective of guests or what-not, Lee banged the glass down fiercely and said, "Wine no good for

95

old woman!" He did this because he loved his master and he loved his master's mother. He must have known in a vague way that there was some relation between high blood pressure, stimulants, brittle arteries and sudden death. Others might contribute to the death of this hapless old woman without protest but he had too much character not to protest —not once, but a hundred times. This little incident provocative of laughter stifled with a tear or two, is very revealing of Chinese character. There is a dogged persistency in the Chinese that never gives up, once their mind is set on a course of action. This is not stupidity but conviction. And there is a strong tie between conviction and loyalty.

The history of China is filled with tales of men whose strong though almost passive loyalty to a cause has led them into the torture chamber and finally to the executioner's block. One of the leaders of a revolt, Chen Kin Lung, is an example. He was arrested at an inn at Soochow. Incriminating papers were found upon him. Tortured in the hopes that he would betray his accomplices he said proudly: "Your excellencies may spare yourselves the trouble and pain to me. I am not the only one ready to lay down my life for this cause. My head, flesh and bones are yours. Take them and end this evil farce. Do not deceive yourself with the hope I will ever betray my confederates, or deny a cause that will bring untold happiness to our country for a thousand generations."

Had he betrayed his comrades a pardon would have been given him. He preferred death to such dishonor. . . . He was led to the block with an iron hook driven through his collar bone.

There was another trait which endeared Chinese servants to their employers, especially those who entertained or who had large families. One of the best ways to soothe the apprehensions of the female cook you are engaging, is to assure her that the family is small and that you rarely have guests. But if you told this to an old-fashioned Chinese cook he would be unmoved by it—he might even refuse the job. A good Chinese cook of the old school wished for a proper scope for his talents. He adored a full dinner table; he liked company. You might have fifteen or fifty—it was all the same to him. And this without engaging a bit of additional help. Not that he did it alone—far from it. If the party were beyond his capacity one always found the kitchen help reinforced by a "cousin" or two. They came to visit and chatter and incidentally "learn the ropes"—invariably young Chinaboys, fresh from the steerage, getting some preliminary training in kitchen service.

Said an old Chinese servant once to a visitor who asked him how things were going: "No good! . . . Nobody home but boss and old woman. Boys all gone to college. Girls go way. Only two for dinner. No good!" Faithful old Sing. He missed the bustle and laughter and keen hunger of the young people. He liked to cook for hearty appetites. He liked somebody to say: "Got another piece of that mince pie, Sing? . . . It's swell!" It was no fun to plan a frugal dinner for two who were beyond the delights of robust feeding.

But it went deeper than that, too. This was *his* family—these boys and girls. He would never have admitted it but he loved them. He was proud of the boys whom he slipped many times through the back entrance when they were feeling a little wobbly after a football celebration. And he liked the girls, too, to the point of sneaking them up breakfast trays in defiance of a stern mother's commands against such practices.

Sing's loyalty to the children of the family is best exemplified in a tale of the son of his employer who married and set up an establishment of his own. At the end of the month in spite of the fact that there was one less mouth to feed under the paternal roof, the mother discovered to her amazement that the bills for food were nearly doubled. Upon investigation she discovered that her affectionate old rogue of a cook whenever he ordered a chicken for dinner had instructed the shopkeeper to send a second chicken to the new ménage with the compliments of the parents—it was the same with a roast of beef, or a can of coffee, or a basket of strawberries.

This same Sing if he liked certain visitors who came for dinner would bow them out and say: "You come dinner next Friday." And many a time the lady of the house found herself with a full table of guests she had not counted on.

But like all loving people, like all efficient people, an old Chinese servant was a tyrant. It was very hard to get him to have chicken broth for a certain dinner if he had set his heart on consommé. He simply would not put the ice cream into fancy moulds if his custom had been to serve it fresh from the freezer. He resented turning over his kitchen to some member of the family for trying out a new recipe. And if this were done in spite of his protest, he ignored the whole proceeding. It didn't matter in the slightest whether the new pudding took six eggs or sixteen. But you may be sure that after a decent lapse of time he would triumphantly duplicate the innovation. And it would be a better pudding.

To any protests, to any suggestions for a new order of things, to any commands he simply grunted, "No good!" If you had ordered him to serve romaine lettuce when he had been in the habit of serving lettuce of the common garden variety, you simply had to wait until dinner was served to see whether your instructions had been carried out. If they weren't and you scolded, he was very bland about it: There was no romaine lettuce to be had. Next time you bought the lettuce yourself. You brought it into the kitchen and dumped it triumphantly on the table. But you had no romaine lettuce that night, either. You looked in on him at the end of the meal. You were furious. He heard you out, patiently. He merely shrugged. "No good! Heap full of bugs!" It was "wine no good for old woman" all over again.

In the end, if you were a wise person you capitulated. Whether you had romaine or ordinary lettuce for dinner was of no importance ranged up against the bigger issues. A really sensible mistress surrendered every detail of the kitchen to her Chinaboys even to the marketing. It was here that he shone. If your bills were too high it was always well to turn the marketing over to Sing. He took a pride in keeping them down. No storekeeper ever slipped bad or indifferent food over on Sing—or overcharged him, or gave him short measure.

And there were never any valuables or money missing in a home in which Chinese help ruled. You could leave a diamond brooch on your dressing table—or a hundred dollars in gold in your trouser pocket and if it disappeared you could be sure that friend wife had appropriated it. At least, your Chinaboy had no hand in its removal.

As we have seen, Mrs. Frank Leslie suspects these paragons of the kitchen "of cultivating the most odious vices beneath a demure and dishonest exterior." Of course nobody can defend himself or anybody else against such generalization. What were these "odious vices?" Visiting bagnios in Chinatown, we have no doubt, was one. But in the seventies, just to mention one decade, San Francisco was over-run with cribs and parlor-houses at which Chinese were not entertained. We shall not accuse the master of an establishment that could afford such a luxury as a Chinese servant, of frequenting cribs but somebody with means supported the parlor-houses where champagne flowed and the entertainment was expensive. Could it be that the Chinese servant was not the only one in the family given to vicious recreation?

Undoubtedly Sing smoked opium. But for the most part, he was very moderate about it. The opium dens in Chinatown were for derelicts both white and yellow, addicts who had surrendered completely to the lure of the pipe, as a small percentage of wine-drinkers surrender completely to the lure of intoxicating liquor. But to the average Chinaman a pipe or two of opium was as pure a relaxation as the drinking of a high-ball to his white brethren.

That he was an inveterate gambler nobody will deny. But this seems to have been a common fault among San Franciscans in the seventies. Sing bought lottery tickets and played fan-tan in the gambling clubs of Chinatown, but his master indulged in a game called poker and plunged into stock-market gambling until, in many cases, the furniture was moved out literally from under him.

No, we are afraid that Mrs. Leslie's "odious vices" is a little too un-specific, or at best, that these "odious vices" had their counterparts in the family circle.

Once in awhile, of course, one woke up to the fact that one had admitted a Chinese gangster known as a "highbinder" into the home. But he scarcely contaminated it. He was apt to be surly from indulging in late hours, and heavy from too much "pipe hitting," and too concerned about the sale of the latest batch of slave-girls he had just imported, to give your household proper attention. But this was a rare situation. The average Chinaboy was sober, good-natured and industrious. As the years went on, and he established himself, he was as apt as not to be the owner of a store or a business in Chinatown. He never surrendered his job on that account, no matter what his profits. Especially if he had served you for years. Your home was his. You needed

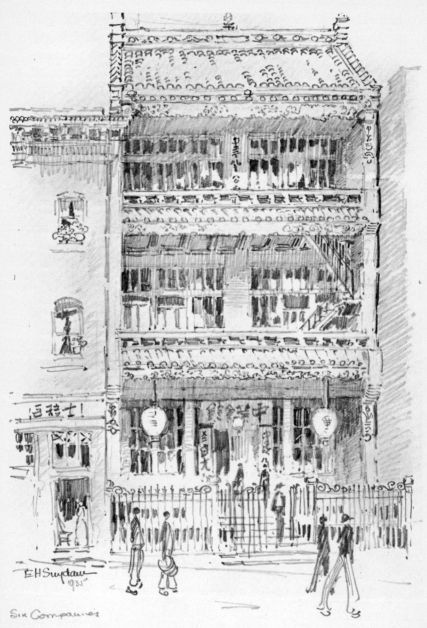

SIX COMPANIES BUILDING,
845 STOCKTON STREET

him. He liked to roast beef and broil steak for you, and make cookies, and sugar birthday cakes for the children. If you had a country place, he adored keeping a few chickens and tacking up the rose bush against the house, or fussing with chrysanthemum beds. At heart he was a homebody. His wife was many thousand miles away—and his sons, and the burying ground of his ancestors. Every five or six years he went back for a few months to see them. But in the years between, he stifled his homesickness by making a home for you, he indulged his pride in sons, vicariously, by making your sons his. He was full of loyalty and real affection, in spite of Mrs. Frank Leslie and other casual trippers to the Coast who went through the dark alleys of Chinatown with a licensed guide and reported hysterical nonsense for home consumption.

It was through domestic service that the Chinaman endeared himself to San Franciscans, and in the other pursuits which brought him in contact with the home. The old Chinese vegetable man who came every morning to your door bending under the cruel weight of wicker baskets piled high with garden produce, became your friend. And the more infrequent but ever smiling "chair-fix-'em" man, who seemed to divine at the precise moment when the cane seat of one of the dining-room chairs had broken through. Or the seller of brooms, or the old flower vendor or the laundryman.

If the Chinese had confined their attentions to mining and railroad building and ditch digging they never would have come within a thousand miles of the American consciousness. But a man cannot live in the same house three hundred and sixty-five days in the year and not incur your love or your hatred. Since there never was a time when Chinese servants were not in demand at high wages in California it is apparent what feelings they engendered.

But even in the capacity of house-boy they had their de-
tractors. "Oh! the man or woman," wails a certain prominent
gentleman of the cloth, "that would dismiss a faithful, virtuous servant because the wages were so much higher to
receive into the family one of those immoral creatures, because he will work at a lower rate—that would expose the
children to be contaminated and ruined by such a wretch
—scarcely deserves the name of human being!"

This statement might have been more impressive if it
had not been founded on misrepresentation. No one ever
hired a Chinese servant because he was cheap. They hired
him because he was efficient and because he didn't entertain
the neighborhood cop in the kitchen while the roast burned
to a crisp. And, if the truth were known, the morals and
even the lives of the children were much safer in Sing's
hands than in the hands of some flighty nurse-maid intent
on keeping dates with the butcher boy in dark hall-ways and
public parks.

It will be seen from the foregoing that dire predictions
concerning the effect of an excess of Chinese help at the
completion of the railroad proved to be unfounded. California was expanding and, moreover, the bonanza days
were soon in full swing. Money was plentiful, more people
could afford the luxury of a Chinese servant. The laborer
of today was becoming the millionaire of tomorrow, with
little concern for such matters as who dug irrigation ditches
or ran up blue denim overalls on sewing machines with
lightning rapidity. Likely as not, he was playing the stock
market—buying shares in Virginia City mines and living on
the proceeds of lucky turns "on change," very much as the
bootblacks and waiters of the nineteen-twenties, risked
their earnings in the firm conviction that with the right
"system" one could live indefinitely without undue labor.

Sandlot Days

Certainly the Chinaman's chief opponent, the Irishman, was not now meeting him on any common ground. Irishmen had no desire to turn agriculturist, or run up overalls on sewing machines, or peddle vegetables. They had other expedients and ambitions—becoming hack drivers, tending bars, wearing fireman's caps and getting fat jobs on the police force. But, the Chinese still rankled the Irishman on two counts—they took away household jobs from pretty Irish colleens and their laundries robbed the widow Murphy of her chance to earn a living by bending over the wash tub. But, on the whole, the Irishman was too busy, himself, to bother unduly about the Chinese menace. Fair weather had settled down on the economic life of California, suspiciously fair weather, with no one taking a thought of getting the old umbrella mended, much less carrying it.

It was 1875 before the first ominous drops fell from the rising clouds of economic disaster—economic disaster that was to end in Chinese exclusion. In August of that year a factional war in San Francisco between financiers closed the doors of the Bank of California and burst the bubble of speculation. This was followed by all the collapses and retrenchments that crowd into the path of such a storm, including an act of Divine Providence known as crop failure. Men began to be thrown out of work—*white* men. But it was plain to be seen that the Chinese still held their own. And even when they felt the lash of the depression's fury they were in much better shape to stand it. Their families were in China and could live on a few cents a day. And the Chinese coolie himself could burrow into Chinatown, get himself a bunk in a small room that housed a dozen others, buy himself a sack of rice which he cooked over a community stove and wait for the storm to blow over.

The white laborer could do none of these things. And even if he could, he was not in the humor for them. He did not care to take the advice of his employers and to learn from the Chinese "how to be better off upon less wages by being more economical" in his habits. And, moreover, at this point, he had no wages at all. Perhaps he *had* been extravagant, perhaps he *had* squandered his money on whiskey, perhaps he *had* speculated in the stock market. But so had his betters. And many of these betters had squandered other people's money in the bargain, the way high financiers and promoters are wont to do when everything is lovely and the goose hangs high.

There began, of course, what always begins in such a situation: the men of affairs thought to turn the disaster to account by beating labor into a corner. If white men would not work longer hours for half the pay, Chinamen could be hired, Chinamen who could rent a bunk in Chinatown for a few cents a day and who could buy a sack of rice that would last them a month.

The unemployed began to organize, to parade, to make themselves a general nuisance. The Chinese were not responsible for the situation and even their contribution to it was grossly exaggerated. But hungry men are not inclined to split hairs and a scape-goat has ever been a more vibrant symbol on which to load the sins and shortcomings of a people than a pack of dry-as-dust facts. Just as Mr. Hitler picked the Jew to bear the sum total of Germany's mistakes and shortcomings, so the Western workingman, in the seventies, chose the Chinese.

Many of the champions of Chinese labor insist that it was "by no means as cheap as was sometimes implied." And this was true, perhaps, oftener than not, about the actual wage per day paid them. But cheap labor is not always measured by the wage—sometimes it is measured by the drudgery, the drive and hours put in from dawn to dark. Mr. John P. Young, an historian of San Francisco, and for many years a prominent newspaper editor, sums up the situation from labor's viewpoint in this wise:

Undoubtedly the influx of Chinese during the seventies gave the laboring element more concern than hours of labor. The burning question with the worker was whether if this movement should continue he would be able to work at all. That his fears were not entirely unfounded is evidenced by the expansion of certain manufacturing industries in which at first the Oriental was employed as a mere helper, but very soon he became ambitious to be his own boss with the result that in certain lines Chinese concerns began to multiply. This was notably true of boot and shoe making and the fabrication of the commoner kinds of clothing and underwear. In these occupations the Chinese became speedily adept, displaying as much skill in the use of the sewing machine as its inventors, and those who engaged in them were as oblivious of an eight hour system as if there were no clock to mark the time.

Mr. Young goes on to point out that the intelligent labor leader saw in this capacity for the Chinamen to master any mechanical device, a menace not only to white labor but to white capital. First the Chinese would displace labor, then, by acquiring greater skill, greater assurance, and greater financial resources they would move in on the white employer of labor and annihilate him with devastating competition. Anyone looking at the matter fairly must admit that this theory was not far wrong. But capitalists of the seventies were like the capitalists of all times: they rarely looked beyond their own noses. Often, of course, their noses have been long enough to carry them to a personal margin of safety, but seldom long enough to carry anybody else.

Occasionally, there was a white employer, who not only discovered the menace of cheap Chinese labor but had the courage to voice it. A gentleman named Aaron Altmeyer, speaking for Einstein Brothers, manufacturers of shoes, had this to say to an investigating committee:

> Any business man who employs Chinese is putting a nail in his coffin. Chinese will one day be his competitors. Einstein Brothers employed both white and yellow labor but Mr. Altmeyer declared that they were willing to pay white men double what they paid Chinamen. "White men," declared he, "do twice as much work as Chinamen and it is of better quality."

As is always the case in any economic revolt, the anti-Chinese movement attracted not only the sober and thoughtful laboring man but all the hoodlums and ne'er-do-wells in the bargain. We have no record of how many village drunkards helped dump the tea into Boston Harbor in the exciting pre-Revolutionary days but there must have been a full quota of them. A cause must indeed be full of vitality to keep its head above water with the rag-tag and bob-tail always doing their best to founder it.

There were plenty of loafers and toughs in San Francisco in the seventies. They hung around corner saloons and traveled in gangs, whiling away their time in attacks on helpless folks, for no reason at all except a desire for vicious activity. Associations sponsoring the anti-Chinese movement pointed to these gangs as the fruit of Chinese competition: They were the youngsters who would have been hired at beginners' wages to accomplish unskilled work, crowded out by Chinese adults. But this was only half the tale. They were the fruits, too, of an impoverished European immigration—a second generation still under the shadow of ignorance, illiteracy and squalor. At this stage in American development they were a problem which every large community faced but which a pioneer city like San Francisco gave additional scope.

One July night in 1877, under the cloak of economic indignation, a mob of these hoodlums bombarded several Chinese laundries and set fire to one on the corner of Turk and Leavenworth streets. Undoubtedly some of the more radical adherents to the cause of labor were also among those present but in the main it was the work of ruffians.

If there is one thing that San Francisco loves to do, aside from putting on trick clothes and having a parade, it is to organize indignation meetings and committees of safety. Next day the vigilante fires which had been smouldering in the blood of San Francisco since the fifties broke out afresh. A Committee of Safety was formed with a leader well-schooled in such stalwart proceedings in the person of William T. Coleman. This gentleman had headed the first Vigilance Committee in 1851, as well as the second and more famous Vigilance Committee of 1855 when Casey and Cora had been hung. But some of San Francisco's hot blood had been tamed, meanwhile, and the *present* committee for preserving law and order—by really flouting it —carried pick-handles instead of rifles, thus earning for itself the name of "the pick-handle brigade."

The unemployed of the town aided and abetted by the inevitable hoodlums answered this challenge a few days later by attempting to burn down the Pacific Mail dock. Owing to the activities of the police and Mr. Coleman's pick-handle brigade—reinforced, it is said, by an occasional rifle—the dock was spared but a lumber yard was fired instead. Mr. Coleman's "pick-handle brigade" was short lived. Arrests in connection with the burning of the lumber yard were made a week later and the Committee of Safety decided to let real law and order take its proper course.

In this "pick-handle brigade," ranged on the side of Mr. Coleman and other distinguished citizens who had wrought themselves up to mild vigilante heat by the attack upon Chinese laundries, was a young Irishman named Denis

Kearney. This gentleman had left home and Ireland when he was a lad of eleven in the capacity of cabin-boy. Just this precocious act alone shows him to have been a person of initiative and courage. At the age of thirty he found himself in San Francisco. He speedily got a job as foreman of a gang of stevedores and later went into the drayage business. What prompted him to take up cudgels with Mr. Coleman's "millionaire gang" in defense of the Chinese will never be known. Certainly racially, temperamentally and economically he should have been on the side of white labor. Be that as it may, his change of policy was as swift as Mr. Mussolini's right-about-face when he switched from socialism to fascism over night: By September of that same memorable year we find Kearney addressing a mass meeting of unemployed denouncing the actions of the "pick-handle brigade" in no uncertain terms, declaring that "those who had organized the brigade had proclaimed that their purpose was to make serfs of the workingman."

Mr. Kearney was just the stuff of which rabble-rousers are made: he was loud-voiced, illogical, had personality and a gift of gab.

Some of his violent traducers say he was also illiterate. But this charge must always remain a matter of degree. Certainly a youth who leaves home at the age of eleven as a cabin-boy could not have had much book-learning at the outset of his career. But this condition is not above a remedy and Kearney must have gone in for self-improvement somewhere along the line. In San Francisco, at least, we know where he trained himself for oratory—at a Sunday debating club with the impressive name of Lyceum of Self Culture. John P. Young calls him a creature of circumstance, "absolutely destitute of originality, but quick to seize upon a suggestion." This in connection with the coining of the slogan "The Chinese Must Go!" which Kearney

FOUR FAMILIES' SOCIETY, GRANT AVENUE

used on any and every occasion until he beat it inexorably into the ears of his hearers.

This effective phrase was the invention according to tradition of a brilliant young newspaperman, Chester Hull. Mr. Hull was a firm believer in Chinese exclusion and it was said that he furnished the telling ammunition of a battle-cry that the rank-and-file man could understand. There were other battle-cries which issued from the Sandlot where Kearney harangued his followers.—"Down with the bloated monopolists!" "Kill the bloody cormorants!" "String up the blood-suckers!" But these were all clumsy and devoid of novelty. Such phrases had been flung by hungry mobs at rulers and aristocrats since the beginning of time. But the cry "The Chinese Must Go!" had a new sound. It gave the rank-and-file man something more than a shrill cry to action—it gave him a living and, what was better, an alien symbol of all his wrongs and prejudices.

Nothing could have smacked more of mob activity than these meetings which Kearney addressed nightly. Not even the restraining influence of four walls tempered their violence. They were held in a space to the west of the built-up portions of the city that had been graded for homes but otherwise unimproved. This space was known as the Sandlot. An ideal gathering-place for unemployed, for hoodlums, for bums, away from police interference, where a man could give his lungs and his prejudices full scope without risking a charge of disturbing the peace.

Whether or not Mr. Hull invented the phrase, "The Chinese Must Go!" the San Francisco *Chronicle* for whom he worked gave this battle-cry and Mr. Kearney a full measure of publicity. Other newspapers swung into line. Denis Kearney found himself a force. A Workingman's Party was organized with Denis Kearney as president. It did not capture the Legislature but it did so well that it threw a scare into the old parties that had been drafting resolutions against Chinese since the fifties and letting the matter rest there.

The result was, as Mr. Young puts it, that "although Kearney's war cry 'The Chinese Must Go!' did not prevail . . . it did crystalize the sentiment against their *coming.*" In 1878 the California Legislature appointed a senatorial committee of investigation to look into the Chinese question. They met in the summer at San Francisco and the evidence which they gathered did much to influence the Exclusion Act which went into effect in the early eighties.

A compromise exclusion act was voted before 1880 by Congress, permitting Chinese laborers to come in small numbers. This was vetoed by President Hayes. There followed a secret ballot in California in 1879 which settled for all time the question as to how the citizens of that State felt on the subject—one hundred and sixty-one thousand four hundred and five votes were cast for exclusion and only eight hundred and thirty-three in favor of admission.

This proved that the laboring class was not the only class opposed to the idea of Chinese immigration. In fact, the opposition to exclusion was so small that the vote *for* exclusion was practically unanimous. Rich men, poor men, beggar men and thieves were all of the same mind. Even the employers of Chinese labor, when it came to a showdown, voted to exclude them. Doubtless they were learning that the Chinese might begin as laborers but there was nothing to hinder them from becoming business rivals.

The amazing returns were from the rural districts where sentiment was alleged to have been all in favor of the Chinese. There was only one answer to this: Californians had begun to realize that baronial holdings worked by contract labor would eventually build up a feudal system not in harmony with American ideals. The new empire had grown beyond the need of cheap labor. What it wanted most was small land-holders who would build up a commonwealth consistent with American traditions.

The forerunner of absolute exclusion was a treaty in 1880 which permitted the United States to "regulate, limit or suspend the admission of Chinese laborers" within its borders. But it also provided that their admission could not be absolutely prohibited. Acting upon this agreement Congress passed a law suspending coolie immigration for twenty years. President Arthur thought the twenty-year suspension excessive, and in May, 1882, a compromise was effected whereby the time limit was reduced to ten years. This was approved, also with a proviso that laborers returning to China could apply for return certificates.

Such a provision was bound to lead to all sorts of fraudulent reëntries. It did. Whereupon, in spite of a protest from China, in 1887 a law was passed and upheld by the Supreme Court, denying laborers who left the United States the right to return.

At the expiration of the ten years, in 1892, a law called the Geary Act definitely prohibited immigration for ten years more. President Theodore Roosevelt was in office when this law ran its course. In spite of vigorous protests from the Imperial Court presented by Wu Ting Fang, then Chinese Ambassador, the President signed an even more drastic bill. This excluded not only laborers but all Chinese from entering the United States. This act had no time limit.

The opposition to the Chinese was not on a personal basis. Many Californians who voted to exclude them had every reason to think of them with affection as individuals. But looking at the issue broadly, or even narrowly as a measure of self-preservation, there was only one course open. But even if there had not been such an unanimity of opinion, the expressions of those who advocated unrestricted immigration would undoubtedly have won the day for the opposition. In all the annals of political movements there has been nothing to equal the puerility of the arguments advanced for allowing the Chinese to pour in.

The ministers and missionaries of the Evangelical churches led the vanguard for Chinese immigration with charmingly naïve arguments. The Reverend Mr. O. Gibson, a worthy man, in his zeal, advanced this interesting theory:

> Remember that we were the aggressors; we battered down China's walls of exclusion; we opened her interdicted ports that we might share her commerce. God permitted us to do this, and the same God, who is no respecter of persons, permitted the Chinese to come here; and shall we war with God?

It is not the first time that God has been accused of putting His finger in the pie of international injustice. God permitted us to "batter down the walls of Chinese Exclusion!" It sounds like the assault of Joshua upon the walls of Jericho! We were "aggressors," backed up by God. At least the Reverend Mr. Gibson has grace enough to call the assault which opened Chinese ports to world commerce by its right name—aggression! But this same God, having been a fellow aggressor with us, now offers the Chinese a sop: He graciously permits them to come to California. "And shall we war with God?" Evidently Mr. Denis Kearney, the State Legislature, Congress, President Arthur, and one hundred and sixty-one thousand four hundred and five residents of California decided that we should.

To realize more fully the sort of racket Mr. Gibson's God was party to, we have only to read the testimony of another minister of the gospel, the Reverend Mr. Frederic J. Masters. Mr. Masters does not insult his Deity by making him an Old Testament bandit indulging in sharp practice for the benefit of His chosen people. He does not accuse his

WAVERLY PLACE

God of being a party to the opium traffic in China. He is more inclined to let the white race take full responsibility for its chicanery. Says Mr. Masters:

> The whole history of foreign intercourse with China has been hatefully cruel and unjust. Foreigners forced themselves upon China at a time when she desired nothing better than to be let alone. Their ports were bombarded to open markets for our Commerce. The most attractive sites were taken as residences for our merchants. Bloody wars were waged with China to force her to legalize a trade in opium which the Emperor To Kwong saw would bring moral and financial ruin to her people. There is no doubt that whatever treaty rights we enjoy in China today have been obtained at the point of the bayonet. We have forced ourselves into the coast ports, into the interior, and even into the very capital. We have talked and blustered as if the country belonged to us. We have stalked through the land, trampling upon Chinese prejudices, shocking their conventionalities and outraging their cherished traditions. For nearly a century we have bullied and plundered China. We have set up our autocratic settlements and our extra-territorial rights; and when China has dared to murmur we have shaken our fists in her face and called for the inevitable gunboat.

Marshall P. Wilder, a humorist, who used to travel over the country entertaining Ladies' Aid Societies and Epworth Leaguers, viewed with "no alarm the Chinese immigration to this country." Why? The answer is simple: Because "the introduction of the Chinese is in accordance with the design of Providence."

J. W. Boddam-Whittman, Esquire, who, as you have guessed, was a visiting Briton with a penchant for writing books to better put his ignorance on record, knows just why California is in such a state. It is not a result of Chinese labor. Oh, my dear no! . . . California is in a bad way because necessities are high priced, because it has high wages and because whiskey occupies too "prominent a position."

But the real enemy of the people is "universal suffrage." He does not say so but he thinks, no doubt, that the Chinese, being denied suffrage, will help counteract this appalling situation.

Our old friend the Reverend Gibson supplements the statements of J. W. Boddam-Whittman, Esquire, by declaring that "free competition increases the price of labor." A statement open to argument, to say the least. And he draws a heart-rending picture of what will happen in the event of Chinese Exclusion. "Let the Chinese go," warns the good man, "and white help would charge more and be more insolent. . . . Many families would leave the country or break up housekeeping!"

But John Codman, a traveler from the Eastern states, paints an even more horrifying picture. Mr. Codman is quite sure that without Chinese competition the Irish waiters and chambermaids will demand such wages that families of moderate means *will be compelled to do their own work!*

But these, you are doubtless saying, are the expressions of emotional clergymen and visiting nonentities. There is plenty of this sort of testimony from residents. One stalwart pioneer weeps unashamed at the thousands of families on small incomes, "enfeebled mothers, helpless children, daily suffering from want of domestic help," if the Chinese are excluded. Another makes dole about the poor women who can't hire white "ladies" for housework at thirty dollars but who can get a Chinaman for ten dollars. There were doubtless hundreds of such poor women who would have been glad to know just where the author of these lines hired a Chinese for ten dollars a month. These servants are as legendary as the seven-foot silk-worm of Hui Shên.

Still another writes voluminously to the paper about the woman whose husband works and whose children are ill.

Sandlot Days

What will she do when the old Chinese vegetableman no longer comes to her door? Only one course is open—*she will have to go to the store for them, herself!*

To read these protests one would imagine that California had been settled by an anaemic, resourceless, neurasthenic breed. The women, especially, are so enfeebled that if they can't get servants they will be compelled to break up housekeeping, do their own housework, go to the store for vegetables! This sort of twaddle went on way past exclusion. It was still being peddled in the nineties by those with a vague hope that the bars would be lifted. In these later days the burden of such songs is taken up by no less a person than Joaquin Miller, the red-blooded, two-fisted, masculine-whiskered poet of the Sierra. Says Joaquin tearfully:

"The man with a home, whether he has a little shop or a little farm, does not want his wife and growing children to cook, wash and do chamber work, when he can get a silent and submissive little Mongolian to work for a song."

Aside from the fact that there is very little record in the nineties or in any other period when farmers were not perfectly willing to let their wives cook, wash, hoe the garden patch, milk the cows and put up quarts of currant jelly and blackberry jam, on the side, Mr. Miller's lament, considering its source, is a classic. Here is the poet of the wide-open spaces who went over and made London gasp at his seven-league boots, his ten-gallon hat and his bandana handkerchief tied under his virile whiskers, who sings of the primal sweep of the western country, of the hardships and perils of the Oregon trail, a creature of covered wagons and Indian wars, shedding tears at farmers' wives who must cook, and growing children on a farm who must help mother make beds and weed the berry patch, all because there is no "silent and submissive little Mongolian" to do the work for them. A great humanitarian this poet of the Sierra, but there is infinitely more snobbery than philanthropy in his concern.

But let us get opinions on some broader aspects of the case. Here is the cloth, again, this time fighting along economic and aesthetic grounds. Says the Reverend Mr. William Spear:

"Valuable species of fish, precious shells, and other products of the ocean's shoals and shores, must be always ungathered unless we can employ gleaners and divers from the Asiatic side!"

This is not a mere matter of rescuing farmers' children from "chamber work." This is a matter of providing peddlers of souvenirs with trophies of the sea to sell to "trippers" and maiden aunts with sea-weed to work into fearsome ornaments under glass for the parlor table.

If you want even sterner stuff there is a warning sounded by none other than William T. Coleman. He is the man who led two Vigilance Committees with as much sanity as any man could inject into such rabble-rousing proceedings to say nothing of putting his hand to a pick handle in support of "law and order" in the Denis Kearney days. Mr. Coleman was a man of education and brains yet the message he conveyed to his fellow-townsmen on the Chinese question was even funnier than any that had come before. Here is a portion of one of his speeches:

It is said that in Great Britain there will be put afloat, this year, at least a million of tons register of iron ships and steamers; more probably one million, two hundred thousand tons, or twelve hundred vessels of a thousand tons each. If occasion required, China could buy one-half of this fleet, and with her own, and such as she could put together, she could start a thousand vessels on short notice, bringing two thousand men each, and hurl, almost before we knew it, two million people on our coast. This could readily be multiplied so that five, ten, or even twenty million could be here in a comparatively short time.

Mr. Coleman lived too soon. He should have been the adviser on troop transportation at Washington, during the World War.

And there also was advanced the usual number of fatalistic arguments by the men who could not see, or pretended that they could not see, any way of stopping the flood from Asia.

Reverend Spear was confident that it was "as ridiculous and futile to endeavor to change this law of nature" (the Chinese invasion) as to prevent "the soil of the mountains descending into the valleys." While Governor Cook of Colorado, a rabid anti-exclusionist who was sure that "what the country needed was an abundance of cheap labor," attempted to quiet the opposition by assuring them that the Chinese "would come to us in the future, whether we wished it or not." He was equally sure that the Chinese would solve the problem of populating the "vast unpeopled country between the Missouri River and the Pacific Ocean." The proper reply to this would have been in the words of present-day vernacular, "And how!"

Even the good old London *Times* advised the people of the United States to be philosophical about the situation since "it is impossible to suppose that Chinamen can be kept out of America."

Henry George, writing on the subject of "Why Work Is Scarce," not so much to favor Chinese immigration as to point out other causes contributing to the economic ills of California in particular and the world in general, said:

There are no Chinamen to speak of in New York, yet you may see sights of squalid misery which, as yet, thank God, are not known here. There are no Chinamen in Pennsylvania, yet there in the coal fields are men reduced to a state of serfdom to which Southern Slavery was an easy lot. There are no Chinamen in England, but there in the richest country in the world one-twentieth of the population are paupers.

These are not isolated opinions advanced by fanatics. Hundreds and thousands of such views were expressed and published. For the most part they were admissions of a pioneer people that they were unwilling or unable to prosecute the disagreeable tasks of existence. Had they been true they would have proved the degeneracy of America. Happily, they were not true. Exclusion became a fact. Families did not break up housekeeping or leave the country, "enfeebled mothers and helpless children" somehow managed to survive the lack of domestic help that they never could have afforded in any case; the woman whose husband worked and whose children were sick found time to go to the store for her vegetables; the farmer's wife continued to cook for hired men, milk cows, and let her children help with the "chamber work."

The "precious shells and other products of the ocean's shoals and shores" continued to ornament parlor tables. And, for some unknown reason the Emperor of China did not buy up one-half of England's fleet and start two million men across the ocean, proclaiming the conquest of America.

Even God did not withdraw his favor because the State Legislature, Congress, President Arthur and one-hundred and sixty-odd thousand Californians voted to interfere with designs which went back to the bombardment of Chinese ports and the introduction of opium into that country. Altogether the decade which followed exclusions was a most disappointing one for the prophets.

Chapter VI

THE SIX COMPANIES

IT is said by prominent Chinese in San Francisco's China-town that the various associations which flourish there are peculiarly an outgrowth of American life—that they do not exist in China, nor are they to be found in Canada, Mexico, or South America. These statements should be interpreted with reservations.

Trade guilds have been in existence for centuries in China, and district associations maintained guild houses at Peking in the old Manchu days for the benefit of scholars who went there to take government examinations.

There is no doubt, however, that associations among the Chinese in America, were unique in both variety and influence. One of the reasons assigned for their ascendency, was the Chinaman's need for mutual help in a land that not only denied him the rights of citizenship but, for a long period of time, even the protection of the courts.

Whether the Chinese would have used the courts freely even if the courts had been open to them is a matter of conjecture. For the Chinese were never a people to "go to law," in their own country. Controversies that could not be settled in the family councils were, for the most part, arbitrated by the elders of the village. There were no lawyers, as we know the term. The nearest approach to an attorney in China was what we might call a notary. Official courts did exist but it was accounted a disgrace to be compelled to use them.

Under the pretext that the Chinese did not feel themselves bound by a Christian oath proclaimed solemnly over the Bible, judges in California, until the end of the sixties, in most cases refused to accept their testimony. A snap judgment would set this down as a rank injustice but it must be admitted that the question presented grave difficulties. The average Oriental mind was neither better nor worse than the mind of any average Occidental when it came to facing a profound ethical situation. Oaths are primarily a matter of superstition; the man who swears over a Bible or other religious symbol is moved by fear of an avenging God should he testify falsely. A higher nature is not afraid to lie but it either scorns such an unworthy course or it realizes that the seed of disaster lies in the falsehood itself. Oaths are for the unintelligent—that is why our Quaker forefathers found them degrading.

Naturally, a Chinese coolie was inwardly unmoved by mumbling a promise to tell the truth over a large black book that meant nothing to him. But there were devices which might have reached him, could they have been evoked. When a Chinese was sworn in trivial cases in the courts of China, he was compelled to write upon a piece of yellow paper the fact that he was swearing, before heaven and earth, to tell the truth. The paper was then burnt. Just as the paper effigies which attended a dead body became instantly transported, by burning, into the spirit world, so this oath was instantly transported by flame into the presence of the Supreme Ruler. "Woe to him who has testified falsely," writes a Chinese interpreter, "but happy will he be who has told the truth."

In graver cases, the oath was elaborated. The witness was made to swear "by the sacred oath of his revered Confucius" which translated read thus:

I now appear in this judgment hall, to give evidence in this case pending, do solemnly affirm, that I will faithfully state all that I know concerning such, and keeping nothing secret, and not misrepresenting for the evasion of justice while in your presence; and hereby burn this paper, thereby to be submitted to the judgment and examination of the God of Heaven.

This likewise was burned.

There were other oaths more primitive and symbolic. Cutting off the head of a cock was one favorite method of impressing the witness with the solemnity of his act of testifying. The idea of this ceremony seemed to have been to the effect that if the witness were lying the blood of his family would also be spilt. But this was said by some to be a form of oath used only by thieves and pirates.

The members of the Triad Society, of whom we shall hear more, had a set of oaths peculiarly their own. They broke a cup or an arrow. Or they blew out a lamp. These all signified that if the swearer proved false he would be broken like the cup or arrow, or lose his life suddenly, like the extinguished flame.

San Francisco's Chinatown

An educated Chinese, giving out an interview to the Hong Kong *Register* in the fifties, discredits all these forms. He says:

> In Chinese Courts it is not required to swear, for they know that the people do not care for perjury if they can gain the cause. The Magistrates only make the people confess the truth by threatenings and tortures, and then compare the confessions together to decide the case; or they would find out the truth by arts and private inquiries without calling for witnesses.

There is plenty of reliable testimony concerning heroic methods employed in China in the days of the empire. Flogging with bamboo sticks was a favorite device, although beating the jaws with pieces of leather also had its merits. A particularly efficacious method of extracting testimony from a reluctant witness was to make the victim kneel on pounded glass mixed with salt. Or just the simple device of kneeling on an iron chain had its points.

Unhappily the third degree was not flourishing in California prisons in the fifties or sixties so that torture devices had little or no standing. Therefore, evidence wrung from the prisoner under duress was not available.

The judges were up against a still more subtle difficulty. It was said that "lying in the abstract was not considered a sin among the Chinese." "If a prosecutor," comments an authority, "believes the defendant to be guilty, he will swear to any false collateral facts, which he may consider necessary to prove guilt." Here again the Courts of California in the nineteenth century were handicapped. The devious plans by which district attorneys use questionable methods to bring about conviction had not yet come into fashion.

With all these handicaps it is no wonder that the judges took the easiest course and barred Chinese testimony. It was not until 1869, in October, to be exact, that Judge Sawyer decided the admissibility of Chinese testimony under the Fourteenth Amendment. This was in connection with a suit involving a wood-chopping contract. The first conviction under the new order took place two months later. At that time Judge Provines convicted a gentleman with the belligerent name of Pat Sullivan of throwing a piece of wood at a Chinaman. The witnesses were all Chinese. Justice at last had triumphed but a good twenty years lay between the arrival of the first Chinese in California and this tardy act of fair play. Settling disputes without recourse to California law had become a habit with the Chinese. And, so it continues, in a measure, down to the present day.

When the Chinese first arrived in San Francisco they formed cliques or mutual benefit associations called tongs. Some of these were workers' guilds, others fraternal organizations. But as thousands upon thousands of Chinese arrived, other influences began to assert themselves. Or to put it in the language of one of the present-day bankers in Chinatown, "The family and district associations grew in influence as a result of the encroachment of the tongs."

Family authority was foremost in China and by the same token the family councils became foremost in settling Chinatown disputes. When these failed there was recourse to the district associations, while the guilds and fraternal organizations dropped to third place.

The average San Franciscan has a most muddled idea of what Chinese associations or tongs are. He conceives them as organizations for the promotion of murder. He thinks of them in connection with blackmail and crime. That such organizations have flourished and still do is true enough. But they are only a fragment of the complete picture just as gangster organizations in the United States under prohibition were a fragment of American organization in general.

Perhaps the association that is more often upon the lips

of white citizens of San Francisco and of which they have the most confused notions is the Six Companies. The Six Companies is an organization of districts. It is composed of members from six districts of China. It represents what the Iowa Society, the Sons of New England and an association of Texans might represent, if they banded together under the title of the Three Companies, to promote their interests in the city of Shanghai. In the fifties, there were only five districts in the combine but later a sixth was added. At present there are really seven, but the old name still survives. The names of the companies making up the combination in the seventies when it was at the height of its power and a record of its membership, showing the relative strength of the different factions are as follows:

Ning-Yeung Company	75,000
Hop-Wo Company	34,000
Kong-Chow Company	15,000
Sam Yup Company	10,000
Yang Wo Company	10,000
Yan-Wo Company	4,300

The seventh company added at a later date is the Shen Hing Company.

What went on in the family councils were shrouded in privacy but when differences reached the tribunal of the Six Companies it became more or less a matter of public interest. Which explains, perhaps, why the Six Companies has earned such a large measure of publicity.

At the beginning, the services which these associations rendered were of a simple nature. It was a good deal like a travelers' aid society, looking out for its members in a foreign clime. The first consideration was to build a hall or meeting-place. After this was accomplished, it was customary to add a temple or altar to the local divinities of each district. Hospitalization on a simple scale came next. At one time, the Six Companies maintained an old building on Washerman's Lagoon, where the Marina district now stands, as an asylum for the sick.

But as time went on the problems presented to the Six Companies increased: matters pertaining to hiring of labor, the repayment of transportation money where it had been advanced by private concerns, disputes between families that could not be settled in the family councils, difficulties over debts, rows between trade guilds, fights between members of rival districts which made up the organization of the Six Companies itself. In short, the Six Companies became a tribunal—a government within the borders of the established government of the United States. It was really a court of final appeal. Not that it pronounced sentence or rendered judgment exactly, but that it brought about arbitration of difficulties.

The different district associations which made up the Six Companies each had its own chairman, secretary, treasurer and interpreter. But there was a supreme head over all. It was a confederacy with an overlord, or a municipality operating under the borough system. The Ning-Yeung Company, at one time the most powerful of the group, was founded in the reign of Ham-fung in 1854. It changed its chairman every year and permitted only merchants to vote. The other companies were run more or less on similar lines.

To achieve the presidency or overlordship of the Six Companies was no easy matter. A sort of civil service rule operated and a man had to achieve certain venerable virtues before he was permitted to preside. But to speak of the Six Companies in the past tense is to give out a false impression. The Six Companies is still operating—it is still a force in Chinatown.

San Francisco's Chinatown

As late as January, 1935, there arrived in San Francisco from China the elderly Kwong Shau Louie from Peiping. He was the newly elected president of the Six Companies, the first president to come from the old country for fifteen years. He was to serve also as the chairman of the Ning-Yeung Company, one of the most powerful of the organizations that make up the Six Companies.

This gentleman came from a family of mixed North China and Cantonese origin. In Manchu the family is known as Kwong, in Cantonese it is called Fong. The Fong family is a very influential one in both Canton and San Francisco. Some idea of Mr. Kwong's fitness for his office may be gathered from the fact that at the age of seventy-one he has spent twenty years of his life in study, twenty years of his life as a magistrate, and twenty years of his life in contemplation. This withdrawal from activity in the autumnal years for contemplation is typically Chinese. It is a great contrast to the American method. As a prominent Chinese-American banker in San Francisco said in commenting on this difference: "The years between fifty and seventy would be used by a public-spirited American in activity—for the betterment of others. In China these years are used as years of withdrawal for one's *own* improvement."

However, in Mr. Kwong's case he has emerged from his twenty years of contemplation into activity on the social side, enriched, doubtless, by his meditations. Americans might profit by adding at least a modicum of such withdrawal to their present life pattern.

When Mr. Kwong arrived he was met at the pier by the chairman of the Fong family in San Francisco. In the ramification of Chinatown life, he is, then, first of all, a member of the Fong family, and secondly, a member of the Ning-Yeung Benevolent Society, a district organization, which is a part of the Six Companies. If it were necessary to make a choice, according to Chinatown ethics, his first allegiance would be to the Fong family.

The activities of the Six Companies have been very much curtailed by present-day conditions but its scope in a less happy time was almost unlimited. A great deal of its exercise of power was continually misunderstood by the American public. Legislative and Congressional investigations were always uncovering the belief among those who appeared before it that the Six Companies not only condoned gangster warfare but marked men for murder. If a recalcitrant member of the Sam Yups was slaughtered it was easy to assume that it was the work of a rival organization within the Six Companies to which he belonged. But even granting that this were so, there was no proof that the murder was a definite Six Companies activity or that it even received official sanction. In fact, everything pointed against it. The better class of Chinese, the merchants, controlled the voting and it is not likely that they were concerned with marking men for death or seeing that such threats were put into effect.

If, again, a Sam Yup proved to be also a highbinder and a murderer, it was not difficult to say that he was so by virtue of his connection with the Six Companies. But as well accuse the Iowa Society of Los Angeles of being an association of thugs because one of its members is found guilty of banditry.

In spite of gossip to the contrary, it seems pretty well established that the Six Companies did not import coolies nor turn itself into an immigration association. As a matter of fact, it did not begin to function until its members landed in San Francisco and registered under the proper branch to which they owed allegiance by virtue of the district whence they came. If they were without a prospective job and had no funds the Six Companies advanced them five dollars. Most of them arrived without funds, having exhausted their savings or their credit in paying fare to the promised land. Many, of course, came under a sort of contract to perform certain work. But investigation proved that it was the trade guilds who bargained with would-be employers for the services of their members and not the Six Companies. The Central Pacific imported all their workmen through these guilds, advancing sums of money for transportation which the coolies had to work out before receiving cash wages. Interest was added, of course, to the principal advanced. This system gave rise to all sorts of wild political talk about "contract" labor, which was a synonym for peonage and slavery and other undesirable working conditions. But this was pure fiction. Once the laborer had worked out his passage and paid up other obligations to his tong, or guild, or district association, he was as free as any citizen of California. Except in one particular, the Pacific Mail Steamship Company would not sell him a ticket home without permission either of the Six Companies or a Christian missionary.

When this fact was first discovered a terrible fuss was kicked up in anti-Chinese circles. Here was proof positive that the Chinese coolie was being held in virtual slavery! . . . It proved nothing of the kind. Investigation disclosed that this provision had a most innocent and ethical explanation. The Chinese are great sticklers for the settlement of debts. When a Chinaman applied to the Six Companies for permission to return home, his record was checked up and a clearance paper was not given him until all his financial obligations had been fulfilled. Many critics of this plan declared that the Pacific Mail Steamship Company could have had no vital interest in this question: after all, if the passenger had money enough for his trip home that should have

SIDEWALK SHOP

sufficed so far as it was concerned. But, they forgot that this same transportation company brought hundreds of laborers to California, whose fare had been advanced by the concerns hiring them. In fairness to these business men it was expedient to see that this obligation, at least, had been squared. The word of a Christian missionary was accepted in deference to the few Chinese who had embraced Christianity and cut themselves off from old customs and affiliations. The rule was a very sound one, everything considered, and the Six Companies the best agency for enforcing it. It was by far the most impartial and central tribunal in Chinatown and practically every Chinese in the city was registered with it.

As with every question involving the vices and virtues of the Chinese, the question of their honesty was a much debated point. Mr. James Duffy, an expressman, testifying before a legislative committee declared that "they were all thieves, liars and perjurers." And, if his claims seem rather sweeping and unjudicial, for those who want a calmer judgment, here is a word by Judge Davis Louderback who insists that they are "a very immoral, mean, mendacious, thieving people as a general thing." Visitors from China and especially Canton, often called them a "nation of thieves" and other names not complimentary to their honesty. But it must be admitted that these shafts were aimed more or less at the lower classes. It would have been a tremendous miracle to have found the submerged millions of city-dwellers living close to the edge of starvation most of the time, with too nice a sense of property rights.

On the other hand, men of affairs were almost unanimous in their praise of the business ethics of the Chinese merchant. More than one spoke of him as "a born merchant of probity, ever true to his word."

A marine-average adjuster says of them:

San Francisco's Chinatown

I have never had a case where the Chinese have attempted to undervaluate their goods or bring fictitious claims into adjustments. . . . As a class, I think the Chinese [merchants] are more honorable than other nationalities, even our own. . . . I never had a lawsuit with them or never had a complaint from them in my life. . . .

While another man in the same business returns almost identical testimony:

They can figure very fast and very correctly, and when they are convinced that everything is right there is no trouble. There is no class of people that pay up as quickly as the Chinese. On Saturday we send them notice that the average is closed, and on Monday, by ten or twelve o'clock, all the certificates are paid. I have had fifty or sixty thousand dollars in a case, and they would come straight forward and pay it before twelve o'clock, while we have to send around to the other merchants a month and sometimes two months, before we get it all from them.

Fred W. Macondray, a prominent merchant in San Francisco in the seventies, also gave testimony in which he said, "I do not know of any class of merchants, I think, who are more honest and upright or who have a better reputation for integrity than the Chinese." He went on further to state that his business with the Chinese averaged from five to six hundred thousand dollars a year and that in twenty-six years he had never lost a dollar. Asked how white business men compared with this record he was very emphatic in his reply: "They do not compare, of course, as favorably as the Chinese."

Mr. Macondray was testifying before a Congressional committee. His questioner demanded:

"Are your contracts with Chinese generally in writing?"

"No, sir, I do not know that I have ever had a contract with a Chinaman in writing."

"They are verbal contracts?"

The Six Companies

"Yes, sir."

"Do they comply with them?"

"They do."

Mr. Richard G. Sneath, vice-president and manager of the Merchants' Bank, also lauded the Chinese business man thus:

I have always found them truthful, honorable, and perfectly reliable in all their business engagements. I have never had a single one of them to fail to live up to his contracts.

As a rule, written contracts with white men—a Chinaman's word.

The sacredness of a verbal contract with a Chinaman, is proverbial with everyone who has done business with them. If you owned a vineyard and wanted a crew of thirty Chinese to pick your grapes, you got in touch with a Chinese boss and made arrangements. There was nothing signed—wages, hours, length of service were merely mentioned, agreed upon. That was the extent of the contract. If there was any default, it was on your side—never on the part of the Chinese. . . . A Chinese cook came to interview you about a job. He agreed to stay a month and try it. No matter what happened—the house might burn down, the roof might fall in, he might not like the set-up—he stayed his thirty days. Even the humble "chair-fix-'em" man who came to your door soliciting chairs to mend—you rendered up your lowliest or most prized possession to him. He named the price of his labors and trotted away with it swinging from the end of his bamboo pole. He gave you no receipt, no numbered tag. You had not the slightest idea where his repair shop was located, what his name was, how to trace him if the chair was not returned. But he never failed you. At the moment when you gave up hope, the door-bell rang and you opened it upon his face, wrinkled like a frost-bitten apple, smiling a wide, green-toothed smile. Were these the same people that travelers returning from China called a "nation of thieves," or that expressmen, elevated to the importance of a witness-stand, said were "all thieves, liars and perjurers," or that exalted judges declared were "mean, mendacious and thieving?"

If *our* judgments could have been so biased and sweeping, it makes us shudder to think of what the returning coolie from the mines must have said of us to *his* people. What must he have reported concerning claims sold him and then stolen back again by force; or of illegal taxes, gouged from him at the pistol point; or of the prototypes of the Christian gentleman who sold "nine dollars' worth of bogus tax receipts" so that he could "keep Christmas." Happily, not having peeped into his diary the Chinese could not report the desecration of the religious ideal the thief was subscribing to.

They might even have told about Ah Ching and his countrymen who, in 1853, went in with an association of Europeans and Americans in bargaining to have a flume constructed to serve their several mining claims. Once the flume was built, the claims were found to be valueless. The Europeans and Americans decamped. The Chinese stayed and paid their share of the construction expense.

The answer might fairly be made in explanation of this business honesty that it was fear of the Six Companies rather than an innate honesty which made the Chinese so scrupulous of their obligations. But the Six Companies must have had some foundation in the Chinese social system itself on which to build successfully a law capable of such uniform acceptance. Figs do not grow on thistles. . . . Death, according to the unwritten law of the Chinese, cancels all debts, therefore they exalt the debtor, who, finding himself unable to settle his obligations, calmly commits suicide.

It would be folly to assert that such a human tribunal as

SPOFFORD ALLEY
E.H Suydam

SPOFFORD ALLEY

The Six Companies

the Six Companies operated always on an exalted plane. Human institutions have a way of mirroring, in the long run, the virtues and follies of the members that compose it. Since the only qualification for membership was a birth certificate, so to speak, attesting that one had been born in such a district, the average could not have been too extraordinary. Its deliberations and verdicts were influenced very largely by the quality of its leader. When a man arrived from China of the calibre of Kwong Shau Louie with twenty years of study, twenty years of public service and twenty years of contemplation to his credit, it is obvious matters must have been ordered more judiciously than by a president not so versed in the contemplative amenities.

In thinking of the Six Companies phase of Chinatown organization, one must think of it as the common denominator of the political, the administrative, expression of the Chinese. It was therefore no better nor no worse than the political expression of any mass of people. . . . The family associations were great or obscure, intelligent or dull, rich or poor as their capacities ran. The trade guilds, the merchants' associations, even the blackmailing fraternities were concerned with questions confined within the narrower frames of their special interests. But the Six Companies were colored by each and every one of these strains, they had to grapple with interests both broad and narrow.

The true scope of the Six Companies, or even their limitations, perhaps will never be known. It is still hard to get unfettered testimony concerning what their duties were and what they are today. The Legislative Committee of 1876 were fairly confident that they were expressing a measure of the Six Companies' power when they rendered this report:

These tribunals are formed by the several Chinese Companies or Guilds, and are recognized as legitimate authorities by the Chinese population. They levy taxes, command masses of men, intimidate interpreters and witnesses, enforce perjury, regulate trade, punish the refractory, remove witnesses beyond the reach of our courts, control liberty of action, and prevent the return of the Chinese to their home in China, without their consent. In short, they exercise a despotic sway over one-seventh of the population of the State of California.

They invoke the processes of law only to punish the independent action of their subjects, and it is claimed that they exercise the death penalty upon those who refuse obedience to their decrees.

We are disposed to acquit these companies and secret tribunals of the charge of deliberate intent to supersede the authority of the State. The system is inherent and part of the Chinese mind, and exists because the Chinese are thoroughly and permanently alien to us in language and interest. . . .

The fact remains that they constitute a foreign government within the boundaries of the republic.

This report made the officials of the Six Companies a party to evasions, perjuries and crimes in the process of settling disputes between its members. This may or may not have been true. One might hazard a guess, however, that these flagrant disregards for American law were brought about by individuals rather than by direct connivance between individuals and Six Companies executives. The Six Companies officials, doubtless, many times shut their eyes to these procedures but it seems improbable that they were of their own devising, or done under their orders.

The Six Companies were naturally active in fighting exclusion. Before the enactment of the laws which grew continually more restrictive, their opposition was forthright. But once exclusion became effective they were charged with all sorts of evasions. The first law in the eighties which restricted laborers made necessary the issuance of a certificate from the Chinese authorities to the effect that entrants were not of the laboring class. It was said that the Six Companies forged certificates to enable laborers to enter.

Later, in 1892, when the more drastic Geary Act required all Chinese to register, the Six Companies raised a sum of two hundred thousand dollars to fight its provisions in the courts. They advised non-compliance with the law. Their power in the State is shown by the fact that out of a Chinese population of one hundred and ten thousand only ten per cent registered. When the Supreme Court upheld the Act, the forthright opposition ceased, but the claim was still made that the Six Companies were not above nullifying exclusion by any underhand means at their disposal.

The leading figure in the fight against exclusion was Chun Ti Chu, president of the Sam Yup Company, at that time, risen to the most powerful branch of the Six Companies. He had the reputation of being one of the ablest men in Chinatown and a militant foe of the highbinder tongs. One of the high officials of the police department said of him: "He can fight as well as talk. He is a fine shot and highbinders fear him as much as they hate him. He is brave enough to stand off three or four highbinders."

Chun Ti Chu organized a vigilance committee among the merchants to oppose blackmailing tongs, and this show of resistance plus coöperation with the police, sent the highbinders scurrying to cover for a season. Bagnios were closed and the women lodged in obscure apartments away from police interference as well as the tribute-levying hands of the hatchetmen.

When the Supreme Court of the United States declared that the Exclusion Act was constitutional there was great excitement and consternation among the Chinese who had taken the Six Companies' advice and neglected to register. The highbinders seized this opportunity to stir up opposition against Chun Ti Chu. A few days following the Court decision notices were posted throughout Chinatown offering three hundred dollars for the death of Chun. Other placards appeared denouncing him as an enemy of the Chinese because of his poor advice in connection with registration, citing his opposition to the tongs, and his connivance with the police to drive them from the city. These notices were torn down by the police and measures taken to protect him.

But the highbinders were not silenced so easily. Within a few hours after the first circulars had been destroyed a new batch appeared. These were insulting and abusive. This is what they said:

The President of the Sam Yup Company contains 12 stinkpots which are inexplicable. He has no literary talent. He bought his position with money. His father was a reformed thief. His mother's first husband was Fung and her second Chung. [Tantamount to saying that he was illegitimate.] He shields guilty criminals and tries to free them. He provoked people to anger at a meeting and tried to escape. Therefore all people had better close their noses when passing his door.

Another famous organization in Chinatown is the Four Families. This is an association of four prominent families banded together because of their numerical weakness. The Lau, Quan, Cheung and Chew families compose this deliberative body. The Lau family has, perhaps, the smallest number of members in America—eight.

Next come the fraternal guilds, or tongs. These may be trade guilds, or merchant guilds, or benevolent lodges, or just pure racketeering associations.

The trade guilds are somewhat akin to our trade unions. They regulate the price of labor, arrange terms, boycott "unfair" competition. The merchant guilds do something of the same thing along the line of price fixing and other problems that parallel American marketing associations. The Tea Merchants Guild, to mention an instance, fixes the price of tea. If one of their members is found cutting the rate, or in any way breaking his agreement, he is ruled out, his credit destroyed and he is driven to bankruptcy. But, one might hazard a guess that these activities should be more or less referred to in the past tense, especially the activities of the trade guilds.

The benevolent lodges need no explanation. Which leaves only the racketeering tongs to be disposed of.

There is no more exciting, or melodramatic note in the mosaic of American crime life than that contributed by the Chinese racketeering tongs. They anticipated the Al Capone era by more than fifty years. And, curiously enough, they, too, were a product of American life. The racketeering tong does not exist in China. The egg, as you shall see, may have been laid there, but it was hatched to full vigor in San Francisco.

Chapter VII

HIGHBINDERS

Most Americans are familiar with the word "highbinder." It is a term long current in the vernacular of the country and signifies a Chinese gangster. But it did not always have this meaning. The Reverend Mr. Frederic Masters is authority for the statement that "the term 'highbinder' first made its appearance in the columns of *The Weekly Inspector* for December 27, 1806." The article described "the riotous behavior of a party of Irish banditti belonging to an association called 'Highbinders' on Christmas eve of that year." The dictionary yields the information that the word was formed by combining *high* with *bender*. And, since *bender* is slang for a drinking spree or frolic, the significance of the original term is fairly obvious.

By what devious ways "highbinder" became detached

Highbinders

from a convivial Irish banditry and applied to the sober, cold-blooded assassins of Chinatown is shrouded in mystery such as so often pursues the career of a word that strays far from its source. Some make the claim that it was first applied to Chinese gunmen by a New York policeman. If so, it quickly made its way across the continent to San Francisco and found instant lodgement at the very fountain-head of highbinder activity.

The Chinese have a less obscure and more significant term for the murderous parasites that prey upon decency and timidity. They call them "hatchetmen" and let it go at that.

When the first highbinder or hatchetman appeared upon the California scene would be hard to determine, but before his coming the Chinese took the law into their own hands and attempted to fight out their difficulties in groups. Later on, with the ascendancy of criminal associations that could be retained to blackmail a rival into acceptance of terms, naïve attempts at group adjustments gave way to the cool, impersonal vengeance of hired assassination.

One of the first group-attempts to settle a controversy took place in the mining country near Weaverville in the summer of 1854. The cause of the disturbance and affiliations of the combatants are lost in obscurity. But, according to report, the struggle was unequal—a band of one hundred and fifty facing an equally irate horde of five hundred. The battle began in the early morning and raged until four o'clock in the afternoon, when a halt was made to collect the dead. Between six and eight Chinamen were killed and many wounded. Pistols, pikes and spears—the pikes and spears in the Oriental mode—gave the occasion an authentic war-like turn. One white man was said to have been killed—doubtless, our old friend the innocent bystander. . . . The next day the dead were given imposing funerals—the smaller group quite outdoing the larger unit in the splendor and noise attending the ceremonies. Which would seem to indicate that the smaller group was the wealthier and more influential. At all events, it was proclaimed the victor.

Later in the fall of that same year, a rather unorganized riot took place in the streets of Sacramento. This seemed more or less unpremeditated and took on the aspects of a Montague-Capulet row in approved Romeo-and-Juliet manner. What chance spark ignited the flame is uncertain, but suddenly the streets were swarming with combatants carrying "swords of tin and iron and cutlasses sporting pink handles." Many of the fighters wore tin hats, anticipating trench headgear of a later date, and they carried bamboo shields. The fight was fast and furious, lasting about a half an hour, when the police arrived and carried away twenty warriors to cool their ardors in the unromantic hoosegow. Nobody was killed but scores were wounded.

Outbreaks such as these occurred from time to time in the mining districts, to the intense delight of the white population who always assembled to encourage and cheer the fighters on to bloodier deeds of valor. A cock fight or a bear-baiting could not have given greater satisfaction. But in 1856 a clash of opposing Chinese forces occurred near Sonora that put all previous contests to shame and earned for itself the imposing title in all the newspapers of "The Chinese War in California."

There was nothing obscure about the origin of this row. It had all the triviality of a neighborhood feud, and demonstrated the kinship of the whole world when it comes to a matter of the puerilities. The opening scene was the banks of the Stanislaus River, at a place called Two-mile Bar. At this point, two groups of Chinese were working adjacent mining claims. On the one claim were twelve members of the Sam Yup Society and, on the other, six members of the Yan

TONG BALCONIES

Highbinders

Wo Society. These were district organizations that later came together under the banner of the Six Companies.

One morning, the Yan Wo contingent arrived from Chinese Camp to work their claim and found that the Sam Yups had dislodged a stone weighing about two tons which had been interfering with their operations, and rolled it over on the Yan Wo territory. The Yan Wos protested but the Sam Yups, outnumbering them two to one, refused to remove the stone from their rivals' path. There followed threats, defiances, challenges—culminating in an exchange of notes in the fashion of rival kingdoms declaring war, of which the following from the Sam Yups is a sample:

There are a great many now existing in the world who ought to be exterminated. We, by this give you a challenge, and inform you beforehand that we are the strongest, and you are too weak to oppose us. We can therefore wrest your claim, or anything else from you, and give you notice that it is our intention to drive you away from us, and make you ashamed of yourselves. You are nothing compared with us. We are durable as stone, but you are pliant as sponge. Your force would have no more effect against us than an egg would have against a stone. You want to coax us to come to terms. That we refuse. We mean to fight you, and expel you from your localities. If you do not stand and fight us, we will consider you no better than so many brutes; and, as such, we will harness you to our desires. There are plenty of us, well-equipped and ready, at any time, to meet and fight you whenever you choose; and would make you run into holes and hide yourselves. But we need not go to that trouble. We have only to speak, and you'll become frightened. You won't stand like men; you are perfect worms; or, like the dog that sits in the door and barks, but will not go further. If you won't accept the challenge, we tell you, by the way, to go and buy lots of flour, and paint your faces; then go to your houses, shut the doors, and hide yourselves, and we'll kill every man of you that we come across. Shame! Shame!

San Francisco's Chinatown

Mr. Mussolini, himself, never breathed a more superior or forthright notice of intention to civilize by the process of extermination than the Sam Yups exhibited in this forthright challenge. We presume that the Yan Wos replied in kind. At all events, a date was set for a battle and the field of honor was named.

There went forth from both camps a call to arms—Sam Yups and Yan Wos from the length and breadth of California being ordered to report on the twenty-sixth day of September at Kentucky Ranch, about four miles from Chinese Camp, to demonstrate the honor and glory of their clans. Enormous preparations began. The Sam Yups sent to San Francisco for one hundred and fifty guns and a supply of ammunition. When this shipment arrived, they hired white instructors at ten dollars a day and a whiskey ration to teach them the gentle art of slaughter in the modern manner.

The Yan Wos relied on older and more conservative devices for warfare. They built pikes eighteen feet long, and tridents with equally far-reaching handles. They bought up all the cleavers in Chinese Camp and Sonora and sent to San Francisco for a supply of gongs. They even manufactured coats of mail by hammering out discarded sardine tins and sewing them on canvas.

When the morning of the twenty-sixth arrived, twelve hundred Sam Yups lined up on one side and nine hundred Yan Wos on the other. In addition to their musketry the Sam Yups had resorted to the terrifying device of robing fifteen of their most imposing members in ancient warrior costume, painting their faces a bright yellow and draping horse-hair tails three feet long down their backs. These fifteen blood-thirsty apparitions, plus the one hundred and fifty guns, were no match for the Yan Wos, in spite of their spears, tridents and home-made coats of mail. But they advanced valiantly to the vigorous beating of gongs and the noise from twelve old-fashioned muskets, to meet the deadly fire of their efficient opponents.

When the first smoke cleared two Yan Wos were dead and several wounded. But the wounded had little chance of escape. Once they were down, the Sam Yups rushed upon them, stabbed them all over, and bore their bodies away in triumph impaled upon monster tridents. They then, according to reliable testimony, "cut them to pieces as they would a hog, and afterwards carried the remains out of sight, burned them to ashes, and scattered them to the four winds of heaven." This, we take it, effectively prevented the bones of the hapless victims from ever resting in ancestral burying ground that would have brought such peace and protection to their spirits.

The Yan Wos, terrified at the turn in events, offered to continue the battle if the Sam Yups would play the game without resort to musketry. This the Sam Yups refused to do. The sheriff of the county now intervened and by the next day had disarmed all the fighters on both sides.

This ended warfare on an imposing scale between rival factions. Perhaps the Chinese decided that too much publicity ended in interference by American authorities. They were always loathe to battle openly with the law. There was too much hazard attached to fighting sheriffs and police sergeants. One never could tell when panic or zeal would lay a minion of the White Government low. In this last furious encounter one of the deputies had a horse shot from under him. A lynching party might have been the answer to Chinese defiance if the deputy himself had been killed.

On the surface the Sam Yups were triumphant, and, a week or two later, they celebrated the event in Sacramento with a jubilee dinner accompanied by fireworks and the beating of gongs. But it would not be safe to assume that the issue was settled. It must have taken many moons for the

Yan Wos to forget their dead, hacked and burned and cast to the wind. Vengeance was a sacred obligation to most Chinese. Like the Kentucky mountaineers they met violence with violence, and clan loyalty had the aspects of religious fervor. Even their most reflective and humane philosopher, Confucius, admonished them thus: "The murderer of your father ought not to remain under the same sky with you; you must not lay down your arms as long as the murderer of your brother lives; and you cannot live in the same kingdom with the murderer of your friend."

The Sam Yups and the Yan Wos doubtless went back to their adjacent claims and worked with stolid calm, but even if the district group found it expedient to forget, there must have been blood brethren who remembered their dead, and the indignity heaped upon them—blood brethren who could not rest with honor while the murderers of their brother lived, friends who found it impossible to live in the same "kingdom" with murderers of their comrades.

For years after, many a Chinaman, found sprawling dead upon lonely country roadside or cobbled Chinatown alley, might conceivably have traced his quick demise back to the feud when the bullets of the Sam Yups pierced the coats-of-mail contrived from flattened sardine cans by the Yan Wos.

Whether fear of becoming involved with American authorities was one of the factors in putting an end to mass murder among groups of Chinese, another factor, equally determining, began to work its way insidiously into the growing frame-work of self-government which the Chinese population in California were evolving. This was the introduction of criminal associations that organized primarily to circumvent American laws and finally fastened themselves with a ruthless stranglehold upon decent elements.

One of the first of these organizations beginning in a small way, in 1852, was the Hip Yee Tong. This association was founded for the purpose of importing slave-girls into the country. It became so notorious in a few years that the leading Chinese merchants under the leadership of the Six Companies in 1863 decided to check its activities. They succeeded temporarily, but with the influx of Chinese for the building of the railroad the problem became too great and in three years the Hip Yees were flourishing again like green bay trees. Obnoxious as this association was, it had for its object a more or less restricted field, and, aside from the shadow it threw upon Chinese society in general, it perhaps did not touch all classes and conditions as definitely as an organization called the Chee Kung Tong did, which established itself in San Francisco, a little later. This Chee Kung Tong was thought by many Americans to be a sort of Free Masonry—a conviction that was further reinforced when they heard its name translated into "The Chamber of High Justice."

But the Chee Kung Tong was a bandit organization pure and simple, in spite of its ethical pretensions. Its headquarters were in Spofford alley in San Francisco. Thence it threw out its tentacles so that every city or village boasting a Chinatown felt its grip and paid tribute to it. Even the Eastern States were not immune. There the organization has a different title but it was a shoot from the parent stem, nevertheless. Yee Hing Oey, it was called, which signified "Society of Righteous Brethren."

Curiously enough, the roots of these organizations tapped highly idealistic sources. They went far back to patriots chaffing under Manchu rule—organizations that worked with incredible patience through two centuries to dislodge the invaders. The first of these asociations was known as the Triad Society, holding in mystic veneration a trinity of Heaven, Earth and Man. "Their revolutionary plots," says Reverend Mr. Frederic J. Masters, "were formed with such inscrutable secrecy, and under such artful disguises, that all the vigilance of the Chinese government, and the ablest detective service perhaps in the world, failed to discover the conspirators until the Tai Ping rebellion broke out in 1850 which shook the empire to its foundations and devastated ten provinces with fire and sword."

This was the uprising put down in the sixties by General Gordon, "Chinese" Gordon, so effectively that the Triad Society slumbered for years, or appeared to slumber. At least there were no outward manifestations in China. With the suppression of the rebellion, those who were agile enough to flee the country and escape the executioner's sword, found themselves out of conspirator's jobs and in strange lands. They fled to the Straits Settlements, to Australia, to South America, to California.

Even so high-minded a movement as freeing one's country from the yoke of an invader, does not attract idealists exclusively. Any revolt presupposes assassination and murder, and assassination and murder always draw desperate men, anti-social men, criminal men to its standard. A more or less passive and peace-loving majority usually provide the sinews of war for impulses toward patriotism and freedom, but the leaders can never in the nature of things be passive or peace loving. Thus it was with the routed leaders of the Tai Ping rebellion. They were men of action—plots and war were their business. Such men do not beat swords into ploughshares.

What these men found to do in the Straits Settlements, in Australia, in South America is beyond the point but what they found to do in California—in San Francisco—is of the utmost importance to this narrative. It was inconceivable, of course, that they were of the stuff that ranch laborers and fruit peddlers were made. One could not imagine an active revolutionist settling down and running up overalls on a sewing machine, or squeezing out sugar roses for the greater glory of a birthday cake, or sitting behind the counter of a merchandise shop. After all, any professional revolutionist is a parasite. He must have a host to feed on. In California, the host was ready and *waiting*—in the mining regions, on the ranches, in the market place—thousands of Chinese, in a state of industry yielding them a return almost fabulous in comparison to anything they could earn at home.

How the founders of the Chee Kung Tong went about establishing themselves must largely be a matter of conjecture. But it is conceivable that at the beginning they did not use blackmail methods to wring dimes and dollars out of the bulging pocket-books of their countrymen. It seems possible that at first they insinuated themselves into the good graces of San Francisco's Chinatown on the score of idealism—of patriotism.

The "Chamber of High Justice," the "Society of Righteous Brethren" flowing back to the venerable Triad Society could easily have been the bait that enlisted contributions to support a cause alleged to be not lost but sleeping. On the other hand, knowing the desperate character of the men who later made the word "tong" a thing to be feared and hated, it is also just as conceivable that they began their activities with undisguised threats and reprisals.

Many years after the founding of the Chee Kung Tong, a police raid on the society's headquarters uncovered a manual revealing the secret rites and history of the organization. The history went back to the heroic beginnings of Triadism. The record was turned over to Mr. Masters who gave an able résumé of the contents, in which he characterized the history of the rise of Triadism as "a story that reads more like a legend of King Arthur's days than a sober chapter of modern history."

The narrative begins at a point some two hundred and

fifty years ago when the Manchus first came into power in China and when their rule was by no means upon a firm foundation. A rebellion broke out amongst the fierce barbarian tribes in the south of China and the Emperor despatched troops to quell the disturbance. They failed dismally, and one army after another was sent against the revolters, only to be cut to pieces. The government then issued a proclamation offering rewards and honors to any leader who could subdue these invincible warriors.

Dwelling in the mountains of the Fookien province was a company of Buddhist priests. These priests differed from most inmates of monasteries in that they were of superb physique. In fact, admission to the order hinged upon certain grueling physical tests. When the Emperor's proclamation reached their province, the hundred and twenty-eight priests who made up the monastery of Shui Lum, took counsel together and decided to present themselves before the Imperial Throne and make an offer to subdue the rebels.

The Emperor was so impressed with their bodily strength which seemed little short of miraculous, that he immediately gave them orders to proceed. Then in the words of the Reverend Mr. Masters:

Having received their Imperial commission they set out for Sai Low. The monks divided themselves into two divisions and fought with such skill and intrepidity that the rebels were seized with panic and fled. No quarter was given; the barbarians were cut to pieces till, as the record states, corpses covered the ground and blood flowed in streams. The victorious monks, without loss of life, returned to Pekin. The officials met them at the gates, the laureate sang ballads celebrating their victory, and the conquerors were escorted through the crowded streets to the Emperor's palace. When honors and rewards were offered them their leader exclaimed, "O King, live ten thousand years! What have thy servants done to merit these favors? Poor friars are we, who have renounced the world with its pleasures, riches

E H Suydam
San Francisco 1925.

"WAI SUNG"

"WAI SUNG"

and honors, and have taken vows of poverty that forbid us, O King, to accept thy gifts.

The monks now returned to their mountain convent, the country rang with their fame, but the court of Pekin was perplexed. The success and popularity of the monks aroused the jealousy of the Manchu soldiery; their rejection of Imperial favors awakened the suspicions of the government. One day two ministers of state, Cheong Kin Tsau and Chan Man Yew, sought audience at court, and accused the monks of high treason. "These men of Shui Lum," said they, "have such superhuman power that they can with a word bring down the sky or raise the earth. Hordes of barbarians that your Majesty's troops tried in vain to subdue have been exterminated by these monks; and now what is there to hinder them carrying out their seditious plot to seize the government and overthrow the state?" At these words the Emperor trembled and his "dragon countenance changed color." "Alas," said the Emperor, "these tidings cause me much distress. What remedy can you suggest?"

Cheong Kin Tsau and Chan Man Yew were full of suggestions. They had a nice plan which involved presenting the monks of Shui Lum with a case of Imperial wine reinforced with poison. This seemed fair enough to His Imperial Majesty and Cheong Kin Tsau was dispatched with a body of troops to the monastery to fittingly bestow this royal favor upon the hapless priests. They were a little puzzled at such unexpected recognition, but, since Cheong Kin Tsau seemed determined not only to present the wine but to see that it was drunk before he departed, the abbot ordered a celebration.

Thereupon a feast was prepared, the tables spread, and the jars opened, when lo! a black vapor was seen to rise from the opened jars, filling the room with a poisonous stench. The assembled monks gazed at each other in blank amazement. "What wine is this that hath so offensive an odor?" demanded the abbot. "Bring forth our founder's precious sword, and let the wine be tested." The sword was produced, thrust into the jar, and withdrawn with evident marks of poison on the blade. Then was the abbot filled with rage, and demanded of Cheong Kin Tsau what they had done to deserve such treatment from a government they had served so faithfully. While he was speaking an explosion shook the building, flames and smoke burst forth, while on all sides were heard the sounds of battle horns and drums and the tramp of armed men. Hemmed in by flaming walls and the swords of the soldiers, escape seemed hopeless. Of the 128 monks only eighteen escaped.

Fleeing to the desert, this handful of survivors encountered a storm which took toll of thirteen of their number. The five remaining, still pursued by Tartar soldiers, one day came upon a stone tripod by the road. Upon it were engraved these words: *Fan tsing, fuk ming,* which was interpreted to mean that they were to work for the downfall of the Manchus and for the restoration of the Ming dynasty which the Tartars deposed.

The monks fell to their knees and "worshipped Heaven and Earth." They then took a porcelain bowl hurling it to the ground three times. It remained unbroken which was a sign that Heaven had decreed that they were to be the founders of a movement to see that "a descendant of the ancient kings was placed on the dragon throne."

This, then, was the noble beginning of the Chee Kung Tong. The story, leading up to the flight of eighteen monks to the desert, is singularly Oriental in spirit—the valor of the athletic priests, the envy of the military caste at court, the insinuations of crafty leaders to the Emperor, the smiling delivery of gifts prepared to destroy. *Oriental?* Perhaps that is too narrow a term when one remembers the court intrigues of the de Medicis and Borgias, of Elizabeth, of Louis XVI. In the history of this movement begun two hundred and fifty years ago, there must have crept in a large element of legend. It is unlikely that one hundred and twenty-eight men, however valorous, could have unaided put down a rebellion.

Highbinders

And, yet, there has been evidence where a single man with resolute bravery has faced and cowed a mob bent on his destruction.

But there is usually some basis for even a legend. And the story of the beginnings of Triadism must have had an essential veracity. As was said of it forty years ago: "Whatever may be its character today its original purpose was plain. Its founders set out to revenge a cruel massacre and break off a hated foreign yoke, objects which it has sought to accomplish by methods more secret and infernal than those adopted by the nihilists or Clan na Gael."

Do the mills of the gods grind slowly and with exactness? And did the treachery of the Manchu court against a band of blameless men, start in motion forces which ended in its fall two centuries later? . . . In the interest of poetic justice it is pleasant to believe that such might be the case. But the ultimate result in China of a movement started by five holy men is not so pertinent to our subject as the ultimate result of this same movement in the United States when whatever idealism it possessed had evaporated and left an ugly husk of criminality and murder.

There were other things in the manual, found by the police in the rooms of the Chee Kung Tong, besides a history of the society's heroic beginnings. There was a full record of its initiation ceremonies. It is an account which reads like the stage business of a melodramatic opera founded on a Chinese theme. It includes doorkeepers fiercely gowned and more fiercely painted, at three mystic portals; challenges for passwords; threats of death for betrayal of secrets; indignities and sometimes torture in the name of purification. All this performed against a background of gilded carvings, the murky smoke of a thousand burning punk sticks, the glowering countenance of Kwan Kung, the god of war, and the more benign though equally warrior-like figures of the five priests who discovered the mystic tripod with a heavenly message written upon it.

Having been passed through the first portal, the candidate proceeded to divest himself of his Manchu clothes, taking great pains to unplait his queue. For the queue, in spite of the attachment that the rank and file Chinaman developed for it, was of Manchu origin. Next he put on garments of the Ming dynasty in five colors, with white girdle and a red turban. It was the Ming dynasty that the Manchus had deposed.

Beyond the second portal was an arch of sharp swords beneath which the candidate was compelled to crawl. In this room was likewise the grand master of the organization with the curious name of "Ah Ma" which means Mother, his hair unplaited, his costume in the Ming fashion. Then came a ceremony that crops out in the folk rites of most aboriginal people, another proof of how the Chinese have preserved customs that go back to a dim past. A needle pierced the finger tips of the candidates and a drop of blood from each man was allowed to fall into a common wine cup. This drink was passed to all present, symbolizing a new brother-and-blood relationship. After drinking of the mingled wine and blood, the candidates were compelled to crawl under the throne on which Ah Ma was seated. This was symbolical of having been born again. It also meant that the candidate had renounced his Emperor, his kin and even his father and mother. His allegiance was now to his blood brothers, and the grand master became his father. This was a terrific step to take, for the cornerstone of Chinese civilization is filial piety.

The third portal was concerned with oaths of allegiance to the cause and instruction into the secrets of the society. "Worship," says Mr. Masters, "is offered to Heaven and Earth, to the spirits of the slaughtered priests, and to the spirits of the ancient kings. Incense and gilt paper are burned, candles lighted, and libations of wine and tea poured to the gods. Thirty-five solemn oaths, mostly in rhyme, are chanted before the High Altar."

At this point, we come upon our old friend the decapitated rooster, which was once urged upon American courts taking Chinese testimony as an oath which would bind them to the truth. During this ceremony the neophyte chanted this rhyme:

> From rooster's head, from rooster's head,
> See how the fresh blood flows.
> If loyal and brave my course shall be
> My heirs immortal renown shall see;
> But when base traitor and coward turn I,
> Slain on the road my body shall lie.

At another part of the ceremony he gave expression to these lines:

> By this red drop of blood on finger tip I swear
> The secrets of this Tong I never will declare.
> Seven gaping wounds shall drain my life away
> Should I to alien ears my sacred trust betray.

A further ordeal awaited the candidate. He was compelled to run the gauntlet of two lines of Triad members. If he were recognized as ever having been an enemy of the society he received a sound buffeting on all sides. But this thrashing settled the score. Thenceforth he was a member in good standing.

Whether this ancient ritual was performed *in toto* as the uprooted Triads under the banner of the Chee Kung Tong sank lower and lower in its aims and ideals will never be known. But that its oaths and secrets were terrifying can scarcely be doubted. Among the lesser breeds of hatchetmen there persisted a ritual simpler but just as binding. The candidate was compelled to kneel in front of crossed swords before the god of war. As he swore fidelity and obedience to his tong, a naked sword was held over his head.

Of the final state of degradation of the Chee Kung Tong, Mr. Masters writing in 1892 had this to say:

The character of the society has completely changed since it has been transplanted to this country. While retaining all the old political nomenclature and forms, it is practically dead as a revolutionary center. Its political hopes extinguished it has now degenerated into a rendezvous of assassins and blackmailers. Professing to be a benevolent association formed for mutual protection it is in reality a self-constituted star chamber, an organized band of villains who rule with a rod of iron. It is not denied that there are respectable men enrolled in the association who would repudiate deeds of violence. These most likely joined under a wrong impression; but, once a member, withdrawal is next to *impossible*. The society's manual frankly admits that its members are drawn from all ranks of life,—rich and poor, learned and illiterate, honest men and swindlers, banditti of the mountains, pirates of the seas, and tramps of the public street. The respectable and honest are few and far between. The society is a cave of Adullam,—a resort for all who are in distress or in debt or discontented. The worst desperadoes of the Canton province, whose heads would have adorned the tower over some city gate had they remained in China, find an asylum under our beneficent laws, and procure congenial employment as the salaried soldiers of the Tong.

The powerful Chee Kung Tong was a pattern for all the gangster tongs which came after. Many of them were shoots from the parent stem—founded by rival factions within the original order that seceded but still held to the old allegiance. For, as Mr. Masters pointed out, it was impossible to shake free of the organization after one had subscribed to its tenets. Once a Chee Kung, always a Chee Kung.

Then there were criminal associations founded along more specific lines—the Hip Shing Tong that controlled the gambling clubs; the Wa Ting Shans, who levied tribute on the brothels; or the On Leong Society that dealt in slave-girls. All these titles were high sounding and of impeccable moral intent. The traffickers in the slave-girls, On Leong Society, meant the "Chamber of Tranquil Conscientiousness." Another society founded for the same purpose, the Kwong Tak Tong, was the "Chamber of Far-Reaching Virtue." The gambling fraternity, the Hip Shing Tong, was synonymous with the "Hall of Victorious Union."

Even the hatchet societies, engaged primarily in killing for a consideration, were just as high flown and pretentious in their choice of titles. "Hall of Associated Conquerors," "Hall of Auspicious Victory," "Hall of Realized Repose," are some of the names they chose. There is something ironically humorous about the "Hall of Realized Repose" in connection with an association which put its victims to sleep at so much per head. And what shall we say of the association that lived by taxing brothels under the title of "Flowery Arbor Mountain Booth?" Were they kidding themselves or the American officials? Or were they just putting over a piece of hilarious nonsense in the fashion of a famous club of convivial politicians that flourished in San Francisco before prohibition under the name of "The Indoor Yacht Club," or the one now operating called "The Indoor Surf Riders."

This penchant for flowery and grandiloquent titles is an Oriental attribute and it is possible that these Chinese gangsters saw nothing incongruous in applying such poetic names to their murderous associations. The streets of Chinatown, even today, are hung with signs that would delight or amuse the white visitor if he could but read them. "Balcony of Joy and Delight" is a fitting enough designation for a restaurant, and to label a fine tea, "Butterfly's Eyebrow" has a touch of the exquisite. But when a dealer in cigars calls his shop "The

Fountain of Righteousness" an Occidental might be pardoned if he smiled.

But the poetic touch is always a little incongruous to the practical mind, particularly when it becomes a part of daily life. The Occidental withdraws to enjoy his poetry, the Oriental, particularly the Chinese, takes it as it comes mingled with drabness and squalor. Their approach to art and visual beauty is the same. A dust-clouded, grimy window-pane in Chinatown may look out upon a cluster of exquisitely pink camellias rising from a porcelain pot. At a certain street corner in the Chinatown of today, is a one-story building that houses a butcher shop. The roof is given over to the smelly business of drying squid, and the cooling of greasy sausage. But every spring this same roof is sown with blossoming lilies for the New Year's Trade, and, in the autumn, there are rows of russet chrysanthemums raised for nothing more practical apparently, than the enjoyment of sheer beauty. Is it conceivable that one would find camellias, porcelain potted, on the window ledge of an American tenement or lilies lighting the greasy gloom of an Occidental sausage factory?

This is the philosophy of a people who have for centuries had to conserve, to count grains of rice, to wring dry sustenance and even beauty from remnants. They have had to take what they could grasp by the way. As with the poetry of blossoming lilies among the sausages, so with the poetry of the spoken word. Only the scholars and the wealthy can withdraw for contemplation. The toiler, the shop-keeper, the hatchetman, if you will, must take his poetry on the wing. Perhaps the cigar dealer's business is far from being a "Fountain of Righteousness," but that fiction upon a gilded sign, somehow shines luminously through the monotonous and commonplace. And, if the memory of seeing a butterfly in fluttering motion has been dulled by years of murky toil in alleyways of the city, who can say how much enchantment

LITTLE RED CAFÉ, JACKSON STREET

Highbinders

may be evoked by just the designation "butterfly's eyebrow"
upon a dingy mound of tea in a dealer's window?

It is easy to be scornful of the poetic note in names chosen
for the questionable associations of Chinese gangsterdom.
One grows a little impatient with a "Chamber of Far-Reaching Virtue" or "Flowery Arbor Mountain Booth" in connection with a business that included the sale of slave-girls
and the wringing of a perpetual tribute from their life of
shame. But, to match such an attitude of mind among public
enemies, one has only to translate this inconsistency into the
soft sentimentalism which pervaded the ranks of Al Capone
et al, in the days of their sawed-off-shotgun terrorism: Soup
kitchens for the poor, orchids for the dead, Christmas toys
for poor "kiddies." Or an even more pointed comparison,
the white gentlemen of the gold rush era, whose disappointment at being unable properly to keep the birthday of the
Prince of Peace, caused them to rob Chinese coolies of their
hard won gold dust.

All our amazement at these contradictions are brought
about by the fact that we think of criminals as working
twenty-four hours a day at their nefarious jobs. We never
grant them moments of relaxation. We forget the immortal
words of the Police-Sergeant in "The Pirates of Penzance,"
which informs us that:

> When the enterprising burglar's not a-burgling,
> When the cut-throat isn't occupied in crime,
> He loves to hear the little brooks a-gurgling
> And listen to the merry village chime.

And in further proof of this great truth, we have only to
point out the story of four Chinese murderers, condemned
to be hung, and the newspaper accounts of how they spent
their last hours. They did not call for a turkey dinner, or a
stiff glass of whiskey, or a twenty-five cent cigar. Instead they

diverted themselves by writing poetry. Three of them danced nimbly on the air and one committed suicide in his cell. The first, Fou Seen, welcomed death in this fashion:

> Green spring, I wait you in gladness.
> Who can obstruct or impede the vast harvest of the grain?
> True felicity must come from self, otherwise 'tis nothing.
> After joyful spring, comes tedious autumn.

The second, Teu Ye, wrote thus:

> My body hath gone before me, borne on clouds.
> My youth was coupled with twenty springs
> I was unconscious of it, but thus it was.
> I loved to follow the bridegroom of the Southern hills.

The third, Coon You, said:

Music and the practice of the guitar hath its time.
The spirit will mount, borne by red incense, full of fragrance.
The fulfillment, like a gem, is soon wrought out.

The suicide, Ah Koon See, penned these lines:

Sing and dance; truth is complete.
Evil smoke will again arouse the suspicion of foes and men.
Now let me wear the flowered cap, wrapped in golden garments.
And my brow decorated with gems.

No wonder the editor of the *Alta California* in commenting editorially upon these gangster-poets was moved to write:

Is not this strange language to fall from the lips of these degraded beings? And does it not, after all, indicate a far higher grade of intellectual powers, than common estimation usually gives to them? Point to a single instance of *one* of the Anglo-Saxon race, who, in a like position, and at a like moment, has ever displayed the intellectual capacity and serenity of mind, necessary to enable him to give utterance to sentiments so full of poetic beauty, as these. And yet, here are four men, taken accidentally, as it were, from among their fellow countrymen, each one of whom utters with his dying breath, words vieing in beauty with those of the others. It presents a strange problem. Who can solve it? Does it not go far to prove that the lavish abuse and ill-treatment that is generally bestowed upon the Chinaman, because of the estimation in which he is held, as a lower order of being than the European or American races, is illy deserved, and does it not illustrate that they are possessed of intellect not inferior to the Anglo-Saxon race?

Possessed of an intellect not inferior to the Anglo-Saxon race.

What a concession for one of our grandfathers to have made!

Chapter VIII

BLACKMAIL AND ASSASSINATION

In subscribing to the principles of the first gangster tongs that established themselves in San Francisco, the decent element of Chinese soon found themselves at the mercy of a Frankenstein monster which they had helped to create. The injustice and indifference of California courts to Chinese problems were as nothing compared to the terrorism and rapacity of these self-constituted tribunals. The time came when murderers stood for hire on every street corner, and, when the business of vengeance became slack, the hatchet boys levied tribute for immunity against their sinister activities, or brewed discord among rival clans to promote business.

Just as vested American interests have from time to time consorted with political crooks and thugs to promote an expediency, to their ultimate sorrow, so Chinese trade guilds and district associations and even, on occasion, the more astute merchants' guilds, trafficked with the underworld in pursuit of their desires.

A typical case of how a business association called upon gangsterdom to assist it in enforcing tabus was enacted in Sacramento's Chinatown in the seventies. The Association of Chinese Laundrymen made a rule that no washhouse would be permitted to open ten doors from another. A Chinaman, who made the additional mistake of going into partnership with a white man, defied this order. A representative from the Laundry Association waited upon him, advised him to close his doors, and fined him thirty dollars. The Chinese, doubtless aided and abetted by his American partner, not only refused to pay the fine but went to the authorities with his story.

The Association had another meeting at which they increased the fine to one hundred dollars, presenting this demand with the delicate hint that refusal to pay would mean death. The victim played for time to raise the money and asked them to call the next day. A delegation of three waited on him at the appointed time armed suggestively with knives and pistols. He parted with sixty dollars, whereupon some waiting detectives pounced upon the three gentlemen and arrested them for robbery.

The Laundry Association had a third meeting. This time they passed resolutions ordering the advertising of bids for the stubborn washman's murder. They then had circulated through Chinatown printed dodgers calling for volunteers. One of these circulars fell into the hands of the police. It offered a substantial reward for the murder by one man—or one man and an assistant. If the murderers were arrested, it further agreed to pay counsel fees and three dollars a day for confinement. In event of either the murderer or his as-

sistant being condemned to die, it promised to pay a lump
sum to their relatives.

This payment of money to the murdered man's family by
the murderers seems to have been an old Chinese custom. It
was a rule rigidly enforced even between branches of the Six
Companies. In one of the legislative investigations, a Christian Chinaman named Lem Scham gave the following testimony:

LEM SCHAM: If I should kill a Chinaman, I am brought before
the company and made to pay a fine. They take the money and send
it back to the family of the killed man to support his mother.

QUESTIONER: If you kill a member of the See Yup Company, the
See Yup Company will determine that you should pay so much money.

LEM SCHAM: Yes.

QUESTIONER: If you pay?

LEM SCHAM: All right.

QUESTIONER: If not?

LEM SCHAM: I must go to the American Courts.

This "going to the American Courts" was tantamount to
abandoning the culprit to his fate. But, there was often a
speedier punishment than this for him, if his enemies were
wealthy enough to hire a highbinder to shoot him down.
When the victim was obscure and lacking in influential family or association ties, revenge did not go further than letting him take his chances in the halls of an alien justice.

In spite of the fact that respectable associations always
were protesting that advertising for men to commit murder
did not exist, the police were continually coming upon authentic evidence which proved the contrary. For the most
part the prospective victims named in these circulars were
Chinese but, occasionally, a white man came under the ban.
This was notably so in the case of F. L. Gordon, the publisher
of a Chinese newspaper. A notice was posted boldly in the

Blackmail and Assassination

streets of Chinatown offering six hundred dollars for the death of Mr. Gordon and two hundred and fifty dollars for the death of his Chinese servant. The servant of Mr. Gordon read the notice and cut it down. This, too, emanated from the Laundry Guild.

The Washhouse Association had run up a printing bill for three thousand dollars which it refused to pay. Mr. Gordon threatened to sue. A bright member of the association thought that an admirable way out was to kill off Mr. Gordon, since a dead creditor could not present any bills. Mr. Gordon's Chinese servant got wind of the matter and warned his master, which explains why he too was put on the spot. The notice was couched in brief language or, at least, the Chinese servant put it briefly when asked for a translation of its content: "Him say, anyone want to get rich, come kill Mr. Gordon and me."

Here are at least two instances where murders were coldly planned by an association that was not organized for criminality. The Washhouse Association was a guild to safeguard business—a legitimate company of men, if ever there was one. Yet, it did not scruple to hire assassins to put its enemies out of the way. But, in the nature of things, the average Chinese laundryman of the last century was not a high type. In fact, something of the mental qualifications and stupidity of the Washhouse Association's officials is betrayed in this move to dodge a debt by the simple expedient of killing off Mr. Gordon. Fortunately for the Chinese laundry interests in San Francisco, the plans miscarried. Had Mr. Gordon been killed, it probably would have spelled the doom of the Chinese washhouse. In any event, Chinatown would have been turned inside out by the authorities in tracking down the murderers and the motives back of their crime.

But it was not often that the Chinese carried their warfare into the white camp. They were too sharp-sighted for this.

San Francisco's Chinatown

Yet, curiously enough one of the most authentic evidences of Chinese racketeer methods came to light under a searching investigation into plans for the murder of a white victim. Again, curiously enough, this was in British Columbia and not on American soil. And it was not a product of a respectable tong in search of a criminal to do its dirty work, but a conspiracy of our old friends the Chee Kung Association, the alleged Chinese Free Masons, whose roots went back to the five priests who founded an order to drive the Manchus from China.

The victim they picked for slaughter was the Reverend Mr. J. E. Gardner. The Chee Kung Association in San Francisco does not appear to have been directly concerned with the traffic in women, but in Victoria it appears that this was one of its major activities. The Reverend Mr. Gardner went after this phase of their work and succeeded in breaking it up. Rumor came to this gentlemen that a hired assassin named Lum Hip had been retained to put him on the spot. Mr. Gardner went to the police, who ran down Lum Hip in his lodgings. The room was filled with knives, guns and other implements of thuggery. But the most important evidence was a document found on Lum Hip. This turned out to be the assassin's commission or a general plan of work expected from him. It does not mention specifically the Reverend Mr. Gardner's name but the inferences as to what Lum Hip had been hired to do, is fairly obvious. And, more than this, it gives a general picture of the other duties assigned to the "salaried soldier," which is indicative of the low state to which the once idealistic Triad Society had sunk.

Here is the document:

To Lum Hip, Salaried Soldier:
It is well known that plans and schemes of government are the work of the learned holders of the seal; while to oppose foes, fight

164

JACKSON STREET

Blackmail and Assassination

battles, and plant firm government, is the work of the military. This agreement is made with the above-named salaried soldier on account of sedition from within and derision and contempt from without. You, Lum Hip, together with all other salaried soldiers, shall act only when orders are given; and without orders you shall not act. But in case of emergency when our members, for instance, are suddenly attacked, you shall act according to the expediency of the case, and enter the arena if necessary. When orders are given you shall advance valiantly to your assigned duty, striving to be first, and only fearing to be found laggard. Never shrink or turn your back upon the battle-field.

You shall go under orders from our director to all the vessels arriving in port with prostitutes on board, and shall be on hand to receive them. Always be punctual; work for the good of the State (the society), and serve us with all your ability. If, in the discharge of your duties, you are slain, this Tong undertakes to pay $500. *sympathy money* to your friends. If you are wounded, a surgeon shall be engaged to heal your wounds; and, if you are laid up for any length of time, you shall receive $10. per month. If you are maimed for life, and incapacitated for service, you shall receive the additional sum of $250.00; and a subscription shall be opened to defray the expenses of your passage home.

This document is given as proof, as an oral promise may not be credited.

It is further stipulated that you, in common with your comrades, shall exert yourself to kill, or wound, anyone at the direction of this Tong. If, in so doing, you are arrested and have to endure the miseries of imprisonment, this society undertakes to send $100.00, every year, to your family, during the term of your incarceration.

Seal of the Victoria branch of the Chee Kung Tong.
Dated July 2nd, 1887.

Here again we have provision for the murderer's family in case of imprisonment, but the indemnity for death seems to be a matter of "sympathy money" for the "salaried soldier's" friends. A curious promise. . . . This custom of providing indemnity for imprisonment and even death promoted a unique racket among desperate characters. Many a man allowed himself to be hired out to impersonate a criminal wanted for an offense. The inability of white men in general to identify Chinese, to tell one from the other, led to all sorts of substitutions. A Chinese might be arrested, bailed out, and, when the case was called, a totally different man might answer the charge. If a conviction were obtained the sub-stitute received so much per day for his jail term, with pro-visions for his family. There were even generous provisions for his family in the event of the death penalty being inflicted. This has been denied on the grounds that a criminal charged with murder could not obtain bail money and therefore a sub-stitution was impossible, but such things *did* happen in China-town. A notorious gun-man named Lee Chuck, once openly walked the streets of the city after having been charged with murder. This disregard of law was brought about by shifty white lawyers, generous bribes, and officials who took risks on the assumption that the white population was unconcerned with the administration of justice in Chinatown. In the main, they were not far wrong.

Another perversion of justice was the sending of innocent men to prison. False charges against a hapless victim, plus false testimony, lodged many an innocent Chinaman who had incurred the wrath of the highbinder tongs in jail. In such a case the prisoner stood friendless and alone, unless one of his companions had the courage to step forward and testify in his defense. But martyrs in the cause of justice in the high-binder days of Chinatown were as scarce as martyrs of the same variety in the gangster days which prohibition ushered in. The rank-and-file Chinaman was no more courageous about testifying against thugs than his white brethren in the face of gangster vengeance.

One of the most profitable businesses of the highbinder

tongs was the promotion of gambling. Of all the vices of the Chinese in San Francisco this was the one that least touched the morals and fortunes of the white community, yet it was the one delinquency over which the most pother was raised. Possibly because chopping down doors to gambling dens had a note of the spectacular about it, but, more probably, because a shakedown every now and then was desirable from the point of view of white men who needed the money.

Practically every Chinese is an inveterate gambler. No people work harder and longer and more persistently at their tasks and no people dissipate what the sweat of their brows has earned so swiftly and completely over the gaming table.

The Abbe Huc when he journeyed through China in the first half of the nineteenth century, gave gambling as one of the besetting sins of the Chinese. Even at that time gambling was prohibited by the government. But the law was more honored in the breach than in the observance. On every hand the Abbe saw men playing cards, chess, draughts, dice—and a game called tsei-mei, a game similar to Italian morra, which involves the guessing of how many fingers the players hold up. He also watched them betting on cock-fights, cricket duels, and the jumping of grasshoppers. The country was filled with public gaming houses where the frequenters sat for hours—for days, even, eating nothing, but drinking quantities of tea.

When the gambling insanity was at its height, the Abbe reports that even just men cast aside all sense of obligation. When their money was gone they offered their houses; when that was lost, they put up their lands; if fortune still forsook them, they pledged even their wives.

In North China, near the Great Wall, Huc insists that he saw naked gamblers thrown out of gaming houses with the temperature below zero. They had risked their clothes in a last throw of the dice and lost. Nor was this the worst of the picture. The wretches, crouching beside chimneys for warmth were the butt and jibe of the men who had won from them. When these sportsmen got tired of their raillery they returned to the gaming tables leaving the wretches to freeze to death. Here was a primitive barbarity that even sixty centuries of culture had not emasculated.

Except for the final scene in Abbe Huc's tale, the narrative might fit a picture of frenzied gambling in any age or clime. Certainly the white inhabitants of San Francisco were never in a position to draw the skirts of piety away from the gaming predilections of their yellow brethren. Yet, when its citizens were gambling away everything *but* their wives and clothing on the stock market, the police were beating down the doors of Chinatown's gambling clubs and making great dole over the immorality of the "heathen Chinee."

The vicinity of Dupont street from Clay to Jackson streets was rife with gambling clubs, as were Ross alley and Bartlett alley. The defenses thrown up to mask these illicit dens strangely anticipated the speakeasy era in these United States. Sometimes entrance was gained through the most innocent of shops. On Commercial street there used to be appropriately a pawn shop that screened a gambling club approach. And one of the notorious gambling clubs was reached through the salesrooms of a most respectable and venerable firm. In other words, even the law-abiding Chinese, supported gambling just as the law-abiding white citizens supported bootleggers and blind-pigs during prohibition.

Over the entrance to a dingy-looking hallway in Bartlett alley, there used to be a sign which read, PAY HOY YUH YAT. This informed you that the gambling table was open day and night—a continuous performance, in other words. You climbed the stairs to discover a door with a watchman lolling nonchalantly before it, like as not pulling upon a long bamboo pipe. If you passed his inspection you opened the door to find yourself in a long, narrow hallway lit by a flickering gas jet which disclosed in the distance another door. This was of tremendous thickness, built of heavy oak and iron to withstand the sharp axes of a raiding party from the Chinatown police squad. There was a hole in this door which disclosed, upon close inspection, two furtive eyes peering at you from the other side.

If the door was opened to you, you found yourself in another short corridor with still a third door barring your entrance. This was nearly as thick as the second door. It also had a hole in it, through which a latch string came. Having passed the first two doors it was reasonable to suppose that your visit was a friendly one. You pulled at the latch string, the door opened and you entered. You were now in a room with a long table in the center. At the head of this table sat the proprietor. The customers were ranged on both sides. In the center of the table, was a mound of Chinese "cash"—copper coins with square holes through the middle.

The game being played was fan-tan and consisted of the very simple procedure of betting whether the heap of coins was odd or even. Once the bets were completed the proprietor with a long ivory-handled rake began to withdraw the cash two at a time. If one remained, odd won; if none were left, even payed. . . . It is a game of chance pure and simple without a vestige of skill or science. But it must be played squarely. So simple and obvious a game is not subject to any cheating devices.

Had you looked undesirable to the first keeper he would have sounded a warning through a system of cords and bells strung along the corridors. Next, he would have engaged you in a scuffle. By this time the thick wooden doors were barred and bolted. The table had been cleared of its evidence—the "tan" markers burned in a stove or thrown down the toilet. Customers would have begun to disappear—through trap-doors which led into the shops below. Sometimes, having gained the ground floors, there were additional ladders into underground courts. Frequently the trap-doors led upward, artfully concealed by wall-paper. Again the trap-doors issued from toilets.

If the warning had been accomplished by the time you pounded upon the second door, it would have opened to reveal the obsequious bow of the attendant. Then, leading you through the third and final door he would have shown you an empty and decorous room devoid of the least suspicion of law-breaking.

But frequently the warning came too late or not at all, depending on the quickness and skill of the raiders. Then, in order to halt the intruders long enough to complete the evacuation of the room, it was necessary to let them chop through the oak and iron of the doors.

The gambling clubs were austere or elaborate according to the tastes and pocket-books of the members. Nearly all had kitchens where tea, at least, was brewed. Some hired orchestras. Ofttimes the kitchens were removed from the immediate club room. Under the stage of the old Chinese Theatre on Washington street, was a kitchen which served several gambling rooms and the actors in the theatre, as well.

Charges were made, of course, that the police received tribute from these gambling clubs and that many of the ax-chopping orgies, accomplished from time to time with a great deal of sound and fury, were pure camouflage. Whether the regular police were in the pay of the gambling clubs must always be a debatable point. But the special police made a good living. These men were hired by the clubs to protect them. From just what is not clear. At all events, each special policeman was reputed to have received five dollars a week from eighty-odd gambling clubs. Anyone with even the rudiments of the multiplication table at his command can readily translate this into four hundred dollars a week, or sixteen hundred dollars a month, for a rather "thin" protection. Thirteen dollars a month from each gambling club was reputed to have been paid to what was vaguely referred to as "City Hall representatives." This totals something over twenty-six hundred dollars a month "protection" or just plain "graft" to white citizens.

If this be so, Chinese highbinders were not the only class of people who battened on the illicit activities of Chinatown.

The gambling clubs were not the only sources of revenue for the "special policemen." They watched the brothels, too. Their tribute was fifty cents for each prostitute. With two thousand prostitutes acknowledged in the hey-day of Chinatown, this comparatively small amount gave these guardians of the bagnios a rake-off of one thousand dollars a month.

Another form of gambling in Chinatown was the Chinese lottery. But a large proportion of the white population supported this activity. One could take a chance on the winning number for as little as five cents.

Tribute to white officers was not all that the law-breakers were compelled to disgorge. In Chinatown's hey-day two gentlemen named Wong Woon and An Geo, used to collect thirteen dollars a month from each gambling house and eight dollars a month from each lottery. This was for their personal gratification. In addition, they were said to have squeezed an extra five dollars per month from each resort for paying white lawyers to fight the law. Not only were they tribute leviers on gambling clubs but they were owners of gambling clubs as well. They ran about six big houses and seventy-five small ones, not to mention being the keepers of numerous houses of prostitution.

This pair was hated and feared throughout the length and

breadth of Chinatown. A brief indication of their quality came out in testimony against them by one Ah Chung, in a tong war involving prostitutes.

"What," said the questioner, "happens to a Chinaman who testifies in Court against the women?"

"An Geo and Wong Woon put up money to kill him," came the prompt rejoinder.

Ah Gow, who was a cigar maker and an interpreter on the side, was one of the many who accused An Geo and Wong Woon of seeking his life. But Ah Gow was little better, if as good as the men he charged with plotting his death. In the rôle of interpreter, he blackmailed Chinese by assisting in their convictions and trumping up forced charges against them, when they failed to "come through" at his demand.

But like so many rascals of his stripe, he "pulled" one "fast one" too many. A Mr. Griswold, a wealthy ditch owner of Amador County, was killed one day by a Chinaman who fled to Marysville, where Ah Gow happened to be living at the time. A reward was offered for the murderer's arrest and conviction. Ah Gow had an inspiration. He went to some white men and said: "Mr. Griswold's murderer is in the washhouse across the street. You have him arrested and we will split the reward." The white men did the work. The murderer was arrested, convicted and hung. Ah Gow got his share of the blood money.

Suddenly, word came to Ah Gow that he had been marked for death. Not only had money been posted for his murder but a man had been imported from China to do the deed. Ah Gow was living in Folsom at the time. He went down to Sacramento, in the hope of eluding his would-be slayer. Instead, he walked into him at the first gambling club he visited. Ah Gow wasted no time in indecision. He leaned across the table, whipped out a gun, and shot the highbinder imported

BECKETT ALLEY

from China to assassinate him. After which he walked unmolested out of the building.

Ah Gow fled to China, but returned in a year. The police were looking for him but the police did not get him. A highbinder bullet did the trick even more efficiently, on the eve of his arrest.

Whether An Geo and Wong Woon were back of Ah Gow's death, is hard to determine but the chances are in favor of it. Wong Woon seems to have been the "big shot" of his day in gangster circles. He was reputed to be very rich, making more off the sale of slave-girls than any of his contemporaries. It was said that he bought girls for two or three hundred dollars and sold them for as high as nine hundred. Besides his friend An Geo, he had two other comrades in the slave-girl trade—Bi Chee and Wong Fook Soi. They were known as the Big Four in Chinatown.

Another man who insisted that Wong Woon had threatened his life was Wong Ben, an interpreter. Wong Ben was called before an investigating committee to testify. Wong Woon offered him money to testify falsely. When he refused an order went out from the gangster to "put him on the spot."

The life of an interpreter was not a happy one. If he were called into Court to translate testimony he was between two fires. Whichever side lost, he was blamed by them. . . . If the loser were a desperate group he was threatened and often murdered. An interpreter named Ah Quong met such a fate. A Chinese stole a woman from a house of prostitution in Sacramento. They then fled to a small town, nearby, where they were married. The owner of the woman went after the pair and had her arrested. He then bailed her out. Next day a different woman was in Court to take her place. Because the husband was not convicted of kidnapping, the gangster group lay in wait for Ah Quong. They shot him in the back and cut him to pieces with hatchets as soon as he left the courtroom.

An interpreter, Ah Dan, who innocently explained the workings of the game of fan-tan to a judge, was ordered to leave San Francisco.

Most of the Chinese gangsters were not known outside of Chinatown. The American public, sipping its morning coffee and dipping into news of violence in the Chinese quarter, read such names as An Geo, Wong Woon, Bi Chee and Wong Fook Soi and promptly forgot them. But there was one exception—Fong Chong. And, even in his case, this same American public might have failed to identify him if he had not been known over the length and breadth of San Francisco as "Little Pete." A name like Little Pete, stuck in the Caucasian memory—Fong Chong merely slipped into the limbo of things not worth remembering.

More than that, Little Pete did not confine his activities to Chinatown. He owned a factory that manufactured shoes, manned, of course, by the sweat-shop labor of his countrymen. But when it came to selling these shoes to the retail trade, Little Pete was careful to employ white traveling salesmen. This threw up a proper smoke screen which effectively hid the horrid fact that his merchandise was not the product of white labor.

Little Pete had other white contacts. He was a great gambler, like all Chinamen, but he did not confine his gambling operations to fan-tan in the clubs of Bartlett alley and Waverly place. Instead he went in for horse racing—*crooked* horse racing. His gold bribed jockeys, stable boys, bookmakers. He made over a hundred thousand dollars by "fixing" races and putting up money on the hundred-to-one shots who easily displaced favorites whenever Little Pete had a finger in the pie.

Besides his more or less legitimate shoe business and his

crooked race-track activities, Little Pete was the organizer and head of a blackmailing tong in Chinatown called the Gi Sin Seer. This, by reason of its success, resulted in the forming of a rival tong, the Bo Sin Seer, an organization formed to "muscle in" on Gi Sin Seer territory and incidentally to put Little Pete on the spot.

In order to protect himself, Little Pete hired a notorious hatchetman named Lee Chuck as a bodyguard. Lee Chuck shot down a rival bent on putting a bullet through his heart one morning. Not content with this show of prowess he next took a notion to shoot up a couple of plainclothes men who suddenly appeared at the scene of the murder, but these bullets went wild. This landed him in jail, however, on a murder charge.

Little Pete was nothing if not loyal to his henchman and from the moment of Lee Chuck's arrest he began operations looking toward freeing the prisoner either by fair means or foul. His activities sent him to jail on a charge of trying to bribe the jury. He was convicted and served five years in San Quentin. But Lee Chuck did not hang. There were three trials, commutation of sentences, and final incarceration in the insane asylum—in short, all the sequences which have so often followed the flow of gold in behalf of assassins in these United States.

It was in 1887 that Little Pete was freed from his bribery sentence. It was then that he devised his system for fleecing the gambling public. . . . When his operations were discovered he was banished from the track.

His rivals in Chinatown were still after his scalp. But Little Pete was a match for them. He hired an American bodyguard this time, secure in the belief that any yellow highbinder would think twice before shooting down a white man.

But one cannot remain vigilant forever. One day, Little Pete went into a barber shop to have his honorable head shaved and his black and shining queue replaited. There had been a race run that day that Little Pete had put some money on: He might have been excluded from the track but he still could bet with the best of them. So he sent his bodyguard down to the corner to buy an evening paper. . . . Five minutes later, the barber shop was a shambles and Little Pete was lying face downward on the floor in a pool of blood.

His funeral a week later was the most elaborate ever held in Chinatown, if not in all San Francisco. Thus, again were the Chinese before white men in a matter of procedure— apparently innovators in the matter of expensive and overwhelming funerals for gangsters!

Superficial folk lay the murder of Little Pete to highbinder rivalry. But there are those who have gone more deeply into the issue. These investigators say that opposition to Little Pete was primarily a matter of resentment against his preference for the society of white men. Little Pete was suspected of disloyalty to his own people. A white bodyguard was the crowning perfidy.

Chapter IX

DAUGHTERS OF JOY

DURING one of numerous legislative investigations into the Chinese question, a Mr. Duffield of the San Francisco Police Department made this statement: "I have never seen a decent, respectable Chinese woman in my life." And another witness, too unimportant to even name, referred to the Chinese as "a people who had no respect for chastity, most of their women being prostitutes."

Mr. Duffield probably told the truth. The few Chinese who had had the temerity to bring their wives to California were not sending invitations out to the police force to call and inspect virtue. Mr. Duffield's duties led him exclusively amid the bagnios in Sullivan and Bartlett alleys and way stations. And, when he was on the scent of crime, his path was more apt to pass that of the Hip See Tong, that dealt in slave-girls, rather than the path of a bridal procession wending its way toward a restaurant for a wedding banquet.

San Francisco's Chinatown

The testimony of both Mr. Duffield and the unnamed witness was part and parcel of most half-truths uttered for and against the Chinese by partisans anxious to prove their points. They rendered sacrifice to truth with offerings flyblown with lies. A Chinese visitor to San Francisco in the early days of the gold rush might have said the same thing of American womanhood.

Since the family is the foundation of Chinese society, it is obvious that chastity among Chinese women is the rule rather than the exception. In China, public opinion forces men to marry, and the rural districts see little of the vice and immorality that flourishes in the cities. "Marriage," says a former resident of China, "is the privilege, duty, and fate of Chinese girls." In proof of which he points out that "elderly, maiden ladies—a most useful and worthy class of people in any country—are entirely unknown in China."

This absence of "elderly, maiden ladies" is due to a system of concubinage. A man may have as many concubines as he can afford. But he has only one wife, and the concubines and their children are subject to her. "The children all acknowledge her as mother," writes an authority, "and the secondary wives acknowledge her as such. They are her servants and associates."

A civilization that finds "elderly, maiden ladies a most useful and worthy class of people" will balk at any such arrangement, but the system has its points in caring for an excess female population with some regard for their normal functions in life.

Nora Waln in her revealing book on modern China, *The House of Exile,* quotes thus from the lips of an aristocratic wife and mother on the subject of a woman's duties:

Adultery is only a feminine vice. Copulation on the man's part is not his wife's concern, unless he sires a child. Then she must accept the child as one of her household. All a man's offsprings inherit equal rights in his homestead. It is a wife's duty to have all his children fed, clothed, and educated in accord with his property. She must stand sponsor for all of them in his clan and to the world. In the event of his death or his absence, she must assume custody of all his children's share in the property and speak as his voice to defend their rights. *No child in China can ever suffer bastardy, as no man's offspring is an illegitimate child.*

This is very far from a Western woman's sense of her place or her duty. But whatever may be said for or against this double code, the last provision is ahead of anything we have devised for the comfort and well-being of children born into a hostile world.

Divorce is the exception in China. Adultery on the woman's part is punishable with death by strangulation. But, not until after the child is born, should the woman be pregnant. There is another eminently sound ground for divorce —"a persistent habit of loquacity on the part of the lady." Happy Cathay!

After reading the foregoing, an American woman would vote China a man's world *par excellence*. But a prominent Chinaman once said in an interview in San Francisco: "Many Chinamen laugh at you and the English people because women rule in your country; but women rule China, too. Women rule the world. Men have the name of ruling them; but they don't."

Which proves, again, the wisdom of the Chinese.

Marriage from the male point of view is a decided duty. There is little or no romantic nonsense about it, since, in most cases, the event is arranged by the young people's families years before the children have any interest in the matter. The first consideration is children—male children. One must have the proper amount of reverence after death to be completely happy in the spirit world. As the female after marriage becomes part and parcel of her husband's clan, it is a male child that assures this tranquillity beyond the grave. There is a notable example of this in *The Good Earth.* The father loves his daughter, but he never sees her again after the day she is given in marriage, in spite of the fact that she lives in his vicinity. Once or twice, he has a moment of sentimentality—of brief longing to look at her face once again. But it is quickly stifled. She is of another household and as dead to him as if she were laid in her tomb.

There are economic reasons, too, for marriage. Time and again, in the old days, one's house-boy would announce that he was going home to marry a wife so that his mother might be provided with a daughter-in-law to help with household duties.

How much of all this lies in the past, so far as the present generation of Chinese in America is concerned, is hard to determine. Much of it is doubtless being scrapped under the pressure of a new environment and fresh ideas. But even at this late date there is record of a young servant bemoaning the fact that he would shortly have to pay a visit to China to marry, because his aging grandmother needed a servant to wait upon her. And not long ago, in Seattle, a family who had had more than its share of disaster and trouble met in council to determine the cause and the remedy. They decided that most of their ills were traceable to the fact that their ancestors were not receiving the proper reverence. They, therefore, appointed one of the stalwart males of the family to proceed to China, seek out the ancestral shrine and offer up fitting prayers and incense. Tradition dies hard.

The romantic aspects of married life in China come into it, for the most part, through the rule of secondary marriages. The head of the house—the first wife—may hold the scepter of family authority but, many times, it is one of the secondary

BALCONY, GRANT AVENUE

wives—one of the "green-skirts," who holds her husband's heart in thrall. Yet, some of the "arranged" marriages evoke an exquisite bond between husband and wife that is charming. A great deal of the poetry of China, when it does not deal with nature, is filled with the tender longings of husbands and wives separated. There are more passionate longings too, but one suspects these of being written for wives of the heart's rather than of the family's choosing.

The North China family of which Nora Waln writes, was founded by a green-skirt wife who stole the affections of her lord away from a Cantonese mate taken on the eve of his departure for duties in Peking and left behind. He never returned to his first wife or to the city of his birth but lived a happy and fruitful life with the wife-of-his-heart. Sometimes "green-skirts" are chosen for very practical reasons by the head wife. One official's wife was said to have picked a "green-skirt" for her husband because she was reputed to be good at keeping household accounts! . . . That such a system does not lead to jealousies and heartaches would be too much to claim but, after all, every system has its problems, and jealousies and heartaches seem to defy any plan that has been so far devised by man.

Sometimes the very institution of marriage provokes a romantic approach to the ideal. Thus, a woman bespoken in marriage gains great *kudos* if her fiancé dies and she decides to follow him into the spirit world via the suicide route to avoid the temptation of marrying another. An outstanding case occurred in Foo Choo in the last century. Here the heroine of the drama was of high position and the affair was conducted with great éclat and made a tremendous impression. The lady decided to commit suicide publicly and invitations to the ceremony were sent out. Friends, magistrates, everyone of distinction in the district responded. The victim was carried through the streets in a litter to the platform erected for her tragic purpose. Upon this platform she strangled herself, picturesquely, with a scarlet crêpe scarf.

At the time Mr. Duffield made his sweeping statement concerning the depravity of Chinese womanhood, there were said to be only a hundred wives in all of Chinatown. But a hundred wives are a hundred wives and one might suppose that a member of the police department could have used some strategy to obtain a glimpse of one. But he would doubtless have remained unconvinced in the face of any proofs short of an actual marriage ceremony. Even then, he would have had misgivings, for there are no forms so empty as the forms we do not understand much less subscribe to. Had he stumbled upon a wedding service he would have seen a ceremony brief but as binding as any performed in a Christian cathedral at high noon.

First the pair would have offered sacrifices at the altar, after which both would have knelt and touched the floor with their foreheads many times. Then a glass of wine would have been poured for each and they would have stood before a priest who burned the wedding contract, putting the ashes in the wine. Then the couple would have bowed three times to the east, spilled a little wine on the floor and burned incense to their ancestors. Finally they would both have drunk the wine and the marriage would have been consummated.

Mr. Duffield, having viewed all this, might have gone forth and issued the following statement: "I have seen hundreds of performances that were reputed to be wedding ceremonies. But there was nothing in any of them that convinced me of that fact. The rites consisted for the most part of drinking wine which proves conclusively that the Chinese are a nation of drunkards and have no idea of what constitutes a sacred contract."

An influx of males in large numbers without family re-

Daughters of Joy

straints, be they American, Chinese, or natives of Zulu, always is followed by prostitution. Armies, logging camps, mines, construction work, breed cosmic urges and loose women to satisfy them. This was the sort of thing that flourished in a big way in California among its white population in the first days of the gold rush. The men were no worse or no better than the average run of males. But they came for the most part to gather their quota of gold with the idea of returning home as soon as this was accomplished. The set-up was temporary. Therefore, they left their wives and sweethearts at home. The substitute for decent female companionship was the substitute that has been made since the world began—*in*decent female companionship. Dance halls, gambling hells, bawdy houses flourished.

When these men began to think in terms of settling down in the country that had bewitched them with its opulence and beauty, they thought of wives and sweethearts and homes. Decent women made their appearance and the scene changed in proportion to the extent of their arrival. The high point in this fury of license was comparatively brief for it did not take the gold seekers long to make up their minds to transfer their allegiance to the new land. Even then, the influence of these first wild days lasted for many decades. But by the sixties the fury had abated, and a headlong civilization founded on impermanence began to give way to conservative stabilization.

But this was not so of the Chinese population. For a good forty years, and even beyond that, they continued to think of themselves as living in a temporary world. They stood with the left foot on the Western shore and the right foot still planted squarely on the shores of their forefathers. Their wives, their children, their ancestral altars were all in the Far East. They did not think of the new world as even fit to receive their bones.

San Francisco's Chinatown

This attitude of mind was caused by the opposition to their coming, the continued agitation against them, the underlying hostility to their race. One might plunder and even enjoy a land that was filled with scorn and persecution but one did not think of it as home—one did not plant a hearthstone or set up a permanent altar there.

Curiously enough, it was the condition that the Chinese had fought most diligently that brought about a change of viewpoint. With exclusion came a gradual dying out of rancor. The Chinese had ceased to be a menace and so the public at large began to see their good points. Then, the hazard of reëntry into the country made a trip home a risk. More and more, the Chinese had to make a choice. Should they abandon this rich, vigorous new world for the venerable land of their forefathers? Most of them decided not to—they sent for their wives, their children. Homes sprang up. Presently a young native-born race came into being—citizens of the country. The revolution in China widened the breach. At last the Chinese felt themselves at home.

This is not to say that gun-men and slave-girls and viciousness in Chinatown died suddenly. Or that any of these things are to be mentioned in the past tense. The oldest profession in the world does not surrender in the face of an exclusion act. But, the traffic in bootleg commodities always diminishes in free competition with the legitimate article and the traffic in bootleg women is no exception. In spite of numerous exhibits to the contrary, wives still have an ace up their sleeves.

The few Chinese women officially reported as resident of San Francisco in the fifties leads to a suspicion that perhaps many of the females engaged in beguiling males for a consideration escaped the census lists. But in any event, they could not have been present in overwhelming numbers. The authors of the *Annals of San Francisco,* published in the fifties, reports a sprinkling of Chinese prostitutes on Dupont street—now Grant avenue—and on portions of Pacific street. They, likewise, mention a notorious "Miss or Mrs. Atoy" whom they designate as "that famous or infamous character, who was alternately the laughing-stock and the plague of the place." She is undoubtedly the Madame Ah Toy who haled miners into court for paying with brass filings instead of gold dust for the privilege of gazing upon her "countenance." This scornful reference to the lady more than throws suspicion on her mode of life. She was perhaps unique in one particular—there is no trace of bondage in any picture of her that has been presented. She was her own free agent and her earnings of pure gold or spurious brass went to no master.

But since the Hip See Tong for trafficking in Daughters of Joy was founded as early as 1852, it seems pretty well established that others of Madame Ah Toy's ilk—we hope we do not wrong the lady—were not so fortunate. Certainly, the hapless Lee Lan was not. She was the first woman to be given an elaborate funeral in San Francisco and the tale of her kidnapping and sale mentioned previously in this volume is a pattern for hundreds who followed her to a life of exile and lascivious slavery.

A large portion of these women were recruited from the poorest inhabitants of Canton—the wretched people who were forced by economic pressure to live on river boats. It was said that many of them never stepped ashore once in their entire lives. Among these people, infanticide flourished and especially when the new-born child proved to be a girl. Those that were permitted to live, were granted the dubious boon of life only in the hope that they would bring a fair sum of money when they came of saleable age. Other slave-girls were of higher birth, frankly stolen, as in the case of Lee Lan. Still others, of greater sophistication and charm, came from the Tai Ping Shan district of Hong Kong. This translated means "Exceeding Peace Hill" which is quite too spiritually sublime for any particular good. These ladies were graduates from what was known as the singing class—"singsong girls" they were sometimes called in pidgin English—and their early lives had been spent on "flower boats," an appellation likewise too full of the breath of spring and innocence to deceive even a plainclothes man. Some of these Hong Kong ladies were the cast-off mistresses of Europeans.

Occasionally, there was offered for sale, a "big-footed" woman from Tartary. These women apparently were not particularly esteemed of the gallants of Chinatown, since they brought very low sums. In China they were reputed to have had a certain amount of decent treatment but in California it was said that they were used "worse than dogs."

At first, the entry of slave-women into the country was fairly easy but as the scandal of this traffic in human flesh became public they were examined and questioned. But in most cases, evasion was easy. The girls came, usually, in the care of hideous old duennas who vouched for them and coached them all the way across the ocean in a line of defense: They came to join brothers, fathers, friends—the hag-like procuress with them was a mother or sister. When they landed, apparently respectable countrymen came to take them away. In most cases white lawyers were on hand to vouch for the authenticity of everything that was said. If they were denied admittance, long legal wrangles delayed deportation. White attorneys-at-law, the courts, legal technicalities, all conspired to assist highbinders to continue their nefarious trade. The Chinese population was not alone in contributing to this scandalous traffic. Many a shifty American lawyer waxed rich on foul money poured out by the fetid channels of Chinese gangsterdom.

The sprinkling of ladies of dubious virtue acknowledged

Daughters of Joy

by the historians of the fifties, grew to such proportions that an estimate of prostitutes in the seventies came to two thousand. Between forty and fifty brothels were listed in Spofford and Sullivan alleys and vicinity.

There is one phase of this yellow slavery which will always remain inexplicable to the Occidental mind. This was the elaborate system of agreements signed between the victims and their owners. It is impossible to discover whether every girl entering a life of enforced prostitution signed an agreement but there was enough evidence of such transactions unearthed to prove that they existed.

Perhaps these agreements were survivals of an arrangement that had some force and validity in China but which, for obvious reasons, in an alien country were mere empty and tinkling symbols of business form. The following known as "An Agreement to Assist a Young Girl Named Loi Yan," is typical:

Because she became indebted to her mistress for passage, food etc., and has nothing to pay, she makes her body over to the woman Sep Sam, to serve as a prostitute to make out the sum of five hundred and three dollars. The money shall draw no interest, and Loi Yan shall serve four and a half years. On this day of agreement Loi Yan receives the sum of five hundred and three dollars in her own hands. When the time is out Loi Yan may be her own master, and no man shall trouble her. If she runs away before the time is out, and any expense is incurred catching her, then Loi Yan must pay the expense. If she is sick fifteen days, or more, she shall make up one month for every fifteen days. If Sep Sam shall go back to China, then Loi Yan shall serve another party until the time is out: if in such service she should be sick one hundred days or more, and cannot be cured, she may return to Sep Sam's place. For proof of this agreement, this paper.

(Signed) LOI YAN

Of course, the agreement, in spite of Loi Yan's signature, is really an agreement between the tong or individual who sold her and the brothel keeper who bought her. But, why such a silly subterfuge? All this talk about Loi Yan being put to the necessity of raising any such sum as five hundred and three dollars for passage money and food to reach America is the most palpable fiction. Even if she were acting as her own free agent in the matter with no procurer or association as a go-between, the cost of her passage would have been in the neighborhood of forty or fifty dollars, food included. That is what the male immigrants paid and it is inconceivable that the females were charged a greater sum. The size of the loan, then, betrays the Ethiopian in the wood-pile.

Another piece of fiction is that, on a certain date, Loi Yan would be her own master or that men should cease from troubling her. On a certain date she might become free of her mistress Sep Sam but not of the villains who camped on the trail of slave-girls with fictitious freedom ahead. On that certain date, Loi Yan probably received a red slip of paper saying that she was free, but you may be sure that a gentleman from the "Chamber of Far-Reaching Virtue" or the "Flowery Mountain Arbor Booth" was on hand to guide the flutterings of the released bird into another bamboo cage. Sometimes she went willingly, sometimes she was abducted, sometimes under extreme necessity she was legally married and then farmed out for another period of shame. These marriages were usually the result of Christian missionary interference. The woman fleeing to a mission for protection was turned over by a white judge to her despoilers who came before him with a marriage license and protestations of virtue. The terrified woman, in much the same position as a gangster's moll of these later days, supported their testimony. White attorneys contributed to the debacle. The judge, under the circumstances, was powerless.

The last provision is a piece of obvious silliness with

DUNCOMBE ALLEY

LITTLE SHRINE IN DUNCOMBE ALLEY

touches of grim humor. It is provided that if Sep Sam closes up her establishment and goes to China, Loi Yan may be farmed out to another House of Joy. In the event, however, of her falling sick with an incurable disease, she is free to return to Sep Sam's place! Anybody, it would seem, would be free to return to an establishment that did not exist.

The plight of the prostitute who became sick beyond the capacity for earning money has been the subject of many harrowing tales. Matt Karcher, one time Chief of Police of Sacramento, once submitted this testimony:

I have seen them thrown out on the street on the sidewalk, and I have seen them put into little rooms without light, bedding or clothing. They were left to die—not only the slave girls *but the old and sick.*

Unconsciously, Mr. Karcher in his final statement more or less admits that this abandonment of doomed slave-girls was in no sense discriminatory. The indifference of the Chinese of previous generations to people marked for death has been fairly well established. But there is something particularly poignant about these birds of bright plumage, drooping and bedraggled, turned out to die, victims for the most part of disease incurred in pursuit of a profession, the profits of which they had no share in. Even a tepid sportsmanship, one would think, could have spared a few pennies to make their last hours bearable.

In the issue of the San Francisco *Chronicle* of December 5, 1869, under the sub-title of "How They Are Murdered," there is this portion of a lurid and we suspect rather overwrought article:

As the consequence of an expressed desire, with officer Woodruff, we now revisited the dens which are located in the vicinity of Cooper's alley. The place seems even more disgusting than our first visit;

the stench more intolerable; the rough board flooring more uncertain and dangerous. We wind in and out, along narrow passages and through low doorways, until our topography is as uncertain as that of the compilers of the early maps of California, or of the engineers who originally laid out the streets of San Francisco. The officer has lighted his candle, for everything is dark, dismal and depressing. We arrive at a miserable door not more than five feet high, which opens into a room some nine feet in length and not so wide; it is the "hospital" where the decrepit and those diseased past recovery are brought to die. The place is loathsome in the extreme. On one side is a shelf four feet in width and a yard above the dirty floor, upon which are two old rice mats. There is not the first suggestion of furniture in the room, no table, no chairs or stools, nor any window through which some stray, enterprising beam of sunlight could find admittance by day. The atmosphere was close and seemed clammy, deathlike and impregnated with the vapors of disease and pestilence. And to this place are brought those women who have become so infected by disease that they are no longer money-making creatures and have become burdens upon the individuals or companies who own them; and here these poor creatures, deserted by both friends and owners, with no one to turn to for help, nor any god to pray to for consolation in their hour of distress, terminate their miserable lives.

When any of the unfortunate harlots is no longer useful and a Chinese physician passes his opinion that her disease in incurable, she is notified that she must die. She knows too well that protestations and prayers are unavailing and submits without a murmur to her fate. Led by night to this hole of a "hospital" (how it gained this distinguished title, we do not know), she is forced within the door and made to lie down upon the shelf. A cup of water, another of boiled rice and a little metal oil lamp are placed by her side. The assassins pass out of the death cell, the heavy door is locked and the unfortunate creature is left to die alone. What agonies the poor victims suffer in their lingering death no one knows. The smothered shriek of despair, the dreadful moans with which weakened nature announces its sufferings, may be heard by those who burrow in the immediate vicinity; but they either pay no attention to them or simply curse the victim in uncouth language as an annoyance. No one offers to interfere with the doomed one; all know the law, and there is not enough charity in the whole race to attempt to interfere with the dreadful edicts. After a few days the lamp burns out, the light fails for lack of oil, the rice cup and the water cup are empty and dry, and the joss-sticks which were lighted when the woman was brought to the cell are nothing but charred splinters of bamboo. Those who have immediate charge of the establishment know how long the oil should last, and when the limit is reached they return to the "hospital," unbar the door and enter, that they may remove the remains of the unhappy victim of man's lust, of disease and of unnatural custom. Generally the woman is dead, either by starvation or from her own hand; but sometimes life is not extinct; the spark yet remains when the "doctors" enter; yet this makes little difference to them. They come for a corpse, and they never go away without it. If the victim is not already dead, the circumstance only delays the removal of the remains a few minutes. When they enter the woman is alive; they soon come forth, bearing a body only—only a body; the heart has ceased to beat; the breath comes and goes no more; the soul has fled. How the deed is done—whether blood is drawn, the victim strangled or smothered—none save those in the secret know. The result is past dispute. A woman —helpless, useless, without value to those who claim to own her— is murdered, and this in the heart of a Christian and enlightened city.

There may be a score of these "hospitals" in our midst as yet undiscovered. Those which have been ferreted out by the police are now seldom or never used; but that others exist and are in constant use is more than probable.

Making every allowance for prejudice and exaggeration, there must be a modicum of truth in this record of a newspaper man's glimpse into an inferno of heartlessness—but in this instance even a modicum of truth is sufficiently horrifying.

The Americans who read these accounts pretended they were shocked but they were not moved to the point of doing anything about it. The only portion of the population who were at all concerned were the Protestant missionaries. But

their efforts to change things were met for the most part
with derision where actual opposition was not the rule. The
reaction of the man in the street to any move to change conditions in Chinatown was expressed by a police chief who
once said, "I don't think it is nature for a Chinaman to learn
anything good." And, even a branch of the Christian Church
voiced similar sentiments through one of its priests who referred to the Chinese as "these pagan, these vicious, these
immoral creatures, that are incapable of rising to the virtue
that is inculcated by the religion of Jesus Christ, the world's
Redeemer."

The fact of the matter was that the Occidental races in
San Francisco were the personification of the Pharisee who
contented himself with thanking God that he was not like
other men and walking smugly on the other side of the
street. It never seemed to occur to them that their very
indifference was a contributory factor to the conditions they
took such delight in shivering over.

There were even some of the white population who pretended to be shocked at the institution of prostitution itself.
To hear them talk one would have supposed that this ancient
and honorable calling was an invention of the Mongolian
race. And this, with all the approaches to Chinatown lined
with cribs and bawdy houses occupied by the most abandoned
white types. A very ingenuous doctor endeavoring to prove
the appalling degradation of the Chinese, laid the existence
of these bagnios to the fact that they were "almost entirely
for the Chinese population." Anything more absurd can
scarcely be imagined. Especially, as in the next breath, he
charges that the Chinese prostitutes were infecting with
disease a large percentage of the white population. The
Chinese, at least, were very conservative about breaking
down the barriers of race. A few adventuresome souls doubtless tested the delights of Venus in the Occidental Houses

Daughters of Joy

of Joy but they were so much in the minority as to be negligible. On the other hand, the Chinese prostitutes who yielded themselves to white men were strictly tabu among members of their own race. In the Chinatown of a vanished era there were alleys given over to Chinese women who solicited white men but Chinese males did not frequent them.

Those of the white race who did not roll Pharisaical eyes heavenward because of the simple fact of prostitution among the Chinese, were profoundly shocked at the aspects of slavery which dominated this traffic in women. For this they could have been pardoned; many years was to elapse before Reginald Wright Kaufman, with his *House of Bondage* was to prove pretty conclusively that a like system, with certain modifications, infected the half-world of the good old U.S.A. itself. The term "white slaver" had yet to be coined.

Not all the slaves brought in came as the wards of gangster tongs. Often, an individual with a flair for making a bit of change on the side imported a woman. But every woman who arrived for the purposes of prostitution paid tribute to at least one highbinder association. The Hip See Tong which in the fifties began as an importer of women became in time more of a tribute levier. This "Temple of United Justice" asked forty dollars from her owners for every woman brought in and, forever after, a weekly tribute was demanded of her. Failure to "come through" boded exceeding ill for those who resisted this blackmail. These monthly fees were shared with white men who stood guard over the brothels in the rôle of special police. Showing that the Chinese hatchetmen were not the only citizens of San Francisco who had an interest in maintaining the slave traffic.

When the boat from China docked a flock of people were on hand to meet the incoming females: their owners, white attorneys with well-greased palms, members of the blackmailing tongs. Once the immigration details were settled to everybody's satisfaction the women were whirled away in "deep, sea-going hacks" to temporary quarters bearing the delightfully romantic name of "barricoon." Here they were "farmed out," those who had been previously contracted for going at once to their destination. The others stayed until sales or "contracts," if you prefer, were consummated. This barricoon was in St. Louis alley directly underneath a Joss House. Which would be more or less equivalent to housing prospective prostitutes in the same building with a church, except, of course, that there is nothing in the religious line in China equivalent to a church.

Not all of these women were sold to houses of prostitution. The more choice examples of femininity found ready purchasers among the well-to-do merchants and tradesmen with a longing for female companionship. The cream of this lot was snapped up by Chinese in San Francisco. Those of acknowledged class but somewhat less charm were shipped to farmers and merchants in the interior of the State. These super-slaves were rarely ever natives of seaport towns of China but came almost invariably from the interior. This meant that they were prettier and fresher, having been reared in an atmosphere of rural plenty. In most instances they were stolen, like Wee Lan, the first woman to have a funeral in San Francisco, and, like Wee Lan, many of them were from homes of wealth and refinement.

One might hazard a guess that the lives of a goodly portion of these girls were not tragically unhappy. There must have been a percentage that charmed their masters into taking them for at least secondary wife-ship, their position being assured for all time if their fruitfulness yielded a male child. Others, naturally, were not so fortunate. Their tenure as "kept woman" likely as not was terminated when their charms began to stale. In this case, through the offices of a gangster tong they found a new field for their talents in the

Daughters of Joy

bagnios of San Francisco or Sacramento. As in the case of such arrangements the world over, the fate and happiness of the woman were largely a matter of the disposition and character of the male into whose hands she fell.

The recruits for the brothels came from a lower strata of refinement and attractions. The best of this lot naturally went to the high-class dens—what would be called "parlor-houses" in the best American circles.

"The refuse," says an authority, "generally consisting of 'boat-girls' and those who came from the seaboard towns, where contact with white sailors reduced even the low standard of Chinese morals, were sold to the more inferior dens of prostitution—as were those who suffered incurable attacks of Asiatic scrofula or had the misfortune to possess a bad temper."

Chapter X

SLAVES—DOMESTIC AND OTHERWISE

THE term "slave-girl" in San Francisco's Chinatown grew
to be associated in the American mind exclusively with prostitutes. But female domestic slaves were a common occurrence. Charges of male slavery in California, also, have been
hurled but these proved to be without foundation. Certainly
there was never brought to light any individual cases, and
wholesale male slavery, implied in the "contract-labor" agi-
tations emanating from the American workingman, were
equally false.

The Reverend Mr. Gibson insisted publicly that male
slavery did not exist even in China but there is other testimony which disproves his assertion. The most authentic of
these instances comes from Hong Kong where John Henry
Gray, Archdeacon of Hong Kong in the fifties, was offered
two youths at three hundred and fifty dollars apiece. Their

profligate father wished to sell them to obtain money for further debauchery. Visitors in China, in that same decade, and later, mention instances of boys and girls sold into slavery for as little as fifty dollars.

One of the most interesting stories along this line coming from Tsing Tau in the seventies has a direct connection with the immigration of the Chinese to America. A Chinaman desiring to settle his debts and raise money for passage to California decided to mortgage his family to a money broker. With the consent of his wife, he went to the elders of his village and presented his problem. The elders brought out the Mandarin of the district and gave their united bond for the amount. The Mandarin in turn gave his note to the money lender. The money lender put up the amount, and the man embarked for America.

The note became due and the borrower neither put in appearance nor sent money to square it. Demand was made on the Mandarin who promptly paid the note. This he presented to the elders, after adding a substantial fee for himself. The elders paid the Mandarin and, likewise, adding a goodly fee, presented their claim to the family. The family was without funds. Since its members had given their bodies as security, nothing remained to be done but to surrender themselves. They were put up for sale a few days later at the City Gates.

The eldest girl was sold to a brothel keeper for thirty-three dollars and seventy-five cents. A son eighteen years old was bought by a sea-captain for seventy-six dollars. A young boy, twelve, brought sixty dollars from a silk manufacturer. The other children, being small, fetched low prices. The mother, too old to be a concubine or mistress, was bought by a man who hired out servants to European families.

Another such tragedy took place in Canton. A family of six was sold to satisfy a note for three hundred and fifty dollars. Here, too, the defaulter was a coolie who had set sail for the Promised Land of America. The eldest girl was sold to an Italian profligate for seventy-five dollars, the boy, next in age, brought fifty dollars. The others, who were younger, brought proportionate prices. Both these instances, brimming over as they are with heart interest, are pertinent at this point in proving that males *were* sold into slavery in China. If, after the sale of a family, the full amount of the loan remained unsatisfied, it was customary to seize the signer of the note, himself, in the event that he returned. If he was without funds, he, too, was put on the auction block.

Some authorities insist that this borrowing of money and putting up a family as security was a common occurrence. In most instances the ticket broker put up forty dollars for passage money. This, by the time interest and fees were added, sometimes went as high as four hundred dollars. The percentage of defaulters under this arrangement was said to have been as high as five out of every ten. But this sounds suspiciously like exaggeration. The proverbial bond between a man and his family in China, be he high or low, would indicate that failure to redeem them from the shadow of bondage must have been traceable to some extraordinary situation over which he had no control, or that he was an exception to the well-established rule. Neither case would have yielded such a high percentage of defaulters.

But all these happenings in China are beside the mark. That human beings were given as security for loans in San Francisco, itself, is attested by a suit brought by a money lender named Ah Chuen against Madame Ah Laon, the proprietor of a bagnio. The suit was tried in Justice Lawrence Ryan's Court in the spring of 1856. The contract between Ah Chuen and Madame Ah Laon speaks for itself:

Slaves—Domestic and Otherwise

Whereas, feeling myself in want of funds, and being hard pressed, I went personally to the place of Ah Chuen, and borrowed from him the sum of two hundred and fifty dollars, with the understanding that the total sum shall be repaid within the limit of one year, bearing 6 per cent interest per month; for the security of which I pledge the person of one of my girls; it being hereby mutually agreed between us, that if the said amount is not paid at the expiration of the time aforesaid, the said Ah Chuen can and is empowered to sell the said girl and pocket the proceeds.

If the proceeds of the said sale be insufficient to cover the whole amount, Ah Chuen will still be privileged to make further demands until the whole be paid.

I this day do acknowledge the receipt of two hundred and fifty dollars, and in witness thereof I execute this instrument as proof of the same.

Ham Fung, 4th year, 8th month, 25th day. (Ah Laon's mark)

The date of the contract is the fourth year of the reign of Emperor Ham Fung which corresponded with our year 1854. Madame Ah Laon's mark was made by sticking the thumb of the left hand in ink and stamping it upon the paper. This device was said to have been by decree of Emperor Ham Fung himself for the benefit of women who could not write. Thus, again, do we find the Chinese before us in shrewdness. The marks our illiterates made could have been duplicated a hundred times over—but a finger print was unique. Thus did they anticipate our modern identification system.

It appears that Madame Ah Laon had engaged passage for China and secretly placed her girls in another establishment. This caused the worthy Ah Chuen to charge that she "had concealed her property with intent to defraud her creditors."

The defense objected that the contract was illegal because

the money loaned was "for purposes derogatory to good morals." The prosecution tried to prove through witnesses that the money had nothing to do with moral questions. The money had been loaned to defray Madame Ah Laon's expenses in crossing over to China. The question of putting up a human being as security seems not to have been raised. But this was in America's slave days therefore the slavery aspect of the case seemed not so monstrous.

It was charged by some that gangster tongs in California had agents all over China, not only for securing female slaves but male slaves as well. One device that was said to have been used in recruiting male slaves was a poor father arrested on false charges. An agent of the tongs would wait upon the victim while in prison and promise to secure his release if he would sign over his son to the organization. The only concession to justice for the youth was the provision that in case of death his bones be returned to China. But, for the most part, the good old device of kidnapping seemed to be the order and the barricoons in the seaports of Chinese cities were filled with males—sometimes even of the merchant class—who were shipped into virtual slavery to Cuba, Mexico and South American ports. The idea was that they were being engaged to work under contract for a number of years, after which they would go free. In most cases, their chances for freedom were as slight as the prostitute's who received her red paper only to be snatched back into the life again. The peril of interference with a traffic in males was too great, apparently, for its introduction into the United States, although the system gave the labor agitators in California plenty of ammunition.

But in spite of the protests of the pro-Chinese group that there was no such thing as male slavery anywhere, an incident in San Francisco, more than proved the contrary.

Slaves—Domestic and Otherwise

In the latter part of July, 1856, there sailed into the harbor a bark named the *Theresa Terry*. This vessel came from Macao, a Portuguese colony on the south coast of China. She had on board several hundred Chinese on their way to Callao to dig guano. A group of Chinese merchants were advised that in this crowd were Ah Coa, Ah Chy and Ah Lion, belonging to a family group with representatives in San Francisco. The entire cargo of human freight had been purchased for something like four dollars a head and was to be sold in Peru at a handsome advance.

The merchants appeared in court to obtain a writ of habeas corpus for the bodies of Ah Coa, Ah Chy and Ah Lion. They were met at the gangplank by a piratical gentleman by the romantic name of Captain Doublais, flourishing a pistol. When he found that he was dealing with the State of California, however, his ferocity subsided and he invited the delegation to look over his cargo of males. But they could not identify the property they had come to rescue so they were obliged to hide their chagrin and bow themselves off the ship.

The next move was to secure a warrant for the arrest of the Captain. Whereupon, he hoisted sails without further ceremony and put to sea, minus his clearance papers. The last item in this comic-opera encounter in the columns of the *Bulletin* was to the effect that the look-out station at Point Lobos had telegraphed that the good bark *Theresa Terry* had passed the Golden Gate and was eight miles out. The steam tug *Martin White* was sent in pursuit and the newspaper hazarded the prophecy that it was impossible for Captain Doublais to escape. After that, there is a suspicious silence on the part of the press. Which leads one to suspect that either the *Theresa Terry* was too swift or Captain Doublais's pistol too bright and menacing. . . . We are driven to the belief that the three Ahs—Coa, Chy and Lion —spent the rest of their lives digging guano on the bleak islands off the coast of Peru.

But however hard and cruel the fate of prostitute slavery in America and contract slavery *out* of it—for the most part, these forms of restraint, at least, dealt with adults who could bring cunning to their aid either to escape or ameliorate their condition. This, the children sold into domestic slavery, could not do. Sometimes their condition was tolerable enough if Fate led them into the service of kind masters or mistresses. But how often has this been the lot of strange children taken into a household to be the family drudge? "Orphan Annie" gets the same treatment in any language and the little Chinese slave-girl was no exception to the rule.

The stories that came to light when this traffic in small children began to receive publicity were as pathetic as stories of American children "bound out" in the earlier days of the republic. There was the story of the child sold to a "bound-foot" woman with a fiendish temper who beat her until she fainted and, when she came to, pulled her around by the hair of the head, and there were stories of children burned for disobediences, or starved for mistakes, or cruelly set upon and beaten by an entire household. But everyone knows such tales. To repeat, Chinatown never had any corner on such experiences. They occurred and will occur wherever there are brutal adults and helpless children. But there is one thing worthy of note—it is rare for a Chinaman or a Chinawoman to be accused of brutality to his or her own flesh and blood.

The domestic slave-children who were farmed out in sweat-shop work were the most pathetic of all. Children were found who were compelled to sew from seven in the morning until long after midnight. If they fell asleep their ears were cut, their hands were burned, or they were beaten. Sometimes the eyes were propped open with all sorts of gadgets. One child who was rescued from this inhuman toil was found to have inflamed eyes as a result of their being kept open with pieces of incense wood.

The stories of the lives and experiences of prostitutes and domestic slaves in Chinatown came to light with the founding of rescue missions for women by evangelical churches. However much one may oppose the idea of missionary work among a people with a well-defined religious code of their own, the fact remains that it was through the efforts of the men and especially the women, engaged in this work, that reforms were accomplished.

Missions for men had begun almost with the coming of the first Chinese. In fact, the first movement toward Christianizing Chinatown might be said to have commenced on that windy midsummer day when the China Boys marched to the Plaza to have their "risibilities stirred" by the account of a heaven too droll for their belief.

The first of the missions to get started was in 1852 when a citizens' committee organized a mission for Chinese at Stockton and Sacramento streets. Later the Presbyterian Board took over the mortgage and gave the transient foundling a respectable Calvinistic name. After laboring twenty-five years in the Lord's vineyard this organization reported only one hundred and forty converts. Other missions followed—Methodist, Congregational, Baptist, Episcopal, even finally a Catholic mission. But the most militant of these soul-saving groups were the Presbyterian and Methodist.

The slowness of results to convert "the heathen" met with all sorts of quips and jibes before investigation committees and in the daily press. But however edifying the several denominational attempts to "save the souls of the yellow brethren," their joint performance was a sorry spectacle. Conversion of a people who had built up a very complete code of ethics to a new dispensation would in any case have been a laborious task if all had pulled together. But public exhibitions of difference of creed made the task infinitely slower.

Father Buchard, a Catholic priest with a decided antipathy for the Chinese, publicly made the sneering statement that with all the labor of protestant forces not one newspaper of the city "had heralded the baptism of a single Chinaman."

To which the Reverend Mr. Gibson replied irrelevantly, with characteristic evangelical choler, that "Popery is more dangerous to Republican institutions than Paganism."

No wonder an Episcopal clergyman was moved to say: "What the Chinese see of Christianity here, from their standpoint must impress them unfavorably."

But in spite of these childish differences Christian influence did move slowly forward. Presently there began to be inevitable testimonials of conversions. Here for instance is the record of Lan Hok Han. It seems that in his heathen condition Lan Hok Han used to "hit the pipe," make cigars, and play the flute. His recorder seems to have set down these delinquencies in a diminishing ratio. After seeing the light, he abandoned even the flute and instead, he discoursed nightly at the mission in a voice "clear and loud" that could "readily be heard by persons in adjoining stores and lodgers above and below." Naturally, one's enthusiasm for Lan Hok Han's new estate would be colored by the fact of whether or not one was a lodger "above or below."

Other testimonials of a like nature were advanced from time to time for public consumption but few of them, fortunately for the neighbors, were about converts with "loud, clear voices." The night schools and the Sabbath schools at all the missions reported full attendance. Which moved the sceptical to "opine" that the Chinese visited them to learn English and not because they cared a tinker's damn about a new brand of salvation. But pretending piety to learn a language certainly was not too ignoble a subterfuge. The State of California provided no facilities for breaking down, at least, the barrier of language between its citizens and its fantastic guests. The mission heads acknowledged quite frankly the truth of this sneer and declared themselves ready to bait their hooks with education in the hope of more profound results.

If, sometimes, the methods of the proselytes seemed trivial and immature to the scornful the intolerance of the scornful seemed equally trivial and immature to the man with an open mind. When the editor of one of the leading weekly papers said in connection with converting the Chinese that he "didn't believe that the Chinese had souls, or, if any, that they were worth saving" a great contempt tinged with shame swept over just minds. The man making this statement was no ignorant rabble-rouser. He was a man of alleged intellect, the head of a periodical important enough to have an international reputation, a force in the community. Incredible as it now seems, there were hundreds like him— men with background and education, who advanced arguments for Chinese exclusion that would have made a Hottentot blush.

There were even those who charged that Chinese turned Christian so that they might kidnap women more easily. . . . This may have been true in some cases. But the rumor doubtless was started to discredit the rescue of Chinese slave-girls by white missionaries, since more than one such rescue often was made, as we shall see, with the help of enamored swains who wanted to marry.

The first movement in the interest of Chinese women,

came in 1869 and was instituted by a Mrs. H. C. Cole, who was a member of the Methodist Church. She went about pushing her way into the few homes that existed, interviewing wives, primary and secondary, stumbling on occasion into brothels to the indignation of the house "mothers" and the terror of the girls. Mrs. Cole was a determined woman, given to making statements in the best King-James Biblical manner. Said she, in speaking of what she considered the forgotten woman of the human race, "They die here and are buried as the brute that perishes."

Following up Mrs. Cole's indignant peregrinations, the Methodist Church, in 1871, founded a "Mission for Women"—a shelter, a place of refuge, it might more aptly have been called. The matron in charge waited a year for an inmate. The girl's name was Jin Ho, a slave-girl in a den on Jackson street. The life grew more than Jin Ho could bear so she escaped one night, ran down to the wharves and threw herself in the bay. A negro with a boat hook fished her out more dead than alive. She was turned over to the police. Captain Clark sent for the Reverend Mr. Gibson to interview her. It all ended by her being sent to the Methodist mission. . . . A year later she was converted to Christianity and joined the Methodist Church. By 1874 the mission housed eighteen rescued slave-girls. All this activity spurred the Presbyterians to action. They opened a mission of their own in the same year.

The gangster tongs began to worry. Here was a pretty state of things. It was easy enough to deal with mere males in the immigration sheds, in the courts, on the police force, in getting their contraband goods into the country and preserving them for the delectation of customers—but with women in the field! That was something else again. In some matters women had much more determination than men.

Slaves—Domestic and Otherwise

Then, in America, their sex protected them against physical violence. One had to be very careful in dealing with a woman.

So the highbinders gave a new set of instructions to the duennas who transported their charges overseas. They were to fill their "girls" with horror tales of the "white, female devils" who lay in wait for little sing-song girls trying to make an honest dollar for their keepers. These "female devils" caught little sing-song girls and pulled out their fingernails and scratched their eyes to sightlessness and even boiled them in oil! . . . The same instructions were given to the "mothers" of the brothels.

The bulk of the girls believed these stories and even when they didn't, like most people, they shrank from any change. Then, the majority had grown to like the life. They wouldn't have run away if they could. In most cases their lives were easy enough. And not so many were locked up in a room to die as one might imagine. Like prostitutes the world over, there was always a chance that some male might come along and take them out of the life by marrying them. This happened fairly often—as often as it did in white circles in San Francisco. Many a Chinaman bought a secondary wife via the brothel route and lived happily with her ever after—deserting her only when he made his periodical trip to China to visit the chief wife of his ancestral courtyard if not always of his bosom. . . . A great many unnecessary tears are shed daily the world over about the wretched state and horrible endings of Daughters of Joy. Thus it was in the seventies—with particular reference to Chinese ladies of light virtue.

But there were, of course, the exceptions. Occasionally, as in the case of Jin Ho, the life grew too hard or too distasteful. How hard may be gauged by the desperation that must have moved those who did escape, to even consider such a thing. The penalties for detection or re-capture were pretty horrifying.

In the annals of both the Presbyterian and Methodist missions were tales of rescue work that make a Drury Lane melodrama seem tame in comparison. The soldiers in the front rank of these onslaughts against female slavery were women. For one thing the women were more convinced of the righteousness of their cause than men and for another they were fairly sure that their sex would protect them against undue violence. The woman propagandist, the reformer, always presumes upon her sex in such matters. In riots women dare male policemen to strike them down. If they are forcibly seized they bite and scratch and scream, and try to shame their retainers into deflection from duty. Not that the rescue workers in Chinatown used such methods—they were not compelled to, but they knew that only the direst of accident would bring about any physical harm to themselves. But they would probably have gone the limit without such an inward assurance. They were women imbued with what they considered a sacred duty and any woman with such a conviction is better than a whole squad of officers of the law in breaking up iniquity.

At the beginning, the police department treated them with an indulgent tolerance. But the day came when admiration for their courage and intelligence won the allegiance of the entire Chinatown Squad. Whenever there was a particularly hard nut to crack, these women were called in as allies. They rarely failed in achieving a rescue they set out to accomplish. When they did, it was apt to be through some loop-hole, some obstruction upheld by the courts by the intervention of shifty white lawyers. In the end, even the courts were inclined to lean in the rescuers' direction.

Among the first tales on record is the story of little Yoke

Slaves—Domestic and Otherwise

Yeen. Yoke Yeen was an orphan ten years old. She had been sold into domestic slavery at a very early age to a master who owned several houses of prostitution. She was, for the moment, a "slavey" in his establishment but it is pretty obvious in what capacity she would ultimately have served him once she became old enough to exert physical charms upon predatory males.

Through some mischance little Yoke Yeen was taken to see a Fourth of July parade. Between bands and drum corps she heard the women who came with her talking about the Methodist mission. Little Yoke Yeen's lot must have been a hard one, for she treasured every word that fell from their lips.

One night, trembling with fear, she fled from her master's house and stood before the door of the mission. But to her horror the door-bell was too high for her to reach. She beat upon the door in desperation. What if her master had already discovered her absence and was at that moment in hot pursuit? She began to cry. A white boy passing by, saw her plight and rang the bell for her. Half-fainting she fell across the threshold when the door was opened.

Her master tried every means, legal and otherwise, to get control of little Yoke Yeen again. He even came to the mission and tempted her with rings of jade and strings of seed-pearls. He brought bolts of silk—azure blue and apple-green—for her to choose a new jacket from. He promised her candied melon rind and sugared strips of cocoanut if she would return. He even promised her a rich husband. But Yoke Yeen would have none of any of these things, so he returned to his ménage empty-handed.

The news of these havens of safety began to reach not only the byways but the highways of Chinatown. Even respectably married women on occasion sought sanctuary within their walls. There was the wife of Ah Ong, for one.

San Francisco's Chinatown

Ah Ong was a thrifty soul who thought to supplement the family fortunes by compelling his wife to take in sweat-shop sewing. But there was a sickly child who claimed some of her attention—too much according to Ah Ong. Then, Ah Ong had another grievance. He suspected his wife of winning money in a Chinese lottery. One day he demanded three hundred dollars of her. "Give me the money or I sell the child!" he threatened. The child was six years old and although there is no record of its sex, we may with a fair amount of safety assume it was a girl. The distracted mother fled to one of the missions. There followed a tremendous battle for possession of the wife and child. Consternation was rife in Chinatown. The "white devils" were striking at the most sacred tradition of China—*the family!* The mother, in the end, won her right to order her own life. But it was not an easy victory. Ah Ong had influential friends. In his behalf even the Chinese Consul-General in gorgeous silk robes made a visit to the mission, in the hope of persuading the matron of Ah Ong's respectability and good intentions.

Here is a typical story of a prostitute of sixteen who came from Canton. She is nameless but her tale could have been duplicated by hundreds of girls picked at random.

This child's father died when she was two years old. Her mother supported the family by sewing. At the age of fifteen she was betrothed to a man in Hong Kong. One day, while the mother was away from home, this gentleman from Hong Kong showed up in company with a woman. He was anxious to take his prospective bride away at once to the home that was waiting for her in Hong Kong. The child was confused and a bit frightened at this sudden demand. She suggested that they wait for her mother's return. But the man would not hear to delay. He had left his business in confusion to make this trip, and it was imperative that he return as promptly as possible. The ship sailed within the hour. Stifling her misgivings, the girl went with them.

Once in Hong Kong, the man faded out of the picture. But another male showed up who promised her a far richer and more influential husband in San Francisco. She and her new keeper sailed away on the *S. S. Belgic.* All the way across the blue Pacific, she was coached in immigration-inspection technique: She was already married—her husband was a boot and shoe manufacturer on Jackson street near Dupont. This was to be the burden of her lay to any and all who questioned her. As soon as they landed a white man showed up. He sponsored her admission and, after she had answered the questions put to her by the officials, she was permitted to land.

The first few days were spent innocently enough—in the bosom of a family. Then, one day, the woman of the household broached the matter of the advantages of life in a bagnio. Home life was dull compared to it! At home one sewed and cooked and listened to the grumblings of one man—in a house of pleasure a grumbling male was soon exchanged for another who was complacent and sometimes merry. A wife wore drab clothes—a Daughter of Joy was given jackets of apple-green and sky-blue ornaments for her hair. A wife went nowhere—a Daughter of Joy went weekly to the theatre.

It must be admitted that the girl's keepers were not ruthlessly inhuman. At least, they tried to prepare her for the life she was to lead. Most traffickers in flesh were not that considerate.

When she realized what was in the wind, she began to cry and beat her breast. But to no purpose. A man came and paid to her captors, in her presence, fifteen hundred dollars. Then he took her away and gave her into the keeping of the "mother" of a "house."

She sulked and resisted the embraces of her transient lovers. They sought to break her spirit. They began by starving her but without success. Then they sought to aggravate her hunger by bringing trays of tempting food into the room and tying her just out of reach. Then they beat her. Finally in desperation they threatened to kill her.

How she escaped is not recorded.

Let us go back to another drama involving domesticity. Ah Lan was born in Sun Ning, China. She was brought to San Francisco and sold to Yue Ka Sheung for one hundred and eighty-five dollars. The wife of Yue Ka Sheung drove a good bargain so her husband let her take Ah Lan and offer her for sale in one of the river towns of California. A merchant named Woo Clue bought her for six hundred dollars and married her. He was a good man and fortune smiled upon the union, for, eventually, she bore him two children.

There came the day when Woo Clue decided to make a trip to China. He departed leaving his wife in the care of his brothers. The ship which bore Woo Clue back to his native land had hardly passed through the Golden Gate when these brothers began to plot to sell Ah Lan. Somehow, she got wind of their intention and her resistance was so great that the brothers began to think that they were getting into deep water. A wife has very definite rights which Chinese society recognizes and it would have been an unpleasant piece of business to have been found guilty of such a social crime. They feared the wrath of their brother when he got home and heard his wife's story.

So these worthy brothers of Woo Clue decided that the easiest way out was to have Ah Lan put on the spot. They hired a man to kill her. Instead, he collected money for the deed and shipped her to Oakland, where he realized a handsome profit on her sale. Then he took passage on the next boat to China. Meanwhile, one of her babies died. The other,

NUM SING LANTERNS IN STOCKTON STREET

only fifteen months old, was sold by the brothers. Their intention was, when Woo Clue returned, to tell him of the death of his wife and child and report that the other child had been stolen. . . .

Here is the story of a slave-girl told in her own words. Apparently she was a domestic slave or else modesty forbade her to uncover a greater shame. Her name was Sing Kim.

I was born in Sin Lam, China. My father was a weaver and my mother had small feet. I had a sister and a brother younger than myself. My father was an industrious man but we were very poor. My feet were never bound; I am thankful they were not. My father sold me when I was about seven years old; my mother cried. I was afraid and ran under the bed to hide.

My father came to see me once and brought me some fruit; but my mistress told me to say that he was not my father. I did so, but afterward I felt sorry. He seemed very sad, and when he went away he gave me a few cash, and wished me prosperity. That was the last time I saw him.

I was sold four times. I came to California about five years ago. My last mistress was very cruel to me; she used to whip me, pull my hair, and pinch the inside of my cheeks. A friend of mine told me of this place, and at night I ran away. My friend pointed out the house. I was very much afraid while I was coming up the street; the dogs barked; and I was afraid my mistress was coming after me. I rang the bell twice, and when the door was opened I ran in quickly.

These stories are by no means the most sensational that the traffic in slave-girls afforded but they are fairly typical, and they are chosen because they have an air of authenticity. There is something very moving about the simple little tale of Sing Kim. We cannot but like the father who came with fruit and a few pennies and wishes of prosperity to his little daughter after she had been sold into slavery.

Sing Kim's story goes beyond the open doorway through which she ran to a new life. But the rest of it is obviously inspired by her protectors. It is filled with the usual Christian-convert platitudes about rejoicing that Jesus died for her—and sorrow at her own unworthiness, in which she admits living a life of sin in those benighted days of slavery. She has "seen the light" and "is now saved" in the most accepted revivalist phraseology. She ends by assuring her readers that "straight is the gate and narrow is the way which leads to eternal life." These poll-parrot testimonials from "saved souls" did more to alienate the sympathies of worthy citizens of San Francisco from Christian efforts in Chinatown than any other single agency. They smacked too much of insincerity and coercion.

In time, the mission became the help of lovelorn swains who had difficulty in achieving their hearts' desires. Frequently a youth would become enamored of some inmate of a brothel. If he had money enough he bought her. But often, if the girl was a money maker for her masters, purchase was impossible. The lover would then help her escape to one of the missions. But the rules were very strict. A girl was required to live a year at the mission, during which time her admirer was made to pay for her clothing and five dollars a month for board. At the end of the year, the man had to produce a marriage license as proof of his honorable intentions.

Once, a Chinaman named Yat Sang assisted three girls to escape from a bagnio. At the end of the year, he and two other friends married them. Their owners came before the Hip See Tong and asked it to assist in reclaiming the girls or three hundred and fifty dollars apiece. Yat Sang was given three weeks to comply. He replied by having eight Hip See highbinders arrested for extortion. But he lost his case. It was hinted that white graft and not justice decided the case.

Chapter XI

CHILDHOOD MEMORIES

When a San Franciscan writes about the part the Chinese played in the gold rush days, the struggle for their exclusion, the history of the gangster tongs, the slave-girl traffic, he can approach his subject impersonally. But if he begins to write about Chinatown, its one-time sinister beauty, its barbaric squalor, its rain-drenched lily blossoms at the New Year, its dragon processionals, its primly beautiful chemist shops, he must desert the third person singular for a narrative form more intimate.

I cannot tell the day, the hour, the precise minute that I became conscious of Chinatown. In my generation it was a fact that had no beginning. So far as I was concerned it always had been. Even before my eyes beheld it there must have been some strange premonition of its existence which filtered through the personalities of Sing, the cook, Jim, the vegetable man, and Hong, who came weekly for the laun-

215

dry. I must have known instinctively that there was a place apart for these strange creatures, with their braided queues done up into artistic knots at the nape of the neck, wearing curiously fashioned slippers, and light blue denim trousers and jackets which Americans later adopted under the name of pajamas in lieu of absurd nightgowns.

Children are incorrigible materialists. I loved Sing because he slipped me nut-starred cookies in defiance of a rule that we were not to eat between meals. And I loved Jim because he gave me a bunch of grapes or a ripe apricot when my grandmother's back was turned. And I loved Hong because at the Chinese New Year he brought me sugared strips of cocoanut, and a box decorated with butterflies hovering over plum blossoms, filled with dried li-chee nuts.

On still summer mornings before the afternoon trade winds began to turn the red macadam dust of Van Ness avenue into companies of whirling dervishers, I used to slip out the garden gate and stand before the open door of the Chinese laundry, just around the corner. The details of washing were not visible since this activity went on behind closed doors at the back of the building, but the activities of the ironing board were at the front to be shared with any-one who cared to watch. A circular stove stood in the center of the room with a rack running about it upon which reposed sad irons heating to the proper state of efficiency. Around the walls were ranged ironing shelves before which a half-dozen Chinamen, in faded pajamas, and with bare feet thrust into straw slippers, moved the black irons swiftly back and forth over the sheets and pillow-cases, tableclothes and nap-kins, father's "boiled" shirts and mother's starched drawers.

The whole procedure was fascinating! First of all, there was the hypnotic rhythm of the moving irons, then the thrilling moment when a new iron was swung off the stove and tested. I always waited for a cry of pain to issue from the throat of the worker as he brought his spit-moistened finger in contact with the iron's blistering heat. But only a faint sizzle unpunctuated by any evidence of discomfort, rewarded my sadistically juvenile hopes. I decided, then, that these Chinamen were in league with the devil in some way, creatures that the fires of my Presbyterian hell could never prevail against. And it would flash through my mind, very dimly, whether it was such an advantage to be party to a Christian dispensation that could consume me in eternal fires, or to be Chinese and have traffic with a devil who offered protection against them.

On each ironing shelf, at the extreme left, always reposed a bowl filled with water—a huge bowl that was the only note of beauty in the entire establishment. Had it been in a white man's laundry, it would have been a plain, colorless bowl, practical and lacking charm. But it was a Chinese bowl, of a deep apple-green glaze with pink blossoms traced upon the outer surface and yellow birds twittering from cherry branches. In those days, however, this glint of loveliness left me unmoved—it was merely a symbol of a diverting performance that had no parallel in my limited experience. I would watch John Chinaman take a fresh sheet from the pile of clothes, spread it out on the ironing shelf, stoop over the bowl and fill his mouth plumply with water. Then, with one gigantic puff, he would expel the mouthful in a shower that sprinkled the entire sheet. Anyone could have filled his mouth with water and blurted it out in one drenching blob but John had a special and skillful technique that forced the water through his teeth in a fine spray, distributing moisture with a beautiful evenness. . . . In later years, a heartless and sanitary city government displaced the beautiful green bowls and John Chinaman's exquisite water-blowing, with contraptions looking like huge salt shakers. From these, the water was shaken out in a monotonous shower. Another art had perished.

At the age of seven, my education in things Chinese broadened. My mother and I went with an aunt to Fresno to establish a vineyard which my uncle had come by. Fresno was a San Joaquin valley district to which water had been brought, and with it the promise of vine and fig-tree yielding abundantly. The workers on this vineyard, aside from a foreman and his assistant, were all Chinese. They were hired through a "boss" at a wage of one dollar a day and they boarded themselves. My aunt provided a weather-beaten shack at one end of the vineyard in which they "camped."

I think even at that early age, I had a sense of this camp's frugal picturesqueness. It had a certain quality that was unique. Even its odors were different and unmistakable. They were a blend of burning punk sticks, nut-oil, and straw-matting.

The building harbored a make-shift kitchen which was also a dining place, and corridors which led to bunk spaces. The Chinaman's bunk was his sole privacy, corresponding to a white man's bedroom. Here, after the day's work from dawn to dusk, under summer skies that yielded a temperature as high as one hundred and ten degrees in the shade during raisin-drying period, the worker smoked his Chinese water-pipe, or rolled himself an opium pill, and dreamed of rice fields and plum trees and family courtyards.

In front of the camp building was a lean-to with a dirt floor open on all sides but covered by a brush roof. Here on hot summer nights the coolies gathered around a community table and ate their rice flavored with dried fish sauce, and drank gallons of tea. In one corner stood a shrine—a gilded tablet engraved with black symbols. A triangular cluster of artificial blossoms surmounted with peacock feathers crowned the tablet. Drapings of turkey-red cotton cloth fell on either side. Before this shrine, on the bare ground, reposed oblong tin cans filled with sand into which punk sticks had been thrust and often, at the proper season, halves of partially eaten watermelons served as containers for these burnt offerings.

This bunk house which housed from thirty to fifty Chinamen seemed at least to my juvenile imagination little larger than our ranch house which sheltered four souls. And I am still sure that it covered no more ground space. It was a perfect example of how successfully the Chinese could pack themselves into small quarters. Bunk room was all a Chinaman needed and a nail or two on which to hang his scant possessions. His wardrobe was, in many cases, just the denim pajama-suit on his back, his wide-brimmed straw hat, and shoes. His few trinkets, his tobacco-pipe, his opium-smoking outfit, he carried in a bright cherry-red silk kerchief. To his outfit of clothing, might be added a pair of light cotton trousers which he slipped on at night—or on Sunday, when he washed the sweat-begrimed denim suit of his labors.

A bunk house sheltering fifty white laborers in the early nineties would have exuded a foul odor of stale sweat. To begin with, the white man of that day, even under a scorching sun, wore full-length underwear, heavy shirts, and denim overalls. He had thick boots and woolen socks. Shower baths were unknown. The accumulation of bodily odors was overpowering.

The Chinese, on the other hand, wore just his denim suit and straw hat. He went into the fields barefooted. Moreover, he was reputed to have taken a sponge bath every day. The indifference of the Chinese to unsanitary surroundings, to accumulation of garbage and filth under their very noses, contrasted with their personal cleanliness was one of the contradictions which always puzzled Occidentals.

San Francisco's Chinatown

A prominent mine owner once insisted before a legislative committee that at the mines the Chinese "washed their bodies every day." And another employer from the State of Washington testified that he had seen them cut through the ice in winter to get their morning bath.

But even all this lack of sweat-collecting clothing and this penchant for daily sponge baths, did not quite account for the lack of body odors in a Chinese bunk house. The fact of the matter is that centuries of civilization have robbed the Chinese of strong skin secretions. And it is with a note of indignant surprise that whites often are conscious that their yellow brethren find their odor extremely unpleasant.

Fifty white laborers crowded into any such quarters for weeks and months at a time, would, moreover, before the season ended, be in a state of nervous quarrelsomeness. Even the most gregarious of whites has a hankering upon occasion for a rudimentary personal privacy. Not so the Chinese. They learn in the family circle to subordinate their personal desires to the rights of the clan. And it is said, that in a Chinese family courtyard, the one unpardonable offense is for one member of the family to close his door upon the general group. Other elements enter in—poverty, which makes crowding inevitable, the calm of the Oriental, his steadier nerves, his capacity to withdraw within himself, in spite of distractions surrounding him.

There can be no question about how satisfactorily gangs of Chinese coolies met the demands of their employers in agriculture in those pioneering days. The "boss" was responsible for his crew. Sickness, death, dissatisfaction—none of these eventualities ever disturbed the farmer or fruit-grower who hired them. All he knew was that he had contracted for thirty or fifty or a hundred workers in his farm or vineyard and every day when a relentless sun began to flame with anger in the east there were thirty or fifty or a hundred

LITTLE SHOP WINDOW

coolies on the job. Coolies might come and coolies might go but the quota demanded for the job and occasion never grew or never diminished. Nobody ever kicked to the employer about the narrowness of his bunk, or the quality of the rice served, or the cheapness of the tea. That was the concern of the Chinese "boss." But one can safely assume that there were few kicks, in any event. The Chinese accepted what was offered and made no protests. Doubtless many of them thought the arrangement a purely temporary matter, anyway. They were in America to "clean up." Every discomfort, therefore, was colored with thought of the day when they would return to their wives and families in far Canton and spend the rest of their days in opulent splendor.

But with all the obvious advantages that Chinese help offered, there were vineyardists in Fresno ridden with the notion of experimentation. A Southerner conceived the sentimental notion that negroes would be more satisfactory. So he got a number of landowners to import crews from Louisiana. The venture was short-lived. The negroes were homesick for bayous and river-banks. They were not interested in making desert sands bloom like the rose. They missed the heavy, moist heat of the sugar-cane country. They missed nights filled with the scent of magnolia and a levee to dance on. Many of them sickened and some of them died. So the scheme to substitute jig-dancing darkies for placid-eyed Chinamen in the fields and a Southern mammy in a calico gown for Sing wearing spotless white duck in the kitchen failed as all ventures founded on emotion divorced from facts always fail.

Aside from Sing, the ranch house cook, only one other Chinaman stands out in my memory. He was a raw-boned, smiling coolie nearly six feet tall whose name was Jim. So far as I could discern Jim knew only two words which he always directed at me whenever I chanced upon him at work picking grapes, or spreading them out on a tray to dry, or trotting down the road on his way to town. At sight of me, his bronzed face would wrinkle with pleasure, he would draw himself up impressively in the manner of a commoner aping his superiors and say pridefully: "Heap high-toned!" At the New Year he brought me a huge basket of li-chee nuts and some candied melon rind.

What was there in me that brought out this burst of admiring affection? . . . I have often wondered. Perhaps I was the reflection of his own son, in far away Cathay, to whom he would return one day with the wherewithal for advantages by virtue of money saved out of a wage of one dollar a day. Doubtless, when he looked at me, well-fed, well-clothed, well-housed he thought that one day this child of his own heart might be as secure in worldly goods. In his narrow bunk at night he probably dreamed of seeing this son a student, then an official—a man of influence. The son of a coolie, a barefooted worker of the soil, dreaming of a position of power for his son? . . . Even so. For it is a well-established fact that the only aristocracy in China is the aristocracy of intellect, and as Mr. Anson Burlingame said, when he came upon a mission from the Emperor of China, "the free competition of China makes scholarship the test of merit" instead of inheritance and blood. Therefore, the son of the lowliest coolie may rise to the highest office in the Empire.

Also, under such class distinctions as operated in China, smiling-faced Jim was only one step removed from the highest class in the land. Next to officials whose real merit was not so much in their office as their implied education, came the agricultural workers. It was something more than a mere example that the Emperor of China ploughed a furrow once a year at the appointed season. Below these workers in agriculture were the laborers engaged in manufacture. Then came the traders, with professional men still lower and, lowest of all, on a par with actors and barbers, were lawyers. An admirable system of rating when one thinks it over. Saving the men of education, the producers of food coming first in the order of man's need, and working down to professions that might minister to man's delight or convenience but scarcely to his necessity.

I have referred to Jim as a "coolie." Nothing could be more false than this designation. The word "coolie" was imported from India and wished on Chinese workers by aliens who knew little and cared less about its origin. The coolie class in India are a low class socially and little better than slaves. No such class exists in China. The term as applied to men who labor seems to have stuck past all dislodgement. But the Chinese have never ceased to protest its use.

Sing, the cook, curiously enough was not one of my favorites. Which was strange considering that I cannot recall a Chinaman of my early years that I do not remember with affection. But, perhaps, this is due to the fact that he once appeared to me in the rôle of tempter—a bargainer for my birthright, which I squandered for a mess of pottage. My birthright, in this particular instance, was a magnificent bronze rooster presented to me at Christmas by an old German vineyardist who used to take me riding with him on the top seat of his truck when he hauled raisins into town.

As the Chinese New Year drew nigh, Sing began to tempt me. First with a quarter, then with a half dollar, finally with what we Californians still call six bits: Would I sell him my domineering and gorgeous rooster for six bits? I fought him off, wavered valiantly, and finally fell. But I had one justification: I have described my rooster as gorgeous and domineering, as indeed he was—as gorgeous and domineering as a Sultan strutting through his seraglio. And it did seem to me, at the age of seven, that he annoyed the hens unduly.

Be that as it may, I delivered him into Sing's greedy hands, and received a foul palmful of silver. But my conscience troubled me. That evening I persuaded my aunt to walk down to the Chinese camp and ask to have my rooster back. . . . It was too late! Chanticleer was already in the stew pot. But to assuage me they brought out a tray holding a tiny bowl with horse chestnuts painted on it, filled with chicken hash wrought from my rooster's parboiled body—and bamboo sprouts, and two chop sticks. I choked back my tears and went and stood in the shadows, where they could not see me surreptitiously throwing their festal dish to my skye terrier. This was my first battle in the war between God and Mammon. And, the fruits of Mammon's victory were bitter in my mouth.

When I came back to San Francisco I was old enough to make an annual pilgrimage with other neighborhood boys to Chinatown. This was before the Fourth of July, in search of bargains in firecrackers. The approaches to Chinatown were foul with white viciousness. One went through streets lined with little pointed-roof cottages equipped with green shutters. If one peered between the shutters' open slats, one got glimpses of obscenely fat women, sitting on the window ledge, exposing far too opulent charms. I will say this in their favor, when they discovered childish eyes trained on them, for the most part, they closed the shutters with a sharp click. I do not think we really cared to look at them but it is fun for a child to outwit anyone. If they had not clicked the shutters in our faces we would have soon wearied of playing the rôle of peeping Toms.

After we got through purchasing our fireworks, we sought out the dark alley-ways which housed Chinese wantons. For

A STREET CORNER

much the same reason: we peered at excessively painted faces through wickets. This was even more exciting, for these wickets were banged shut amid shrill cries of terror. This was in the district of women for Chinese entertainment, only. In the even darker and fouler alleys, where the yellow slave-girls enticed white men, it was our turn to flee. Here the women were no respecter of ages, and anything in the male line from seven to seventy was their prey. We were at once intrigued and terrified by their beckoning fingers but at our age terror triumphed and we escaped pollution and possible disease.

But there were more wholesome adventures. The poultry shops for one thing. Ranged along the wall, were tier upon tier of shelves which imprisoned, behind bamboo bars, lordly roosters, squawking white ducks swaying upon yellow feet— on occasion, even fat geese stuffed to breathless obesity. We boys always waited for a customer to arrive. It was exciting to see a feathered victim selected, and watch the skill with which its neck was wrung, its throat slit and its blood caught in a sky-blue basin. The counters were filled with bowls of chicken entrails, the scarlet combs of roosters, the heads of hens, even chicken feet. Apparently no part of a fowl went to waste in Chinatown.

In the butcher shops were fat tubs of cold, clammy rice for those who lacked kitchen facilities and in the bakeries cakes stuffed with rice or sesame seed or bits of pork, or chopped hazelnuts. Or there were jewelers working in plain view of a street audience, drawing gold out into a wire, or beating it out into thin plates, or inserting jade into rings and hair-ornaments. They did not use gas jets for heating the precious metal in those days, but tiny lamps fed with nut-oil.

The street occupations were another source of wonder and delight. The cobbler wearing a fur cap with ear-muffs drawn down over his ears. The tin smith heating his lead for soldering over a charcoal brazier. The chair mender weaving thin strips of bamboo into a broken seat or making willow deck-chairs whole again.

But our supreme amazement was the merchants and bankers tracing accounts in paper-covered books with a brush dipped into incredibly thick ink or adding up accounts by virtue of rows of bright balls strung on thick wire such as we had used in kindergarten days. These gentlemen of affairs by virtue of their divorce from manual labor wore their fingernails an incredible length, especially on the little finger. It was enormously diverting to attempt to figure out why these little fingernails did not get in the way of the adding machine or the writing brush; or even get tangled up in the long, full sleeves of their possessors. For sometimes they were of such extreme length that they curled slightly like the talons of an eagle.

Except for the wantons, we rarely encountered a Chinese woman in Chinatown. Those that went abroad were usually big-footed serving women, intent on buying a smoked duck for dinner or a bag of melon seeds for their mistresses to nibble on. They were broad, rather squat-looking females, dressed sensibly in jacket and trousers of alpaca. The trousers were fairly short and displaying ankles encased in white stockings.

But, once in a blue moon, we came upon a woman of quality, teetering on lily feet, swinging her arms out like a tight-rope walker, to keep her balance if by chance she was un-attended—a rare occurrence. In one hand she held a fan of carved sandalwood, in the other a bright cherry-red silk handkerchief. We were told in those days and even in later years that these small feet were a badge of wealth. They were an announcement to the world that the women who possessed them could afford the luxury of helplessness. A woman with a foot three inches long was obviously not built

Childhood Memories

for activity. She was an ornament, an exquisite thing, to be served and petted.

But in these later days, we have it from the best Chinese authority that this binding of women's feet had a sexual basis. The natural foot is to the Chinese a gross and unlovely thing. Binding the foot, then, was primarily to make it dainty and soft and alluring. Granted, but horrible and distorted to the uninitiated—on a par with the wasp-like figures of the Western woman in the gay nineties. But the sex appeal went beyond the foot itself. The small feet induced a sort of lascivious motion to the body when their possessor walked. The high-heeled shoe of the Western woman is said by the Chinese to do the same thing. Moreover, lack of activity in women meant soft, yielding bodies, a highly prized quality in terms of Eastern seraglios. . . . But, was there not, perhaps, another angle? A lily-footed woman was not built for gadding about. One knew that such a wife was apt to keep to the family courtyard.

Later, I was to read an account of the torture involved in such a practice. How the toes of the child were turned under; how the foot was pulled as nearly straight with the leg as possible; how, commencing at the toes, a long narrow cloth bandage was wound tightly around the foot to the ankle and a little above. The pain to the growing foot must have been excruciating!

On Washington street, just above Grant avenue, in a blind doorway, there used to be a man more venerable even than the shoemaker. He made and repaired opium pipes. His kit was filled with drills, burnishers, files, a small saw and a hammer. It was fascinating to watch his primitive drill swinging now right, now left, as he pierced a hole through the hard surface of a pipe bowl. A very grandfatherly-looking soul to be engaged in what we had been brought up to regard as a very questionable occupation. For anything allied with the word opium sent delicious shivers down our juvenile spines.

Then there were the lantern makers and the men who manufactured festival candles. These were indoor trades, naturally, but one could always watch the proceedings by virtue of an open door. The lanterns were of thin varnished cheesecloth stretched tightly on bellying bamboo frames, with characters in black and green and red splashed upon them. These characters were mottoes of goodwill and they shone out boldly when candle-light warmed them into life and made doorway and balcony things of dim mysterious beauty.

The festival candles were made of soft tallow, carved into unnumbered fantasies: dragons and roses and holy pagodas. Red and green—with prickings of gold, if the occasion was one of magnificence. They were for altars and ancestral shrines. And often they burned pallidly at funeral celebrations.

The candle maker operated in a little hole in the wall. He would first take a strip of bamboo and wind paper about it. This paper was the wick. Into a huge pot of either hot green or vermilion tallow he next dipped the bamboo. When the proper amount of grease had adhered to the stick he swung it out and rolled it into shape, hanging it on a wire line to dry. All about him were bowls of red, green and yellow paint, and gold leaf on a pink-and-green platter. His dipping over, he began the task of decoration at which he worked with incredible swiftness.

On one occasion we came upon a funeral celebration with the body reposing under a canopy just outside the house. This was notable because, besides the inevitable roast pigs, a roast sheep with erect head was turned toward the corpse. Amid the beating of cymbals and the wailings of flageolets, five women and five men prostrated themselves on either side of

Childhood Memories

the bier. All this was puzzling to our Christian training, but especially the live duck tied under the coffin.

There were the sinister alleys—not the alleys of women but the alleys of murderers and thieves. I have no way of identifying them now, under their shining electric lights at nightfall. I would have to see them again in flickering light—gaslight preferably made even more ghost-like by the sea's breath blown in a white cloud from the dunes—which also are no more. Nor do the new names mean anything—correctly painted and hung against dead brick walls that once blossomed with red posters bidding for the services of assassins. . . . Where is Murderer's alley? Where is Bull Run? Both foul streets even before the Chinese occupation, and translated thus from the Spanish. "We used to find a man in Murderer's alley," said an old policeman, "almost every morning before breakfast, served up all stark."

And which street, now, was Cooper's alley, where the thieves foregathered—or Rag-pickers' alley, which needs no explanation? The Chinese rag-picker was a familiar sight in my youth, trotting from dawn till dark all over the town, with two small baskets on a pole, and a bamboo wand with a nail in it for picking up stray pieces of rags from pavement, gutter and Sandlot. The old rag-pickers were the only dirty Chinamen I ever saw. They seemed dressed in tatters that they had accumulated in their calling and they had skinny wrists and lean fingers dried like parchment and equally lean and serried throats, caked with grime.

And where, oh, where is the Calle de Rosas—Pike street, to us—that held a fascinating tale of the underworld? I think it is now Waverly place, but no matter. It was once the abode of white women who had trod the primrose path that sometimes led to little peak-roofed cottages in furtive narrow streets. . . . Marie Banier, was one such woman—from Paris, as you have doubtless guessed.

San Francisco's Chinatown

She had fled Paris and her social estate to avoid a scandal. She adopted the rôle of fascinating adventuress in San Francisco—had amassed a fortune and was received in bohemian circles. But, there are some things that even bohemian circles draw back from. Marie Banier's past was one of these things. What it was or how it was unearthed is not material. Her friends fell away and she drifted stratum by stratum down to the little white cottage in the Calle de Rosas.

One night she was found strangled. There was no solution. Sometime after, at a gay party in San Francisco, a diamond bracelet was found. Inside was the inscription:

À notre fille

Marie Banier

A respectable woman claimed it. Next day her husband was arrested for the murder of Marie Banier.

Years after, the white cottage fell into the hands of Chinese owners. They began tearing down the walls to erect a Joss House. Between floors, they found deeds to valuable property in Paris, assigned to Marie Banier's son—as well as a huge certificate of deposit in a San Francisco bank. You can guess the rest—the happy ending for a penniless child on the banks of the Seine.

I think that perhaps the barber shops diverted us more than anything else. We always knew when we were drawing near to one by the four-legged frame with green legs and red nobs on the top which stood outside in lieu of a barber's pole. Every self-respecting Chinaman was shaved once every ten or fifteen days. If that seems infrequent to Western males nearer their cave-men ancestors in point of physical inheritance, I hasten to assure them that a Chinaman is not cursed with an incipient beard that needs daily discouragement. At all events it was not so much the face but the forehead which needed attention. This, to be in the proper mode had to be scraped back several inches, to provide the proper setting for the queue of cherished memory. Nor was shaving the half of it. The skin had to be not only washed but scraped from the shoulders upward. Then the queue had to be washed and combed and oiled and braided. If one were a dandy, red silk was twined in with the black strands to give a note of color. After which, came the process which we loved to watch—the cleaning of the eyes, ears and nose. A slender scoop was used for these last ministrations. Sometimes the eye-lashes were trimmed and often twisted—for all the world like a leading lady's in the cinema.

Then, there were the grave gentlemen looking through eye-glasses in heavy tortoise-shell frames; the boys playing shuttlecock with their heels; the merchants smoking their brass-and-enamel water-pipes. These pipes were a modification of the Turkish hookah. The tobacco smoke passed through water and was cooled. But there was no long coil of pipe. It was a very compact device and could be held in the hand. One filling of tobacco was good only for about three whiffs. Which meant a constant filling and re-filling of the pipe bowl. But, in a leisurely day, what did that matter? . . . They lit their pipes not with matches but with paper quills, ignited at a gas jet or from a charcoal brazier. . . . The only place one sees these water-pipes, now, are in the curio shops. Some of them are very lovely with porcelain designs upon them of exceeding beauty. One of the measures, in the old days, of a man's station in life was the quality of his water-pipe. It was of moderate or elaborate decoration, according to one's purse. Most Chinese tobacco was mixed with Chinese nut-oil and it imparted a curious odor to anything with which it came in contact. One's clothes from a Chinese laundry often reeked of this smell and it took much fresh air or close association with a lavender bag to make them fragrant again according to our standards.

In the outlying districts were the truck gardeners, long since routed by Italians. They specialized in rows of pale green lettuce, green onions and purple cabbages. During the arid summer months they did not resort to either sprinklers or irrigation ditches. Instead, they swung huge coal-oil cans on the ends of a yoke fastened to their necks. A silver shower streamed out of the perforated cans down upon the crisp leaves. It was a tedious performance and one not calculated to stand up against more modern methods.

To the south of the city was Hunter's Point, helping to form a cove, where tiny but delicious shrimps abounded. One of the first pursuits of the Chinese in San Francisco was fishing for these shrimps. They still have a monopoly of this business and their settlement on the south shore is as old as any Chinese settlement in California.

Chapter XII

COMEDY RELIEF

OLD Chinatown always had diverted San Francisco. It was undoubtedly the show place of the town, running the Barbary Coast a hard race for supremacy. But it was its sinister aspects, its delinquent phases which allured. Worthy citizens who would have been profoundly shocked at viewing the depravity of their own kind, made tours of lascivious inspection, over and over again, salving their conscience with the conviction that they were viewing a breed too far removed from rectitude to make any enjoyment of the scene a contributory factor.

Men who held their noses as they walked through the white tenderloin which hemmed in Chinatown, released pressure on the nostrils once they reached streets where vice was dressed in exotic garb. To them, Chinatown was a thing of bagnios; gun-men; underground windings, dark and desperate; opium dens; filth; bubonic plague; leprosy. It was diverting partly because it was none-the-less a horrible example.

Such "refined ladies" as Mrs. Frank Leslie, who would have scorned entering a white bagnio, even for the worthy purpose of describing its inmates and their specialities to stay-at-home readers of pallidly impeccable journals, made no bones about pushing their way under police protection into the quarters of Oriental slave-girls.

Their decision to leave white prostitutes alone was wise. These abandoned ladies would have met intrusions with a flood of billingsgate worthy the impudence which prompted such visits—if not a bit of hair-pulling or a well-deserved slap in the face.

Then, suddenly, it was borne upon a few discriminating souls that old Chinatown was a thing of beauty. The pioneers in this movement were Dr. Arnold Genthe, an Austrian and a stranger to San Francisco, and Will Irwin, a resident Californian. Dr. Genthe was a photographer by avocation and he went about the streets of Chinatown taking incredibly beautiful pictures of things that had been so much a commonplace to the people of San Francisco. Here was the old cobbler with his fur ear-muffs, bending over his last; or a little Oriental miss with her hair in a betrothal knot, buying a cluster of blossoming lily bulbs from a corner stand; or a group of highbinders with pig-tails hanging stodgily down their backs, reading the rewards for murder, posted on a corner building; or a lady in embroidered trousers shading her face with a fan; or just a cluster of huge bamboo baskets with bottle-necked openings, for transporting live fowl.

One saw them first in the show-cases of Dr. Genthe's studio, after he turned professional. Could it be possible that Chinatown was beautiful? Could it be possible that one could find something of interest there in just the simple life of the people, without recourse to obscenity and murder?

While San Francisco was pondering this momentous fact, Dr. Genthe published a book of his pictures, with a narrative supplied by Will Irwin. Then, San Francisco knew that beauty reigned in Chinatown in abundance and they learned to subscribe to Mr. Irwin's dictum that "the Chinese could make art out of rubbish." Yes, even a cluster of brown earthenware gin bottles, and a discarded pickle tub, and an empty rice bag of matting thrown on a pile, in some abandoned lot, had a form, a rhythm, a composition that made a picture. Was it the materials or the arrangement? Something of both. Glass gin bottles turned out by a machine, and thrown on a rubbish pile could never be beautiful, nor a tin tub equally turned out by machinery, nor a burlap sack made at the State penitentiary.

Prior to Genthe and Irwin, maiden ladies, belonging to sketch clubs, had gone down into Chinatown and painted putty-faced children in bright kimonos, and bits of still life which went no further than punk sticks smoking in their pewter ceremonial bowls, or clusters of ravished ginger-jars filled with marigolds. Even trained writers, when they passed up opium and gang murder, painted the scene in pretty words that described not even the surface of Chinese life. But of Chinatown's sanity and vigor there was none.

I, in company with my townsmen, had not troubled to understand Chinatown. In my youth, I had gone there with my comrades for firecrackers and found it diverting and outlandish. Later, I had taken trippers through, watching them shudder at the proximity of community kitchens and stinking latrines in the courtyard of what was called in derision the "Palace" Hotel. I had led them triumphantly into blind alleys that caged women, with all the arrogance of Mrs. Frank Leslie, *et al,* and down into the regions below the street level to look upon withered husks of men dried to parchment by opium smoking. But, until an informing spirit pointed the way, Chinatown had been as empty of substance as the shadowy Mandarin figures that danced about the gorgeous ebony-and-silk lanterns in the restaurants.

Of these old surface phases of Chinatown, the most apparent to the man walking through was its density and attendant squalor. Yet there was an overlay of color, and zest for life which was astounding—a gray, drab surface, pricked with accents of gold and green and vermilion.

This squalor was in the main due to the Chinaman's curious indifference to accumulations of rubbish and filth. Every vacant lot was a catch-all for rotting food, abandoned containers, and the putrefying bodies of dead cats. Even the cobbled streets and gutters ran foul with refuse. But, in this the city government was a contributory factor. On Dupont street, the merchants contributed funds to have their gutters swept once a week, since it was alleged that the street department had attended to this detail only once in five years.

In any other part of the city such a condition would have brought on a plague. But the Chinese through centuries of crowded living and indifference to sanitary conditions seemed to have developed an immunity to disease.

Some of the medical fraternity, puzzled by this hardihood, attributed it naïvely to the amount of smoke which always floated about the streets of Chinatown and made it seem wrapt in a sort of Indian summer haze whenever the winds were still. In the days before the earthquake and fire there was scarcely a stove or a chimney in Chinatown. Everyone cooked over charcoal and the arrangements for these gleaming beds were primitive in the extreme. For the most part, a brick bench laid in mud or mortar, served the purpose. This was usually laid before a window, or on a balcony. The smoke escaped lazily and inefficiently and filled the rooms, and passageways, and alleys and streets of Chinatown with a lovely blue-gray veil that gave them added mystery and a charming odor of captured woodlands in final release.

But there were some doubting Thomases, even in the medical profession. Those who could not reconcile immunity to disease with blazing charcoal beds, explained that this smoke mixed with the smoke from cigars, tobacco, and opium pipes had a fumigating effect!

Perhaps, in its day, the most crowded building in Chinatown was the old Globe Hotel at Jackson street and Grant avenue. This was a three-story building containing about sixty rooms and housing between eight hundred to one thousand souls. In cubicles as small as eight by ten slept as many as fifteen Chinamen, on bunks that reached almost to a ceiling ten feet high. In addition to lodging quarters this structure was said to have harbored three or four gambling clubs and a school where, to the scandal of the exclusionists, white women missionaries conducted classes for children. A building of like proportions harboring as many white inmates would have been a center of disease and a spreader of epidemic. But the Chinese seemed to have developed an immunity to germs which was the puzzle and despair of the medical fraternity. . . . Health officers were always predicting dire consequences as a result of this crowding together but nothing very much came of it except a bubonic plague scare in the late nineties. This was effectively checked by drastic measures and the wholesale annihilation of rats in the Chinese quarter as well as the city in general.

The penchant of Chinamen for herding together like rabbits in a warren, once led to a civic comedy that assumed the proportions of a Gilbert and Sullivan musical farce. Officials decided to enforce in Chinatown what was known as the cubic-foot ordinance. This provided a sleeping space allowing five hundred cubic feet of air to any one person.

The first raid was made upon the basement of a lodging house on Jackson street "having," to quote the *Bulletin,* "about the same capacity as the forecastle of a coaster." Fifty protesting Celestials were dragged out of their bunks.

Next morning, the fifty prisoners were hailed into court and each fined ten dollars apiece. A few paid and went free but the majority, acting under the advice of Chinese organizations, decided to become the guests of the city and went back to their cells. Arrests continued. The jails were filled to overflowing. Since practically nobody paid fines it soon became apparent that in order to keep up the drive against violators of the cubic-foot ordinance, the city itself was being led to ignore its provisions. In the words of the *Bulletin*:

> The Mongols have determined upon the policy of worrying the authorities in their attempt to enforce the ordinance prohibiting the unwholesome crowding of lodging houses, in the hope of rendering the effort futile.
>
> The large gang brought up and fined on Tuesday, with reinforcements today, have completely filled the prison accommodations. And, if the crusade is continued, the cattle pound, or some other spacious enclosure, will have to be utilized for their confinement. . . .
>
> Meanwhile, the police are earnestly engaged in mathematical calculations, with plan and diagrams to determine about the precise space a Chinaman requires while in the flesh.

The officials finding themselves made a laughing stock of the town, began to think of reprisals. They would deprive Chinamen of their pig-tails; they would stop shipment of dead bodies home to China; they would put confiscatory taxes upon Chinese laundries. To a present generation brought up on the notion of the high sense of justice and mental equipment of its forefathers, it is revealing to find them so lacking in even the common decencies. A laundry

Comedy Relief

tax was, perhaps, ethical enough except that it struck at a class of Chinamen who were not violating the ordinance in question. But in the matter of abolishing the queue and the return of a Chinaman's bones to the tomb of his ancestors, the city fathers exhibited a lack of feeling for the proprieties that is extraordinary to the present hard-boiled age.

But, let it be said to their credit, there were some protestors. When these matters were brought up for discussion, a Mr. Forbes, one of the city fathers, declared that "the letter and spirit of these resolutions are illegal, narrow-minded, contemptible and utterly unworthy the sanctions of this body." And most of the newspapers warned law-makers that if they passed any or all of these ordinances they would be violating the Civil Rights Act and furthermore that they might easily find themselves in Federal Courts defending their course. The *Bulletin* advanced the idea that it might be practical to put the coolies, who were having such a good time violating the cubic-foot ordinance at the county jail and getting free board in the bargain, to work cleaning the streets. But this very obvious and simple solution to the difficulty went unheeded. The officials resented being put on the spot by a company of yellow aliens and they were out for their pound of flesh.

Of the three projected ordinances to bring the unwelcome guests of the city to their senses, the queue ordinance provoked the most discussion. The "antis" pointed out that the "Chinese pig-tail was a national badge of honor, filled with religious significance." To which the proponents of the measure answered, "Rubbish!" They insisted that whatever significance the modern Chinaman attached to the queue, it was originally a badge of servitude and nothing else. When the Tartar Dynasty came into power in 1644, it decreed that all Chinese subjects should wear the Tartar sign of submission to the conquering Emperor—a queue formed by

239

shaving the front part of the head and braiding the hair. The august Emperor assured his new subjects that of course there was no compulsion to conform to this edict, but it would be expedient to do so, since non-compliance might lead to the loss of one's head. . . . In any event, those who complied, were favored at court and could take the literary examinations which were the foundations of all prestige and progress in Chinese life. In time the "mark of derision became the badge of honor" and thus the Chinamen of the nineteenth century regarded it.

The proponents of the queue ordinance won. Not to the extent of decreeing that all Chinese in San Francisco were to submit their lovely queues to the barber's scissors. That apparently was too great a job in spite of the fact that it was argued that no one residing in the land of the free and the home of the brave should be permitted to wear a badge of servitude. But a law was passed which provided that all male prisoners, "under conviction should, upon arrival at the County Jail . . . have the hair of their head cut off or clipped to a uniform length of one inch from the scalp thereof."

Of course, this did not discriminate against the Chinese in word but it did in fact because nobody but a Chinaman cared whether his hair was clipped one inch from the scalp or not —at least not to the point of legal protest.

Consternation reigned in Chinatown and the newspapers began to make jokes about the sheriff in the rôle of Chinese hairdresser.

The next day a gentleman named Ho Ah Kow was arrested for violating the cubic-foot ordinance. He was fined ten dollars but as he had no money to pay the fine, or pretended that he had none, he was imprisoned in the county jail. Then the sheriff ordered brought out a bright and shining pair of

ROSS ALLEY

scissors and Ho Ah Kow was shorn of his badge of submission to the Manchu dynasty.

Whereat, the worthy Ho Ah Kow sued the sheriff. He declared that the loss of his queue was a mark of disgrace and was attended, according to his religious faith, with misfortune and suffering after death. He alleged that the act had caused him "great mental suffering, disgrace in the eyes of relations and friends, and had ostracized him from his countrymen." He asked for ten thousand dollars damages.

The sheriff replied that he had merely carried out the law and passed the buck to the Board of Supervisors that enacted it. Then, Ho Ah Kow went after the honorable board. He accused it of having exceeded its authority, of "imposing a degrading and cruel punishment upon a class of people who were entitled, with all the other people in the United States, to equal protection under the law."

The courts sustained Mr. Ho Ah Kow and the sheriff in the rôle of barber made his exit from the scene.

The severe laundry tax was killed by a boomerang. Its provisions under the law could not discriminate between Ah Sing, who ran a bona fide laundry and Mrs. Murphy who "took in" washing at her own home. . . . The plan to stop the shipment of bones back to China died of discouragement.

Students of religious customs will be interested in Ho Ah Kow's contention that loss of his queue would bring misfortune and suffering after death. If we assume his sincerity, it is indicative of how easily even a distasteful law may by general acceptance be exalted. It took only two centuries to convince the average Chinaman that a badge of submission to a conqueror had elements of spiritual significance.

This Chinese queue, for the benefit of a generation who have never seen one, was formed "by separating unshaven hair on the crown of the head, three or four inches in diameter, into three strands and braiding with a coarse silk or false hair." A truly impressive queue would sometimes, when uncoiled, reach within three inches of the ground. But it was rare to see uncoiled queues in San Francisco's Chinatown. For the most part they were worn in a coil under the hat. Critics of American manners have insisted that this was a precaution against indignities to this sacred though compulsory institution.

There is some truth in the charge, undoubtedly. Small boys as well as hoodlums were apt to find a queue a tantalizing object of investigation. But, on the whole, except for the merchants, the Chinese population were workers, and whether one worked in kitchen, factory, or orchard an imprisoned queue was more convenient. It didn't fall into the soup, get tangled in the sewing machine, or caught in the branches of a fig tree. It was, however, a mark of disrespect to have a queue coiled in the presence of a superior—a point which white employers missed.

The last man to continue wearing a queue was Quan Hoy, a merchant, who died in the spring of 1936. He was loyal to the old Manchu idea, apparently, and he wore his queue to the last, tucked up under his hat. But, this precaution, undoubtedly, was directed against his countrymen who in a few short years had developed a fanatical opposition to a custom that once had held them in thrall.

If one were interested in looking over the "alleys of painted women" it was well to go in charge of a guide or a special policeman to get more than a glimpse of what went on behind the wickets. The alleys that harbored women who catered to white customers were, of course, open to any and all who cared to enter, but these were scarcely typical. Such women were rated as beneath the pale by their countrymen. As one commenter says: "With the white-men prostitutes

Chinese will have nothing to do. If she degrades herself so, she is too low for the Chinese." Which was a pretty good fistful between the eyes, for a member of the "superior" Occidental races to swallow.

The bagnios that received white men were tricked out in all manner of atmospheric trappings. Silk embroidered draperies hung on the walls, pale yellow Chinese rugs covered the floors in the most elaborate ones. The air was heavy with the smell of blended perfumes.

The houses that served only Chinese were bare to the point of austerity. Bright cotton hangings hung in the doorways leading off from the main room or were sometimes used to break a large room up into smaller compartments. The beds were mere shelving set against the wall. Cheap matting covered the floors.

In the daytime, when business was slack, the girls sewed between engagements. Their masters were thrifty souls and were firm believers in the theory of utilizing by-products. The work was farmed out by sweat-shops specializing in women's underwear and cheap male garments for the white trade. There was, at least, no air of the vicious idleness which hung over white crib houses in daylight hours.

At night things were gayer. If one arrived early enough, one could catch the inmates at the evening meal, which usually consisted of a huge mound of rice and a stew of pork, mixed with hard-boiled eggs, liver and kidneys.

Later, about the same table that was used for dining, the one-time sing-song girls sat and played dominoes with their admirers, or sipped daintily at little green and yellow cups filled with Chinese gin, or puffed at miniature pipes. Their faces were powdered and rouged to a state of expressionless vulgarity. The costumes of the prostitutes were simple enough but their hair was slicked back into fantastic forms held in place by gaudy combs. Artificial flowers and strings

San Francisco's Chinatown

of seed-pearls and ornaments contrived from feathers of
the sky-blue kingfisher, heightened the grotesqueness of the
bedaubed faces. Two characteristics of these ladies of easy
virtue have been adopted by their modern white sisters—
hennaed fingernails and plucked eye-brows.

A smooth face was considered a thing of beauty and there
were several men who made their living doing the rounds of
the bagnios plucking any and every stray hair from face and
forehead, leaving only the thinnest line of eye-brow to be
penciled over. Since fashion decreed a very high forehead
effect, the process was sometimes long and painful.

On shallow shelves about the main room were the inevitable tea-pots, with here and there an opium tray.

Chapter XIII

DENS

THE feature of Chinatown which gave visitors the most terrifying and dark-brown thrill was "underground" Chinatown. Actually an ingenious labyrinth contrived out of connecting basements and narrow passageways one level below the street, it grew in legend until practically every stranger as well as most of the natives of San Francisco repeated marvelous tales of how it burrowed down five, six, seven, *eight* stories underground. It took an earthquake and fire to smash the greater part of the myth and halt this subterranean city's progress downward to the infernal regions. An earthquake of even small proportions would have collapsed underpinnings weakened by any such intensive burrowing. But Chinatown stood up valiantly built upon firm ground and compounded of brick buildings made with the honest labor and honest mortar of a by-gone day.

The fire which swept the quarter twenty-four hours after the earthquake was the great disillusioner. All that it revealed of those marvelous eight underground levels were basements as prosaically shallow as any basements in the white quarter. But the fantastic tale still persists. As late as 1926, when I was doing a daily column of San Francisco life on the old *Bulletin,* a statement by me that the depth of underground Chinatown was mostly fancy brought indignant protests from spinsters who treasured their descent into hell as one of the crowning delinquencies of their lives, loyal native sons who liked the story, and even police sergeants who probably had been regaling bar-flies and the home circle with tales of their explorations into the bowels of the earth.

But underground Chinatown was none the less foul and sinister because of its shallowness. It harbored filth, disease and murder. It was sanctuary for fleeing assassins, opium addicts, and even lepers. Most gambling clubs had trap doors which led into passages that finally achieved this nether world. Stolen slave-girls were hidden there and dead bodies were flung into its depths. It was the scampering place for huge gray rats foul with vermin that carried bubonic plague germs. A White population would have been devastated in a month's time had they conceived and populated such a noxious quarter. But Chinamen fled to it and even lived in it, strangely immune to its menace.

A portion of this labyrinth under Bartlett alley was so foul that it earned the name of "Dog Kennel." It boasted a murky sort of courtyard through which trickled an open sewer. One of the approaches to the underworld was down a flight of steps dug out of the ground. It led to a habitation of thieves. Water seeped down its sides and trickled from the roof. The planks which formed a crazy flooring all but

Dens

floated in a slimy ooze of moisture smelling mightily of sewage. Filthy bunks lined the walls and wooden boxes served as tables. It is incredible that human beings could have used it even for a temporary rendezvous much less have lived in it. Eugene Sue, himself, never conceived anything more loathesome. Nearby lived an old blind hag with a roomful of cats that waxed fat in such a happy hunting ground for rodents.

Underground Chinatown was a great place for pawn shops. Particularly those that dealt primarily in arms. Heaped upon their counters was every conceivable kind of weapon. Stilettos fashioned to simulate a fan, made more particularly for the use of ladies; curious pen knives whose open blades could slash a man to pieces; a device which at first glance looked like an innocent poker but which was really a device for braining an antagonist. This was curved to fit close to the body and was worn under the blouse. Pistols, revolvers, axes, hatchets—one could find anything needful for a good, clean murder.

Barber shops flourished underground, for even refugees and derelicts had their artificially prolonged foreheads shaved at least once in every fifteen days and their queues replaited.

In Chinatown, what most people descended below the level of the street to see were opium dens. My generation had been brought up on melodramas based on the rescue of beautiful young white women from opium dens. This always made us hopeful that we would one day run across some females tricked out in the décolleté gowns and striped stockings affected by the "ladies" who enlivened every issue of the old *Police Gazette*. But our quest always ended in futility. Not only were white women missing from the opium dens of Chinatown but white men as well.

In an earlier day, there was much talk of white addicts lolling on silken divans and drawing in great draughts of

opium smoke, but the nineties saw little of such open delinquency. All opium dens were known to the police. In view of
the repugnance of the average white citizen to the idea of
opium smoking, the keepers of the dens doubtless found it
better policy to exclude whites from the hospitality of a
shelf-like bunk in one of their establishments. Yet, even in
my day, there was talk of opium dens exclusively for white
addicts—on Pine street and on California street. But both
these streets were merely on the fringe of Chinatown and if
dens existed, they were doubtless run by white proprietors
under the greatest secrecy.

But this did not mean that white addicts could not get the
drug. If one could read the Chinese sign which proclaimed
the sale of opium, it was easy enough to obtain it. All that
was necessary was to enter a shop, take out the little horn
box looking like a pocket ink-stand that betrayed your need
and place money on the counter beside it. The merchant
would slide from his stool, deserting his counting machine
for the moment, open a drawer and lift out a jar with a large
mouth. From this he dipped a small amount of fluid which
looked like black molasses. This he deposited into your horn
receptacle, gave you your change, and you went on your way
rejoicing. Speech was not necessary.

Naturally, there were tastes in opium, just as there were
tastes in tobacco. If the shop's sign read "Precious Opium of
Patna Sold Here," you knew that you were on the trail of the
very best in opium brands. This came from India, contained
less morphia than most brands and had a superior flavor. On
the other hand, the Persian and Turkish opium was said by
experts to be much higher in morphia content and left a
bitter taste in the mouth.

In earlier days, the Patna opium was imported into San
Francisco via Hong Kong. Here the crude product was boiled
and prepared for the pipe. As time went on it became profit-

able to import crude opium also, and do the boiling locally. But a tax for importing the crude opium and a second tax for manufacturing it for pipe smoking made its local manufacture theoretically impractical. A year after these two taxes went into effect scarcely any crude opium came into the country. That is, not legally. But smuggling grew apace and illicit opium kitchens flourished like green bay trees. In those years gorgeous opium bowls of brass mellowed to green-gold by extensive boiling of opium were to be had at any second-hand dealer in Chinatown. And there was scarcely a living-room or studio in San Francisco that did not have a dark corner enlivened by a brightly polished opium bowl that had seen yeoman service. Later, these could be bought in any importing shop on Grant avenue which catered to the tourist. But they were harshly new and unlovely.

Much opium was smuggled in on a large scale but there were continuous dribblings through personal channels. One of the most popular ways for extensive smuggling was in cans with disarming labels. Sometimes it was hidden under the coal piles in the steam-room of ships from China; sometimes between the soles of shoes; again in the seams of clothing. Between the toes was a popular place for concealing small quantities.

The hold that opium had on the Chinese of a by-gone day was extraordinary considering that it was a habit acquired from India and developed at the cannon's mouth by the British government. Two hundred years or more, in the history of a people that had existed as a civilization for sixty centuries resisting outside influences, is insignificant. Yet it was in this short time that opium smoking rose from the exclusive plaything of privilege to the proportions of a national vice. But viciousness breaks down barriers more easily than virtue.

However, one must grant that the Chinese seemed admirably suited to stand up against the insidious effects of the poppy seed. It was easy to exhibit horrible examples of the opium-smoking habit in the dank-green dens of underground Chinatown just as it was easy to pick horrible examples of gin guzzling in any Inebriates' Home. But, the fact of the matter was, that among the Chinese an enslaved drug addict proved to be the exception and not the rule. The gravest charge against "opium eating" was that it "had a particularly destructive effect on the powers of procreation."

But the Chinese seemed to have successfully resisted this menace if vital statistics may be trusted. This was for the most part a bogey reared by a self-righteous opposition very much like the bogey against wine drinking which William Jennings Bryan once flourished. He used to say that a third generation of wine drinkers was always sterile. But he died before Mr. Mussolini was forced to go to war to provide lands for his wine-drinking subjects to expand in.

David Colton, vice-president of the Central Pacific, in battling for Chinese labor before an investigation committee, once said, "I have heard of the Chinese smoking opium, but of the three or four thousand on the road, there are no opium smokers." This was, of course, as nonsensical as if he had stated that out of an equal number of Irish laborers in the railroad's employ, none of them took a glass of whiskey. But it was typical of the loose and prejudiced statements of the times. The truth of the matter probably was that every mother's son among the Chinese contingent smoked an occasional pipe of opium and profited thereby. Their work was hard and prolonged, they had little or no diversions. An hour or two under the relaxing influence of opium doubtless renewed their energy. The white man's release was through a positive stimulant—whiskey. The Chinaman's release came through a passive agency—opium. Both of these relaxations were typical of the temper of the races indulging in them.

Dens

The Reverend Mr. Frederic Masters, while constrained to shake an ominous head at the vice of opium smoking in general, was fair enough to give this testimony concerning the effect of moderate opium smoking upon men doing hard work:

Years ago when in South China I made a journey of thirty-five miles in one day borne in a sedan chair by three strong Chinamen who took nothing but opium till they got to their journey's end. They would carry me at a rapid pace for three hours till they came to a town, then dump me down in the crowded market place and deaf to all remonstrance, rush off to an adjoining opium house, have a quarter of an hour's smoke, and start again with lightness and elasticity in their tread. I have had boatmen who have towed, rowed and poled my boat up rapid streams from sunrise till dark on three meals of coarse rice and salt fish, yet every night these hardy fellows retired to the stern of the boat and smoked opium for an hour or two before retiring, maintaining in the face of all my good advice that they could not do their work next day without it. It would appear therefore that used moderately and with proper bodily nourishment opium smoking is a stimulant like strong drink and is not attended by any immediate debilitation or any visible physical infirmity as is generally supposed. This is no doubt the case with the great majority of smokers in California. With good food, comfortably clothed and housed and wages sufficient to procure the best opium we do not so frequently meet with the hollow eye, ashen complexion and enfeebled body usually regarded as the marks of the opium smoker.

But having quoted Mr. Masters' grudging brief for opium it would not be fair to pass up his picture of the reverse side of the shield:

Yet who will dare to maintain that even a moderate use of the pipe is innocuous or that the fumes of a deadly poison can be taken into the lungs even in small doses, with perfect immunity from disease? There may be no injurious effects to the system visible for the time being but the man is not what he was. He becomes idle, dirty in his person and habits and generally down-at-heels. He loses all capacity for business, and interest in his work. No one in China has any confidence in an opium smoker's word or honesty. If a member of the Christian Church in China persists in smoking even the smallest dose he is expelled. If you discover your domestic servant to be an opium smoker, go and count your spoons at once, and send him off. He may only smoke a few pipes a day but the love of the pipe means moral degradation and you can place no more confidence in him.

These last statements may not be exactly false but in my opinion they are exaggerated, in spite of the fact that Mr. Masters proves himself on most occasions to be as fair and impartial a recorder of Chinese as one could hope to find in a man burning with Christian zeal. I am sure that most of the Chinese servants I knew in my youth smoked an occasional pipe of opium and nobody missed the family spoons. Moreover, it has been amply proved that the Chinese merchant was the soul of honor and integrity and yet in the nineties there was scarcely a shop or business house in Chinatown that did not boast a room where one could retire and close a business deal over a pipe of opium. All of the restaurants had divans where one could recline and take a long pull at an opium pipe during the progress of a banquet. In short, the hopeless addicts were few and far between. Something in the racial set-up of the Chinaman made moderate indulgence possible. Not so his white cousins. White men did well to steer clear of the whole seductive business.

The ability of the average Chinese to withstand the worst effects of opium is illustrated in a newspaper account of the arrest of Wong Foon for having opium in his possession. Wong Foon was ninety years old when he was arrested in 1936. His defense before Judge Lile T. Jacks was as follows:

I have been in California seventy years. I smoke opium seventy-two year. My mind is clear as crystal. Can remember day in Ogden, Utah, when Governor Stanford he hammer last spike for cross-country railroad. Judge, you put me in jail, I die. Wong Foon, he know.

The judge with true understanding gave him a six months' suspended sentence. Wong Foon was probably one of the "three to four thousand" Chinese workmen on railroad construction that Mr. Colton alleged *never smoked opium.*

Of course, there were the exceptions and harrowing stories were repeated of the lengths to which Chinese addicts went to secure opium—notably the one about the wretch who sold his concubine for a few dollars to satisfy his cravings. This would not have been so bad except that she was with child and he was selling the fruit of his loins to indulge his passion. When the money was gone, he had the grace to commit suicide.

There was nothing glamorous about a Chinese opium den either above or below ground. Those underground were reached by narrow passageways lit by flickering gas jets which increased the sense of mystery. Often the den itself did not even boast a feeble gas flame. The light from opium lamps fed with nut-oil, before each bunk, was sufficient. Someone has spoken of these opium dens of a by-gone day as being like "sepulchers filled with dead." I can think of no better description.

Nor can I find a more exact or more clearly worded description of how the opium pill is prepared and smoked than the following one written by Mr. Masters:

The smoker lies on his side curled up, with his feet resting on a bamboo or earthenware pillow. Before him is a tray containing the necessary appliances. There is an opium lamp of cut glass narrowing at the top, the rim being on a level with the tip of the flame. There is a pipe aptly called "smoking pistol," being a polished stem of carved bamboo, often mounted with silver, a ring of ivory at the mouthpiece, and a round, earthenware, flat-faced bowl, with a tiny hole in the center. There is a box about the size of a pill-box, made of buffalo horn containing smoking opium, near which lie a number of slender wire pokers, a cup of water and a sponge to wipe off the bowl after being used.

The smoker now takes up the pipe and warms the bowl over the lamp. Using a wire poker, he dips it into the box, taking out as much opium as adheres to the point. He holds this over the flame, being careful not to burn it. The heat makes it swell up to twenty times its original size, till it looks like melted India rubber. The steam that has been generated inside is liberated by rolling the opium upon the flat surface of the bowl. Again, it is held over the flame, roasted for a few seconds and again rolled over the bowl. This operation is tiresomely repeated for a couple of minutes, by which time it is reduced to a soft, solid state by the evaporation of a portion of the water of the extract.

When the little bolus has been brought into a state fit to be smoked, it is worked into a conical-shaped ring around the wire. The point of the wire is then inserted into the hole of the bowl and twirled round till the opium becomes detached from the wire and adheres to the pipe, the hole through the center of the bolus connecting with the hole of the bowl. If the opium does not slip clean from the wire, it will have to be roasted and rolled a little longer.

The stem of the pipe is now applied to the mouth and the bowl held over the lamp, care being taken not to char the opium by contact with the flame. The smoker takes a deep inhalation, and the heat is drawn over the bolus, converting into vapor all the volatilizable material of the bolus, which frizzles and sputters like a candle burning down in its socket. Fifteen seconds have gone, and there is no sign of smoke. The fumes have evidently gone into the man's lungs, traveling over the respiratory mucous membrane, where the alkaloids cannot fail to be absorbed into the blood. But now the pent-up vapor breaks forth, a dense volume of smoke pours from nose and mouth, the smell of which is enough to turn a horse's stomach. The pipe is empty, the bolus having been smoked in exactly thirty seconds.

There is a short pause, the bowl is sponged off, and the smoker takes another dip into the little box, and the same tiresome process is repeated, until . . . at last . . . the victim sinks back, the pipe slips

Dens

from his hand, and oblivious of everything around him, he drops off to sleep. What is that dismal den to him now? All misery, pain and care are shut beyond his sense. His soul borne on nepenthe fumes is far off in dreamland's Elysian fields.

Above ground, at the old "Palace" Hotel, was an opium den where the proprietor sat before an earthenware jar and ladled out opium to the customers. This had bunks built one above the other and there were often as many as fifteen addicts in the place at once, filling the air with deep-blue smoke that smelled a bit like burning peanuts with a sickly sweet tinge.

Here, one day, an old timer described for me his attempt to break himself of the habit. The first symptoms of distress came with excessive sneezing and shortness of breath. Then a running of mucus from the eyes and nose comparable to a bad cold. Next came the most terrifying and gripping pains in the bowels. . . . If one persisted long enough in abstaining from a smoke a dreadful diarrhea set in which was usually fatal. My old and wizened friend had escaped that stage through quick surrender. He looked like dried parchment that a playful wind might further shrivel up and blow away. He was a little over forty years of age, according to the proprietor sitting before his jar of questionable delight. He looked at least a hundred and fifty.

Even the very poor had access to an occasional pipe of opium. They bought their opium paste from dealers who obtained the collected scrapings from used pipes and retailed them to the lowly.

Chapter XIV

FADS, FANCIES AND FEASTS

THE only thing that is wrong with New Chinatown is the fact that it must forever stand in the shadow of the old quarter. People who knew next to nothing about Old China-town—who, perhaps, never went oftener than once a year to walk between the street bazaars on the Chinese New Year, will tell you emphatically that "Chinatown isn't what it used to be!" Sweet old grandmothers from Ladies' Aid Societies and Needlework Guilds will shake the jet flowers on their bonnets and sigh that the Old Chinatown is no more. They miss the bright costumes, and the lily-footed women, the pig-tails entwined with red silk—the cobbled streets. They miss the dimly lighted alley-ways, although they haven't the remotest idea what these alley-ways har-bored. In short, although they would emphatically deny it, they want the old days back, with the streets of Chinatown filled with lecherous gun-men, the culs-de-sac crowded with painted slave-girls, the underground section overrun with murderers, opium smokers, lepers, bubonic-plague rats. There are even civic organizations which propose that the young clerks in the bazaars, many of whom have University of California degrees, return to pidgin English in dealing with customers, so as to revive a synthetic and bastard "local color," for the benefit of tourists from Grand Rapids and Oskaloosa. To enter the New Chinatown with your heart still enthralled by the past, is fatal. You will find nothing that will beguile you. It will be as empty as taking on a new lover while your affections are still in bondage to the old. But if you enter the New Chinatown, alert and eager, scorning memories, group tours, and licensed guides, you will come into your reward.

The way to see the New Chinatown, is the way to see any quarter, any city, any country—poke about yourself. In the old days, the heartbeat of Chinatown could have been felt by these personal and, for the best results, solitary, excursions. True, unless you were experienced, it used to be well to take along a policeman, if you cared to dip into Chinatown's vicious depths. Not that anything would have happened to you, but because it would have been next to impossible for you to have found your way about. But, even then, a solitary stroll through the quarter was always the most revealing. Those who scorned such a conquest of Chinatown came away with a distorted view of the Chinese, just as the visitor to America goes away with a distorted view if he witnesses only gang murders, Southern lynchings, the contempt for traffic rules, and tipsy young people on hotel dance floors. There is no denying that a people's sins are much more thrilling than a people's virtues. Even the Old Testament is most exciting when the characters in it are breaking the law. Adam and Eve are very dull people until they take matters into their own hands.

If you do no more than walk down the main street of Chinatown, Grant avenue, with your eyes really open, you will find plenty to beguile you. I still think of anything south of California street as being a mere approach to Chinatown, so you will do well to discount the two blocks that lie between Bush streets and old Saint Mary's Church. For one thing, most of the shops within these boundaries are Japanese. Not a distasteful fact except for the mechanized trash which is heaped up in its windows. Imitation seems the watchword here and we have attempts to render Dresden china, Italian pottery, and Venetian glassware in terms of Japanese counterfeit. If one wants a mechanical toy for a quarter that any child can break in ten minutes, this is the place to buy it; or a cheap tin ash tray with Fujiyama impressed upon its face; or a calendar, with the same mountain as a decoration; or a bright yellow kimono, turned out by a factory in Tokio and retailing at two dollars and ninety-eight cents; or some mules made of white cats' fur that will moult all over the house; or a dreadful pottery dog minus a tail that will be supplied by your toothbrush once it reposes on the glass shelf in the bathroom. But in fairness, even here, there are one or two legitimate Japanese shops, whose windows gravely arranged with charming economy of line, exhibit mellowed prints, and lovely bronze vases from which a single stalk of cherry blossoms or toyon berries spring upward according to their season. Here, too, one can see exquisite boxes of gold lacquer—just the thing to set upon the polished surface of a mahogany table; or a bolt of gold brocade; or the iron silhouette of a crane under a bamboo branch to hang against the wall; or a lantern for the garden wrought of stone; or a pine tree, fifty years old, but not over six inches high, as twisted and gnarled as if it had been battling the elements for centuries.

There are even one or two American firms in these two blocks that snare yellow Ming horses with green trappings and white jade bowls for the discriminating at fabulous prices. But one must enter these shops to get any notion of their treasures. They are like millinery stores that exhibit not more than two models in their windows—smart but excruciatingly expensive. They keep carved ivories and agate perfume bottles in containers lined with brocade. And they show you their wares one at a time so that you will not be confused or overdazzled.

In these two blocks the simple Japanese shops are cheap and vulgar, the discriminating Japanese shops—conventional and formal, the American importers profoundly elegant and in perfect taste. But, once you cross California street line, the bazaars grow more exuberant, more colorful, more filled with artistic vitality. The windows are heaped with Canton vases, pink and green having notes of yellow shot through them; with teakwood tables, inlaid with mother-of-pearl; with processional umbrellas of cherry silk studded with sequins.

Here are ebony screens, framing porcelain panels on which mincing court ladies are assiduously watched by pot-bellied eunuchs bearing scarlet fans; vermilion chests upon whose surface a score of fantastic flowers bloom; robes of state, embroidered in apple-green and old rose, and lined with white fur.

Here are figures of the smiling God of Wealth with obscene belly and obscene breasts; Buddha in gold shrines; Goddesses of Mercy, in white porcelain or ivory, chaste and serene. Here are trays of red lacquer with carvings an inch thick on them; paintings of mountain peaks dripping cascades of water; round ivory balls containing two score of thin layers of carvings within, all movable but imprisoned in the outer shell, equally carved.

All this, not exhibited decorously with an eye to single effect but heaped together, with careless prodigality, achieving a curious harmony in spite of the confusion. What a wealth of artistic outpouring! What a riot of creative imagination! What a sweep of line allied to an infinite capacity for detail!

But all these things are exotics, things to ponder over after one has exhausted the more human avenues of approach to an understanding of Chinatown. Embroideries and ivory carvings and Ming horses heaped up for emptying the purses of tourists are all very well but we shall come nearer to the daily life of a people if we poke about the shops that minister the needs of the Chinese, themselves.

On the corner of Clay street and Grant avenue, is a shop that deals in delicacies to tempt the jaded palate. It makes a particular speciality of dried food. In the shallow window a half score of sun-dried eatables hang in long rows on a wire. First of all is dried duck. Here is a food that even a tourist from the corn belt cannot mistake for though it be boned and flattened, the outline of a duck is the same the world over. It has first been salted, then hung out to a leisurely cooking in the sun's slow oven, then pressed in oil. Next comes a cluster of dark brown, almost black, shapeless masses of food—dried pig livers. Then pork spareribs, first barbecued, dipped in soya-bean sauce, and sun-dried as a finishing touch. The little shriveled brown objects strung upon a bamboo stick are not dates, as you first supposed, but dried oysters. And the dried frogs would be unmistakable, except that at first glance they look in their shriveled state a good deal like dead water-dogs.

Just across the street there is a shop that seems to spe-

HANG FAR LOW

cialize in fish products: Dried abalone, looking fairly un-appetizing; brown fish dipped in oil and sun-dried; fish balls that have only to be heated and served in the most approved delicatessen shop manner; dried squid; dried fish-skins, silvery and transparent; dried shrimps; dried seaweed for use in soups.

Where they sell vegetables and greens you will come upon beans in sprouting condition, Chinese parsley, a turnip that is peculiarly Chinese, shaped like a dirigible; the bark of a bush which is fried with pork until it is crisp. If you chance to see a basket of lily bulbs in a food shop do not imagine that they are for spring planting. They are to be eaten, after they have been chopped fine and fried.

There are miscellaneous things—dried mushrooms, which come nearer to our understanding; pork and dried greens, cooked in soya-bean sauce; a white fish looking like cod, boiled and ready for serving, floating about in oblong pans filled with water. There are Chinese chicken, cooked in soya-bean sauce, bean cakes fried in oil, and rows of brown-glazed jugs, filled with herb wines.

If you do not like the smells or the look of any of these eatables, try to imagine how a Chinese would react if he were turned loose in one of our delicatessen shops for the first time. The dried fish, the smoked hams, might not make his gorge rise. But he might find sauerkraut scarcely to his taste and blood pudding far from appetizing. And he would certainly find any and all of our cheeses hard to take. In fact he would leave them severely alone. For there is one edible food, and one edible food only, a Chinese does not know at home and which he will never acquire a taste for—*cheese*. A curious omission, until we remember that the Chinese are not a pastoral people. Yet, it is surprising that the Mongol invasion with its background of flocks and herds, did not introduce the cheese-eating habit.

San Francisco's Chinatown

I went in London to a dinner which included a young Chinese student among the guests. A huge cheese was brought on at the end of the meal. I saw the Chinese turn pale. But when someone cut a slice and a series of transparent white worms fell squirming to the bottom of the plate, he excused himself hurriedly and left the room. I must confess this last demonstration tested me severely, too. I am passionately fond of cheese but I want to see the life which gives it flavor and quality only under a microscope.

There is never any beef or lamb sold in Chinese butcher shops. It is said that in the old days, a very special torture was devised in hell for the man who slew a buffalo for food. These Oriental buffaloes were beasts of burden and were guarded and revered as such. Sheep, doubtless, require too much grazing land to secure an economic foothold in China. There is a small butcher shop on Waverly place that seems to specialize on pig's "innards." Large pans of the pig's intestines and what the Chinese call "tripe" fill the window. This last has something to do with a pig's stomach. But, allowing for the momentary recoil which any strange food gives one, these swinish agents of digestion look flabby and uninviting on close inspection. Even their color, white, tinged with pinkish lavender, is not overly tempting.

There are certain old-fashioned delicacies which seem to have lost their vogue in the new era. One used to stumble often upon tubs filled with ancient eggs encased in mud, sharks' fins, and Chinese terrapin. But there is one delicacy which still appears in the shop windows during the New Year's season—birds' nest for soup. It comes, now, packed in fancy boxes and looks like old-fashioned gelatin.

The earliest records of Chinese banquets always mention this soup and to a person who had not seen the crisp, clean substance from which the soup was made, the idea sounded

262

Fads, Fancies and Feasts

foul. The encyclopædia yields the information that this soup ingredient is "a gelatinous substance forming the greater part of the nests of certain swifts, consisting of the mucus secreted by their salivary glands." And, if you are in doubt as to just what a swift is, you will find from the same source that it is a "micropodoid bird of swallow-like form that preys upon insects and has highly developed salivary glands." If the word "micropodoid" affrights you, another glance at the book, will assure you that a micropodoid is a "true swift" and you are right back where you started from.

But you may discount this information entirely and take one of my Chinese friends' assurance that the substance which forms the nest is not manufactured by the salivary glands of the swift but is the spawn of fishes gathered by the birds. The best hunting ground for these birds' nests, is the island of Sumatra, in almost inaccessible caverns along the sea coast. Gathering them is a dangerous business and makes the price of the luxury mount into the upper brackets. The most expensive nests are, for obvious reasons, those gathered before the birds are hatched, when they are still a pure white. But, less virginal nests must go through some sort of sterilization process before they reach the market for the ordinary eye cannot detect any uncleanness in them. I have never tasted birds' nest soup, but my informants tell me that it is delicious. Pressed to declare what it tastes like they can only answer: "Like birds' nest soup." Which means, of course, that the flavor is indescribable.

Shark fins, I am informed, have a rank musty flavor. Apparently they are an acquired taste.

Other dishes which old restaurant menus once yielded were stewed ortolans, a dish called Taranaki fingers contrived from the fruit of a New Zealand tree, fish brains, Chinese quail, reindeer sinews, scorpion's eggs, and stewed moss. But even if some of these are missing from the shops and eating houses in modern Chinatown, there is still enough interesting and exotic food to give one's palate a new thrill.

As late as 1935, I went with my friend Zee Min Lee, to a dinner which he gave for me and a group of friends at the Shanghai Low. We began by sipping draughts of herbal wine out of tiny porcelain cups, by way of an appetizer. Then a melon was brought on the table. It was a species of watermelon, hollowed out, cut in half and standing upright. A lid, contrived from the rind, was lifted and revealed a smoking hot soup. This soup had been steamed in the melon, gaining a subtle flavor thereby. It was a soup made from chicken stock, reinforced by lotos seeds, mushrooms, bamboo shoots, and shredded ham. It was delicious.

The next course was known as Pekin grilled duck. To achieve this, the skin has first to be painted with peanut oil and grilled many times. This was served with a sauce of red plum jam mixed with spices, herbs and soya-bean sauce. Our first helping was a slice of the delicately browned skin, which proved to be the most savory part of the bird.

Then came walnut chicken, chicken cooked with walnuts, as its name implies; roast pigeon; barbecued pork with cabbage hearts; ducks stewed with nuts; and fried shrimp balls. There was a main course for every guest—a rule which sets the length of the feast in Chinatown.

At some of the banquets served in an earlier day, where the attendance was large, over a hundred courses were reported. The invitation to one of these feasts is very brief and deprecating. It merely states that "This noon a slight repast awaits you at the Hang Heong restaurant." The "slight repast" in this instance proved to be one hundred and twenty-five courses.

One of the most interesting dishes was Chinese ravioli. These were not steamed as the Italian ravioli is, but fried crisp. They were compounded of paste stuffed with minced pickle, cuttle-fish, pork and peppers. My host informed me that the Italians got the idea for ravioli from Marco Polo and modified it when he returned from China. The same thing was true of spaghetti and all Italian pastes. These were merely variations of the Chinese noodle. We had noodles instead of rice at this feast, stamping it with the seal of North China. For it appears that the Southern Chinese eat rice—those from the North, noodles. Noodles are likewise a birthday dish. They are a symbol of long life.

I am not sure, but I think this occasion was a birthday feast. At all events, the matter of age was brought up and we Westerners bemoaned the passing of time and the gray hairs that were appearing in the heads of those who retained enough hair to make such a condition obvious. Our host reproved us. In his country, it was not polite to mention anyone's youth. Age alone was to be commended. The greatest compliment you could pay a man was to remark upon his venerable years. And it was flattering and a pleasant gesture to address a young man as "elder brother."

At the end of the meal, we sat about for several hours amid a litter of empty platters, unwashed dishes and a crumb-strewn table. It appears that it is impolite to clear anything away. That is tantamount to hurrying the guests, hinting to them to be on their way. While there is something pleasant in a clean board after one has done with food, this gesture of consideration for leisure has its points, too. With modifications it might be commended to Occidental butlers and waiters who go about snatching food from under one's very mouth in a mistaken zeal for service.

It is perhaps unnecessary to state that with this meal we drank quantities of clear unsweetened Chinese tea. Tea is accounted a great digestive agent by the Chinese. It serves them not only at meals but all through the day. Its vogue, like all age-old customs, is passing slowly but surely with the younger generation. One scarcely ever sees a table in the business houses devoted to the inevitable tea-pot, any more. It used to be a feature. When one entered a home or a place of business, one poured a cup of tea not only to refresh oneself but as a ceremonial. The pot reposed in a wicker basket padded and covered with a quilted lid. Only the spout was visible, sticking out, inviting you to tip the basket and fill one of the tiny bowl-like cups which reposed at the side.

All shades of breeding were betrayed by the manner one drank one's tea. There was a language built around tea drinking—a thing of subtle signs, of positions of the hands, the fingers, the gesture with which one raised the cup to the lips. The old anti-Manchu Triad Society, for instance, had a complete set of tea-drinking rules which revealed membership in the society to a stranger who was also of that persuasion. Even the position of the tea-pot upon the table, its relation to the number of cups and their position with regard to it was fraught with meaning in tea-drinking circles. Were the cups placed in rows or pairs? Was the tea-pot in the center with the cups grouped around it? Were the cups in front of, or behind the tea-pot? Which way did the spout point? Every one of these arrangements was subject to interpretation.

Western civilization owes an incalculable debt to the Orient for introducing tea drinking into the Occident. Marco Polo seems to have been the first to bring it to the notice of Europeans in the thirteenth century. But the Italians apparently took less kindly to this innovation than they did to noodles and ravioli. . . . Three hundred years later, some Jesuit missionaries brought tea into use in church circles. The first tea to come into England was said to have been in the form of a present by the East India Company to the King in 1667. Up to that time the dames of old England were sipping a brew made from sage. It took Catherine of

Fads, Fancies and Feasts

Braganza, the wife of Charles II, to make tea drinking fashionable. But the price was too prohibitive to make the English matrons give up their sage-tea drinking. In those early days, tea cost from six to ten pounds a pound. This was equivalent anywhere from one to three hundred dollars in gold. But when it did get a foothold in England its conquest was complete. Lecky in his *History of Civilization* says:

The effects of hot drinks, tea and coffee upon domestic life has been even greater in England than on the Continent; checking the boisterous revels that had once been universal, and raising women to a new position in the domestic circle, they have contributed very largely to refined manners, to introduce a new order of tastes, and to soften and improve the character of men.

The question of a tax on tea, also helped to bring about the American revolution, so, all in all, its three hundred years of life in the West has been fraught with influence.

In 1852, there was an agitation started to grow tea in California. The San Francisco *Herald* published a long editorial proving that California was in a position to "furnish the labor, experience, climate, soil and character of country, necessary for the production of tea."

"Who," inquires the newspaper, "will be the first to import the plants from China and commence the experiment?"

The answer, apparently, was, "Nobody."

Every year the rumor goes about that the Old Chinese New Year is to be abandoned in favor of the New Year which begins the Roman calendar. But every year, happily, there seems to be just as many blossoming lilies for sale in the temporary stalls along Grant avenue, just as many sweetmeats to tempt one's palate, and just as many firecrackers exploding far into the night as there ever were.

San Francisco's Chinatown

. . . The younger generation do not ignore the New Year of the Occidentals, but, they are loathe, like all young people, to abandon any excuse for a holiday. The Roman calendar and all its feasts have been incorporated into their general scheme very much as every god that they have ever known is made a part of their religious experience. Thanksgiving, Christmas, the Fourth of July are celebrated enthusiastically. And, to the great unrest, we are sure, of the shades of Denis Kearney and all Irishmen who orated and threw bricks in pursuit of their conviction that all Mongolians were of sinister origin, there are even young Chinese Social Clubs who not only have dances on St. Patrick's Day, but advertise the fact with posters fashioned of emerald green cardboard in the most approved shamrock shapes.

The white residents of San Francisco are continually lamenting that the Chinese New Year "isn't what it used to be." But what holiday ever is? Somehow the years rub the bloom off recurrent celebrations. Anniversaries, in the end, come to be tinged with notes of sadness. Sometimes it is because the spirit of the occasion has grown thin, but, more often, it is our increasing lack of capacity to be thrilled as the years roll on, by the innocences implicit in fête days.

Since the early fifties, whenever the new moon entered the sign of Aquarius, there have been stirrings in Chinatown as unmistakable and prophetic of a seasonal goodwill to even the white residents of San Francisco as the stirrings of Christmas cheer that precedes Yule-tide. The premonitions of impending festivity come always with soft February rains, and the vagrant perfume of a Chinese lily, blossoming before its appointed time, or the flame of quince blossoms lighting a window ledge in Waverly place. Unmistakably, it is a hint of spring, an awakening of life heretofore stale and unprofitable.

Then, suddenly, overnight, there are stalls set up along

SONG KEE SHOP

the length of Grant avenue, with crowds bargaining for sprigs of cherry blossoms, or bags of salted plums, or boxes of candied cumquats. Greeks peddling gay balloons, invade the quarter, and the fathers of families are seen hurrying home, carrying branches of almond trees in bloom or a pair of ceremonial candles for the family altar, dyed a deep vermilion, with trappings of gilt-and-silver paper made into fabulous butterflies.

In the bakery shop windows there are pastries and cakes unending flavored with various and sundry bean pastes. The beans are black or brown as the cook's fancy dictates, boiled, ground and sweetened into a thin paste for a filling. There are cocoanut cakes and almond cakes and pastries stuffed with Chinese brown sugar.

The stalls are filled with mounds of li-chee nuts, lily seeds and the seeds of melons. There are dates looking curiously unlike any dates which the Near East produces. There are tiny dried figs, equally unrecognizable. There are pickled almonds that look like plums. But there are still plenty of plums in divers shapes and forms if your appetite leads you in that direction—dried purple plums, candied green plums, pickled plums, both purple and green in plum syrup. Strips of winter melon, candied, overflow cornucopias of thick brown paper, and there are thin slices of sugared cocoanut piled in snowwhite mounds.

At midnight of the appointed day, the streets are suddenly cleared of stalls and hucksters, the shutters are put up before every shop window, and bellying lanterns are lit in the doorways glowing pallidly past the sunrise. Through doors swiftly opened and as swiftly closed, one can get glimpses of family altars contrived from teakwood tables, set with incense jars of pewter surmounted by Buddha lions. Lily bulbs shooting up heavily scented blossoms of cream and gold, platters of mandarin oranges, mounds of yellow cumquats, are arranged upon the table with an uncanny sense of composition. Amazing bouquets of paper flowers, combining every color and every form that in Occidental hands would scream to heaven, rise from pink-and-green vases and are translated by some magic into forms of perfect symmetry and beauty.

Toward late afternoon, the barrage of firecrackers begins, continuing all through the night. Not firecrackers set off singly and alone in frugal American fashion, but firecrackers exploded by the package in dim corridors, firecrackers exploded by the hundreds at street corner and curb, firecrackers exploded by the thousands from tong balconies. These last are of gigantic size strung together on a central fuse and lowered as the sparks run gaily upward and tear them to pieces. In the morning, the sidewalks are two inches deep with red, green, and yellow husks of shattered firecrackers, like butterflies overtaken by a storm.

There are missing glories, naturally. The faithful no longer parade through the street, carrying one of their gods in a lacquered chariot reputed to have been worth thirty thousand dollars. The flag poles no longer blossom with the standard of the Imperial Court—a black dragon upon a yellow field. Red flags with crescents or yellow flags with white dragons do not unfold in the afternoon breeze. And "merchant princes, in dark blue silk tights, and long flowing sky-blue gowns" are no longer seen going about with "red slips of paper in their hands," making ceremonial calls. Nor are the male children of the wealthy tricked out in crimson and gold skull caps from which their diminutive queues, more red silk than hair, fall arrogantly. . . . Nor does one see anything as gorgeous as the Tartar official who used to put on his festival clothes at the New Year. He was taller, more lithe than his Canton cousins, with skin "like old-gold satin." He wore tunic and trousers of rich brocade, green and red and purple. And a heavy gold chain was about his neck. His stockings were of white silk and his sabots of white, pale green and gold. . . .

Nor does the Chinese dragon writhe through the streets as of yore. Instead, the Buddha lion dances nimbly before every doorway that lures him to it with a lettuce leaf dangling on a string. This lion comes out of his lair about the third day of the New Year feast and his quest is really money for some charitable purpose. Of recent years, it is the Chinese Hospital that has benefited by his voracious appetite for lettuce leaves and five-dollar bills; for, if you inspect the lettuce leaf closely, you will see that it is merely a ruse for concealing currency.

The advance of the lion is heralded by an orchestra, full of beating drums and crashing cymbals. Behind the automobile carrying the musicians comes the lion, prancing and dancing. He is a very venerable lion with a rainbow body and a white beard. He has four legs, two near the head and two at the other extremity, which, if you look sharply, are very human and trousered in pantaloons of cherry, blue or green silk. Youths with palm-leaf fans attend him.

The lion sniffs the air proudly shaking his mane and keeping a lookout for lettuce leaves which are his consuming passion. He sights one spinning in the morning breeze at the entrance to a chemist shop. He halts shivering and shimmying with delight. A barrage of exploding firecrackers sending out blue clouds meets his gyrations. The attendants blow the smoke away from his nostrils with their fans. The orchestra plays a dance tune, the firecrackers subside, the lion's body undulates and plunges, circling round the lettuce leaf with rhythmic anticipation. Then, drawing near to the feast, the insatiable monster leaps upward, closes his jaws over the lettuce leaf, the string snaps, and he moves on to the next doorway.

San Francisco's Chinatown

At the last New Year, it took two days for the lion to make his way up and down the length and breadth of Chinatown. Then he moved over across the bay to the Oakland side and spent another day devouring lettuce leaves and currency. It may not be as efficient a way of collecting money as the method adopted by the community chest but it is certainly more picturesque. But the procedure is very exhausting and many legs swathed in cherry silk are used up before the lion's appetite for lettuce leaves is satisfied.

This is one practical aspect of the New Year season. The other, which is foremost, is the rule that all debts must be paid. In the old days, social ostracism was the fate of a man who neglected this detail. Many white merchants can remember the Chinese residents coming with sacks of gold at the New Year and squaring their accounts. They did this, too, with the money lenders. They would pay up their score and, once the festival had run its course, return to borrow the money all over again.

The feast which used to rival the New Year was the Feast of the Dead which came in April. Sometimes it was called the Feast of the Hungry Ghosts. It was then that the spirits were reputed to come forth from their graves to visit the earth. Visits were made to the burying ground with food which was placed at the heads of the graves in the fashion of a funeral feast. But this food was largely symbolic for the returning hosts brought back the roast pork and the dried duck with them and had a feast. It was really a memorial day with the exception that food was used to manifest affection for the dead instead of flowers. Who can say which is the more expressive method? Our forefathers with customary smugness referred to the rites at the graveyard as the performance of "a variety of droll capers." This feast seems to be a thing of the past.

MANDARIN THEATRE, GRANT AVENUE

Fads, Fancies and Feasts

So, too, is the Feast of the Dragon Boat, which was performed annually on the river at Sacramento. This was in reality a boat race and took place in the middle of March. From ten to fifteen boats manned by Chinamen wielding paddles used to assemble for a prize-winning contest. One of the newspapers of the day described the historic background of these races as follows:

Many years ago, a Prime Minister of the Celestial Empire was drowned in one of the canals of the flowery land, and a great reward was offered for the recovery of his body. Sympathy for the loss of a ruler who was universally beloved, but a still stronger motive, probably the desire to obtain the reward, drew together an immense concourse of watermen from all parts of the realm. The struggle which took place for precedence in the attempt to recover the body was accompanied, it is said, by some of the most exciting races ever known in Chinese history, both to and from the scene of the search, and in memory of the event, the day has ever since been marked by regattas and boat races.

Will Irwin, writing the text for Arnold Genthe's photographs, gives a charming picture of a festival that occurs once in every seven years:

Once only, in my recollection, came a day when all the women, high and low, virtuous and lost, had free run of the streets. This was the Good Lady Festival, celebrated every seven years in honor of that illustrious Chinese woman, princess and martyr, who was raised for her virtues to godhood. Her symbol is a little shoe, the tapering shoe of the lily feet, which she threw into the river before she died. And on the day of her festival, woman was raised to the level of man. She was free to walk the streets, to sacrifice, to bow publicly before the outdoor altars where priests in white robes and white fillets tapped their little gongs and sang incessantly to the joss. The "Prayer store" on Dupont street where one might buy anything and everything sacred to the Chinese religion, banked its counters and filled its windows with tiny shoes, from a thing of gold which one might hang on his tunic as a souvenir to a valentine thing in pink rice paper, large enough to clothe a proper lily foot.

Another day on which a female divinity was honored was the Feast of the Goddess of Heaven, in April, but in what manner, I have never been able to discover.

Then there was the inevitable Feast of the Lanterns so esteemed as a motif for Christmas pantomimes in which buxom ladies in tights were wont to parade up and down the stage, carrying lighted lanterns on their shoulders. But, I never saw aught of this pageantry except on the American stage. However an old newspaper file assures us that it was one of the main festivals of Chinatown and was celebrated with a procession preceded by an orchestra beating cymbals and tom-toms, followed by priests chanting songs said to be over two thousand years old. Gods were carried out into the streets, sitting upon golden thrones. Every man in the company carried a punk stick but where the lanterns came in is not apparent.

In the middle of September, there is a festival which is still kept, perhaps because it is tied up with the simple rite of eating a special dish. It is called the Distribution of Moon Cakes and is in honor of a famous but bibulous poet Li T'ai Po. He flourished from A. D. 618 to 905. Li T'ai Po went rowing on a lake one beautiful moonlight night after imbibing not wisely but too well. He saw the moon's reflection in the water and thinking it a chastely beautiful woman dived after her and never came up. Whether his quest for beauty was successful none can tell. But every year as the season comes about, the Chinese honor his memory by eating "moon cakes." But they are not as ethereal as their name implies. As a matter of fact they are dumplings made of rice flour, stuffed with chicken or pork and wrapped in green leaves. Thus again do the Chinese use an excessively material symbol to commemorate a thing of airy fantasy.

Chapter XV

THE DRAMA AND THE JOSS HOUSE

THE Chinese Theatre, like the theatre the world over, suffers in these mechanical days, in competition with the movies. But, occasionally, a banner is stretched across Grant avenue announcing, I am sure, in perfect Barnum and Bailey parlance that the "most marvelous, the most colossal, the most engaging show ever assembled under one roof" is about to open.

Drama dealing with modern problems has only begun to rear a rather inadequate head in China, I am told. Certainly it has not appeared in San Francisco. The old classical drama is still the thing—with certain modifications. Now, the female parts are taken by women, there is an attempt at scenery; they have begun to use a curtain. None of these innovations are improvements—at least, not in their present stage of development.

276

The Drama and the Joss House

Chinese acting, as almost anyone knows, is highly stylized. Perhaps that is why the men who were trained from youth in the conventions of female impersonation were so manifestly superior in giving out an illusion of perfect femininity. Those who saw Mei Lan-Fang will know what I mean. He, of course, is the apex of female impersonation. And, yet, impersonation is scarcely the word for the remarkable way in which he translates symbols of womanhood into womanhood itself.

He is the "sublimation of woman" rather than the real thing—a distilled essence of the feminine principle. He is the symbol of all women and therefore an exaggeration. And by this same token a complete product of art, since all art is, properly, exaggeration.

The ladies of the present Chinese stage are at no pains to employ art in their creations. Against a background of males playing even their own sex with true artistic emphasis they are content to be unaccented females. Insubordinate females, I was about to say, for they stand clear of the ensemble at every point. They are a little too concerned with their permanently waved hair, with the modern note which has crept into their costumes. One suspects that they are infected with Hollywood ideals—that they think of themselves as stars.

The scenery is too much of a compromise to be successful. Its over-abundant detail takes away from the figures on the stage. Chinese costuming is too overwhelming to stand competition. What it needs is a neutral background. As for the curtain of silk, drawn across, instead of descending to screen the stage, it might beguile us with its purple-silk softness if it did not bear in perfect advertising-English the glad tidings that a certain remedy manufactured in Canton is excellent for bloated stomach and kindred internal troubles.

There are other "improvements." The actors when they

277

are not occupying the center of the stage do not loll about the side-lines in full view of the audience smoking, chewing on sugar cane or eating strips of candied cocoanut, as they used to at the old playhouse on Jackson street. The men do not sit with their hats on in the orchestra leaving the gallery to the women. The gorgeous robes are no longer kept in equally colorful chests on either side of the stage. One cannot, now, see the manager peering through a circular window at the rear to mark the progress of the show, or catch glimpses through this same aperture, of members of the company at supper.

It was these variations from the routine of Occidental show-house behavior that diverted our grandfathers much more than the plays themselves. But, of course, they thought even the plays outlandish in the extreme.

The first dramatic company came in 1852 but San Francisco's curiosity was unaroused. The newspapers commented on the "terrible noise, like the wailings of turkey-cocks plus the drum poundings of small boys" which issued from the theatre building, but were otherwise unmoved. In 1853 when a more elaborate dramatic season was inaugurated the town flocked to the innovation.

Knowing nothing about the conventions of the Chinese theatre the white auditors completely missed the point. They were trying to reconcile their own puerile drama in which "Fashion" and "The Drunkard" were shining examples—or at best the classical dramatic art of Shakespeare and Sheridan—with a completely alien form of expression. It never occurred to them that the Chinese drama was more in the nature of an opera than a play. But, perhaps, this would not have helped them since Chinese music was equally unintelligible to them. In fact, San Francisco refused to accept Chinese music as anything but a meaningless accumula-

The Drama and the Joss House

tion of noise, until in the late nineties, Paderewski came to town.

Paderewski was the musical matinee idol of his day. Strong women wept and weak women swooned when he played Chopin on the piano—anything he did or said was above criticism. Mr. Paderewski was taken to the Chinese theatre. Next day, in an interview in one of the papers, he declared that he had never heard any music so dramatically moving as Chinese music. The musical sections of the town buzzed. Could it be possible that what had once been described in San Francisco as the blended noises of "a man mending pots, another filing a saw, another hammering boards, another beating a gong, and two boys trying to tune fiddles" was really music? The great Paderewski had said so. That settled it. After that, high-brow circles affected a belief in the superiority of Chinese music. Since then, San Francisco has had concerts featuring the music of Schoenberg which makes it hopeful that some day Occidental music will overtake its Oriental rival in the matter of discord.

It was the stage conventions that handed our parents the biggest laugh. The first absurdity was lack of scenery and the sign hung out to indicate the background. They had forgotten or perhaps had never heard of the Elizabethan days when the same device was used by a gentleman named Shakespeare. It also tickled their risibilities to see a character die on the stage and after lying still a few moments, get up and make an exit. But they were not moved to laughter when a dead hero of their own drama stepped out from the wings to take a final curtain call.

In mob scenes where contending armies fought but did not bleed it seemed the height of absurdity for an actor to indicate that he had been beheaded by inclining his head slightly and retiring from the stage. But how about defeated Roman stage generals who threw themselves upon swords that clumsily came through the cleft between arm and body?

Our forebears were more than disconcerted at having their Victorian sense of propriety outraged by frank birth scenes depicted in the course of a drama, although these were stylized past all offense, if not actual recognition. And, you may be sure that when a writer remarked in the best eyebrow-raising mode of the period, "It is reported that the grossest indecencies are represented in some of these plays," that he had such gross indecencies not by report but by actual observation. He was merely twittering like some old maid who had witnessed an assignation but had not the courage to give direct testimony concerning it.

In short, the conclusions reached about all this dramatic exoticism were summed up by a dramatic critic who dismissed the whole matter with the smug remark that "the Chinese are not a histrionic people—their dramatic instinct is not strong."

Of course to really analyze the Chinese drama would take a volume in itself. Suffice to say that it has elements of music, poetry, prose and bodily rhythm. It is at once a play, an opera, a ballet and an acrobatic performance. It might be called, for want of a better designation, a classical extravaganza.

Since these plays are classical in point of age as well as manner their content is known to the rank and file in the audience. The public goes to see the same repertoire again and again. They know all the big scenes, all the outstanding musical numbers, as we know the soliloquy from *Hamlet* or "Caro Nome" from *Rigoletto*. This explains why the audience is in constant flux, coming and going all during the performance, and why one can purchase a seat for an hour, or two hours, or for the entire evening. Some of the historical

The Drama and the Joss House

dramas last for weeks. But one may miss several consecutive performances if one knows the opus. If one has seen repeatedly *The Ring of the Nibelungenlied* one may miss *Siegfried* or *Die Walküre* without being too disturbed. If one wishes simply to hear a new prima donna sing "Une poco voce" it is not necessary to sit through all of *The Barber of Seville*. This is the spirit which apparently informs the attendance at the Chinese Theatre—this and the state of one's pocket-book. In the early days the price of admission was fifty cents for a full performance. But after midnight it was possible to purchase a seat for as little as five cents. Thus was the poor man given an opportunity to catch at crumbs from the table of artistic plenty.

This of course is all understandable once it has been explained to an Occidental, but, there is one thing that will always remain inexplicable to him—the confusion, the inattention, the distractions throughout the audience. Spectators wishing to leave by the stage entrance no longer cross the stage with little or no concern for the importance of the scene being enacted. But every other known form of disturbance which amused and puzzled our forebears is still in force. Indeed, the disturbance is increased, if anything, because, now, swarms of children accompany their parents to the play. These children come, not to see the performance, but because it is the easiest way of disposing of them while their elders enjoy a bit of recreation. They romp up and down the aisles, talk without restrictions, make innumerable, and I am sure for the most part, unnecessary excursions to the dressing room. They wriggle past you on their way out and return in due time to assure Papa and Mama that everything is all right again, only to tread your toes a moment later on their way to fresh excursions in foyer and lavatory.

All this, mind you, does not take place during intermissions for there are none. The house lights are never dimmed and the stage is in competition during the entire performance with all that is going on in the audience—the vendor of newspapers, for instance, peddling an extra concerning the latest uprising in Hankow, or the seller of sweetmeats, or the greetings of two friends stopping to give the gossip of the neighborhood on their way out.

Perhaps, a boy martyr of ten or twelve, tending the family baby that does not look a day over two months old, comes in from the lobby to talk with his mother about certain necessary attentions to his charge. We expect to see the mother rise with a show of impatience at having an important scene interrupted. But, bless her heart, she is not impatient. She is really not very much concerned. She merely gives her son instructions and a safety-pin, and the boy departs without any visible signs of rancor, to minister to his young brother.

As the theatre is not heated, and mother is bundled in fur, we cannot help speculating whether or not little Hung Gow-of-the-needful-attentions will have pneumonia tomorrow, since he is in very thin calico rompers and minus any head covering. We even wonder whether elder brother will not drop him surreptitiously down the drain. But, after all, we suppose mother knows best.

When we return our attentions to the stage, we find that we have missed an important battle scene in which hundreds have been killed and thousands wounded. Did mother miss this, too? We fancy not. We fancy that some curious Oriental quality of subconscious concentration made it possible for her to discuss the problem of what to do for little Hung Gow-of-the-needful-attentions and not miss the stylized decapitation of one hapless warrior.

For, after all, a stage fight is robust enough to stand up in competition with a minor diaper distraction. But how

The Drama and the Joss House

about an aria, or a bit of exquisite poetry, or tense, emotional scene? Can you imagine the immolation scene from *Die Walküre* in competition with a discussion as to what to do for baby? . . . Can you imagine Lady Macbeth walking in her sleep while a newsboy displays disconcerting news about the kidnapping of the Lindbergh baby? . . . Can you imagine lines from *Cyrano de Bergerac* given to the accompaniment of neighborhood gossip? Of course with the proper amount of concentration one can *see* over noise but how does one hear? . . . The fact that one knew "The-quality-of-mercy-is-not-strained" speech by heart never made it possible to care to miss one word from the lovely throat of Ellen Terry when she spoke it.

But this is just one of the points where "never the twain shall meet." It probably comes down to a matter of nerves. Take their music. It may be dramatic, it may be all the things that Paderewski said it was, but an hour of the din and clash from the orchestra which accompanies a Chinese extravaganza leaves a Westerner irritable if not exhausted. Lin Yutang lays Chinese indifference to sound chaos to their superior nerves, although he is forced, in the same breath, to wonder about the American's nerve-resistance to saxophones and jazz bands. He also lays much of the theatre din to a day when Chinese plays were performed in the open air and theatres "had to compete with the peddlers' cries, the barbers' tuning forks, the malt-sugar sellers' small gongs, the shouting of men, women and children and the barking of dogs." He intimates that while the theatre has moved indoors it has not accommodated itself to confinement of four walls. The high falsetto voice of the singers was also a device to make the sounds carry in the open.

But if the nerves of the audience are proof against distractions, not to mention musical din, what can one say of the nerves of the players? What manner of men are these who can go through their paces, reciting verse, singing arias, dying tragically, with an audience who seems so outwardly indifferent to their art? The last time I went to the Chinese Theatre the spectators in my vicinity all had their noses deep in what I thought were programs of the evening's performance. But my Chinese friend explained that it was a synopsis of the play for tomorrow. There was a very important scene going on at the moment, yet, having paid good money to see it, or perhaps, I should say, hear it—these patrons were concerned with reading about something scheduled for the morrow. A Westerner might conceivably ask why they did not fold up the paper and take it home for future reference. Why miss hearing Richard recite, "Now is the winter of our discontent made summer" because of an impatience to read about the performance of *Henry VIII* at a future date? Or can the Chinese attend to both details at once? The answer must be "yes." But it will never cease to puzzle us.

Added to this apparent inattention there is no applause in the Chinese Theatre. Here again the actor is denied a sense of warmth and understanding from his audience.

There has always been one feature of a Chinese play which even Westerners could enter into with perfect enjoyment—the acrobatic feats Writes a critic of the sixties: "The acrobats or tumblers make their entrance en masse at about eleven o'clock, and the whole stage is filled with all the members of the troupe. Their feats are wonderful." And another, at a later date says, "The play was followed by a tumbling performance, in which the chief feat of the tumblers was to jump off two tables, set one upon another, and fall flat upon their backs with a thud that ought to have broken their ribs." One does not need an interpreter to enjoy this sort of diversion. It is to the Chinese play what the ballet is to opera—a *divertissement,* a relief.

But in these later days the acrobats seem to be missing.

The Drama and the Joss House

The agility of the actors in a battle scene is about all one can hope for in the line of athletic action. They twirl their spears and wands, whirl about, sidestep—as well as side-swipe—the enemy and are decapitated or victorious as the book runs.

To the average American the Chinese Theatre is and must ever remain a curiosity—a museum piece. There are *poseurs* who insist that they find it exceedingly profound and enjoyable. But do not trust them. It touches our racial consciousness at no point except when it turns acrobatic or slap-stick. Of course the performance of a Mei Lan-Fang is another matter. Genius speaks every tongue. But, remember, too, that when we see Mei Lan-Fang we see him in a Western theatre. The house lights are darkened, the aisles are free of romping children, the music is tamed. The real test of our enjoyment of the Chinese Theatre must be made with all its distractions, its incongruities, its incoherences.

Which is not to claim that our drama is more profound. Our drama is less aesthetic and more social, perhaps. But, in any event, it is too *different,* ever to achieve a *rapprochement.*

There is one institution in Chinatown that has remained uncontaminated by modern influence and that is the old-fashioned chemist shop. Visually it is as lovely and formal as ever, except that the clerk wears a Hart Schaffner and Marx suit and an Arrow shirt instead of a softly quilted jacket of plum-colored silk over an apple-green waistcoat. There are the same rows of lacquer red boxes with brass handles, the same rich carvings, the same teakwood chairs ranged against the walls and the same botanical prints hanging just over them that proclaimed the chemist shop of fifty years ago.

The types of remedies go back a hundred and fifty years

—perhaps nearer a thousand. There is a wine brewed from snakes, pickled in a liquid looking suspiciously alcoholic but which is said to be merely concocted from a brew of herbs. There are dried sea-horses; the bark of trees, virginal deer horns. There are withered toads, crucified on wooden crosses. There are even dried mushrooms. But try and discover from any resident of Chinatown the specific use of these wonder workers.

One informant told me grudgingly that the mushrooms were a cure for colds but in what form I could not discover. Did they grind them into a powder? Did they mix them, say, with dried sea-horses? Did they add hot water and serve? Nobody knew. Nobody would answer me.

From an old book I did get a line on the dried toads. They were made into a soup that was an "infallible remedy for leanness." All the other things—the sea-horses, the bark of trees, the virginal deer horns were vaguely described as "tonics" by any and all that I approached on the subject.

But a missionary told me something about the virtues of what he called "Chinese hartshorn." Also its preparation. First of all, like the proverbial rabbit for stew, it is essential that you get your deer. The best results are to be obtained by shooting the animal so skillfully that it dies instantly. This has some effect on the manner in which the carcass stiffens. Or maybe it doesn't stiffen, under these circumstances, I'm not sure. You next hang the animal with his head downward so that its strength goes into the horns. This accomplished, you remove the horns and dry them over a slow fire. It is now ready to be reduced to scrapings and mixed with the juices of certain plants. You may then use it for intestinal troubles, according to my missionary friend.

But I have a suspicion that horns with a virginal velvet on

them restore lost manhood. I once read a book wherein some Korean priests attested that one draught of deerhorn tonic made "the steepest mountain become a plain." Which would seem to be proof positive that it has a potent effect on energy in general. Then, why not in particular?

Apparently *any* deer's horn will not be acceptable. Or, at least, its effect will be largely determined by the province in which it is shot.

So with the snake wine. Just a plain snake is not all-healing. To get the best results a snake that has swallowed a toad should be obtained. After which you slowly drown the snake in a liquid filled with macerated herbs at the point of fermentation. . . . What this is good for not even my missionary friend was able to say. But if you have a mild form of smallpox, blood from a pig's tail is said to be efficacious, especially if you apply it very cold.

The last time I went hopefully in the early afternoon to visit a Joss House and report upon its present-day activities I found a sign on a barred door which informed me that it was only opened between the hours of eight and ten in the evening for the benefit of tourists. In other words, for the most part, this place of worship had degenerated into a mere show place—a sort of racket for the mystification of sightseers. Inquiry revealed that there was only one other Joss House operating in Chinatown. This, likewise, catered mostly to tourists. I questioned the younger generation about this. Their answer was that only a few of the older, conservative Chinese ever visited the Joss House.

Most of the young people had had Christian training. In one or other of the Protestant Sabbath Schools, they had learned about the pastoral heroes of Israel and the story of the Saviour's miraculous birth. At Christmas there had been glittering trees, and bags of candy distributed. On Easter, purple and vermilion eggs had been their portion. Their approach to spiritual truths had been an approach so often used—through the senses. The Salvation Army learned quickly that a hot cup of coffee is a better opening wedge to a hungry man's salvation than a tedious prayer. Christmas trees and Easter eggs fix the feasts of the Church more indelibly upon the minds of children than masses and sermons. Even now, at the Christmas season there is no quarter where the Christmas trees are set up earlier or stay longer than in the newer sections of Chinatown where the native born Chinese have their hearthstones. The colored electric lights entwined in fir and redwood branches wink from the middle of December way past the New Year.

How far-reaching the influence of Christianity will be in the final analysis is hard to say. Certainly most of the young people I talked to in Chinatown admitted that they were drifting religiously very much as the young people with Occidental backgrounds are drifting. They do not use the Joss House and they do not go to a Christian Church. But the force of the new religion is felt sub-consciously—of that I am positive.

It is a far cry from the days when Father Bouchard, a Catholic priest, said openly that the Chinese had no capacity for rising to the religion of Jesus Christ and Mr. Frank Pixley, a prominent editor, insisted that the Chinese had no souls worth saving. The most revered figure in China today is the late Sun Yat Sen—the first President of the Republic *and a Christian*.

You may be one of those people who declare that a Chinaman will never be a Christian. Or go further and insist that all Chinese Christians are thieves and robbers. Or merely be content with the observation that you liked the old "heathen Chinee" best, and that you think it an impertinence for us to force our religion down anybody's throat.

CHINESE TEMPLE, PINE STREET

The Drama and the Joss House

As to this last, do not be so indignant and concerned. The only thing that has ever been forced down the throat of the Chinese people by another nation is opium. And this only because they liked the idea. There is no race so successfully resisting outside influence as the Chinese. If they finally accept Christianity they will put their own interpretation upon it—of that you may be sure. It will go through the mill of their race consciousness and come out changed. In philosophy, Christian principles are not unlike the principles of Confucius. Confucius enunciated this negative golden rule five hundred years before Christ was born: Do not unto others what you would not that others should do unto you.

The Far East when it has been influenced by Christianity has been influenced very profoundly. Witness the Christian element of non-resistance to force that burns like a flame amid the Hindu philosophy of Mahatma Gandhi. And what of the Japanese Christian, Toyohiko Kagawa, who is revolutionizing the conditions of the poor in his country on an economic basis? In both instances we have practical applications of Christian principles that far outdo our own. Perhaps a religion has to be seen with fresh eyes to glimpse its real glory. Perhaps the West has known Christianity too long. It is like a familiar landscape to us—accepted but without thrill until a stranger comes along and renews in us a sense of its beauty by his enthusiasm. It may be that through the Orient, the beauty of the Christian ideal may be revived in us again.

It is hard to define a Joss House in Occidental terms. It is neither a church, nor a temple, nor a mosque. But it could easily have elements of all three. A Joss House is not a thing of sect and dogma. It is, to quote the Chinese themselves, simply a "place of worship." Into it may be poured any and all the religious faiths and influences that the

San Francisco's Chinatown

Chinese have absorbed and modified in the sixty centuries of their civilization. It may contain symbols of a pagan past, with its charming gods of forest and stream, field and farm house. It may contain symbols of venerable ancestor worship, of the philosophies of Lao-tsze and Confucius, of the religion of Buddha. It is conceivable that a Chinese Joss House, a Chinese "place of worship," fifty—a hundred years, hence, might incorporate symbols of the Christian cross into the varied pattern of its religious texture.

The Chinese are geniuses in the matter of conservation. They waste nothing. So with their religious experiences. They have never quite abandoned their old beliefs in the face of fresh revelations. They have merely used these new revelations to augment the faiths of their fathers—to give them greater breadth. The West has not been so loyal to the past; therefore, there are no places of worship that harbor under one roof shrines to Apollo, and Wotan, and Erda, the great god Pan, and the pitiful Saviour. There is no Druid altar side by side with altars to Pallas Athene and the God of Abraham and Isaac and Jacob. One of the outstanding traits of Chinese character, according to a modern Chinese writer, is its reasonableness, its capacity to achieve a "golden mean"—a spirit of compromise which we of the West are too impatient to foster. When we are overcome with a new and profound revelation we let its force sweep everything that went before it into oblivion. We are like Saul of Tarsus, blinded by the vision. The Chinese receive a new outpouring into the broad stream of their racial consciousness and slacken it. Nothing of the past is carried away by the flood.

The derivation of the term "Joss House" is significant of its broad purpose. The word "joss" is a corruption of the Portuguese word "deos" meaning God, and goes back to the days when Portugal was one of the few countries trad-

The Drama and the Joss House

ing with China. It is, therefore, a House of God, with no confining limits as to any special manifestation of His presence. In the old days, these Houses of God were set up in San Francisco as often as new tongs or associations were organized. Especially was this true of the district tongs. The first need was for a general meeting place. A place of worship usually followed, where among other gods, the local divinities could be honored. In the case of trade guilds, gods who favored the craft, were exalted. Our patron saints are an extension of this idea.

In one of the old Chinatown Joss Houses, there used to be a shrine to Ma Chu, the Goddess of Sailors. She sat between two assistants, "Favorable-wind-ear" and "Thousand-mile-eye." Ma Chu, according to tradition, was the daughter of a sea-faring man. One day she fell asleep at her loom. She dreamed that the junk which was carrying her father and brothers on a trading venture was caught in a terrific storm. She did not hesitate an instant: She seized the junk in her hands, cramming her father into her mouth for safer keeping. As she dragged ashore the junk with her two brothers aboard, she heard her mother questioning her. Duty compelled a reply. Forgetting her father, she opened her mouth to answer and awoke. A few days later, word came of the drowning of her father and the safety of her brothers. Sailors call her affectionately "Grandmother Ma Chu" and it is thus they address her when in peril.

The most popular god in these old Joss Houses used to be Kwan Tai, the God of War—a curious choice for an essentially pacifist people. But, on second thought, it was well, perhaps, for peaceful folk to keep a god of war in good humor. Nearly every Joss House had an altar above which he glowered with a sort of genial ferocity. He was a very red-faced gentleman with an impressive black beard.

There was another impressive god called Yun-Ten-Tin,

San Francisco's Chinatown

the "Supreme Ruler of the Somber Heavens." He had control over the elements. A sort of super forest ranger, he sat
in a tree and prevented droughts and conflagrations. Then,
there was Wah-Taw, the God of Medicine. In the old days
when he lived and walked the earth he cured the sick by the
Christian method of the laying on of hands. When Marco
Polo made his famous trip to Cathay, his record is full of
accounts of Christian sects in nearly every city he visited. I
used to wonder when I read of his travels whether or not by
any chance this Wah-Taw was really a Chinese paraphrase
of Jesus. The ancient Christian communities have long been
swallowed up by the inexorable forces of China but it is
pleasant to fancy that their contribution to the religious
scheme is a Great Physician who puts his hand on the lame,
the halt and the blind and makes them whole. Occasionally,
one ran upon an altar raised to an evil spirit—a devil. There
was such a one in a Joss House in Waverly place. He was a
very unpleasant-looking person, as I remember, with a
horse, saddled and bridled, at his right hand, as if in readi-
ness to take him places. Great quantities of food were offered to him every day and it was rumored that they disappeared every night with unfailing regularity. Another one
of these devilish deities was Shon-Ton. He was a god with
a dirty-white visage that one sought to placate with delicate
foods whenever there was sickness in the family. But his approach to food was more spiritual than the approach of the
god with the waiting horse whose name I have forgotten.
He merely imbibed their essence for two or three days,
after which they were removed and distributed to the poor.

There was a surprising amount of goddesses, too, for a
civilization reputed to be for the benefit of males. Chief of
course was Tin How, the Chinese "Queen of Heaven."
There were three temples in her honor. The most impressive was in Waverly place and over the entrance was in-

scribed these words that have been an admonition from every revealer of God since the world began: "Purify thyself by fasting and self denial." Whether there were any temples to the lovely Kwan Kung, the Goddess of Mercy, I do not remember, but she smiled serenely from every bazaar window.

Naturally, amid the female gods, was a Goddess of Love. And there was a Goddess of the Lake, who surprisingly enough came from Egypt to bring the Chinese a code of laws. She was always represented standing upon a lotus flower. . . . I have been told that there was even a goddess who listened to the prayers of the prostitutes. If this seems incongruous, remember that there is a patron saint in the Christian Church, who intercedes for erring women.

In Spofford alley there used to be a Joss House that had a shrine to a deified monkey. His name was Tsai Tin Tai Shing. His chief claim to reverence was that he had learned the language of men.

Naturally, in a land of gold, there was a Joss House to the God of Fortune. He sat upon a throne, holding a nugget of gold in his hand, against a carved screen of great beauty carved from a single piece of wood. It was said that the punk sticks were burned before this shrine very much longer than ordinary and a long row of cups filled with tea were ever filled to allay his thirst.

It would be sheer prejudice to lump the worship of all these aforementioned symbols as crass idolatry. The placation of devils comes nearest to it. But there are grades upward from placating Kwan Tai, the God of War, to a veneration of the serene Kwan Kung, the Goddess of Mercy. It is the progress of "revelation according to capacity" of St. Paul. The minor gods of nature are here, too, in great number. But these are really very pleasant symbols of great forces and a simple belief in them can do no harm. . . .

San Francisco's Chinatown

There are no more passionate believers in the Christian mysteries than the Irish. Yet, their supreme faith has not banished fairies and banshees and leprechauns from the green hills of Erin. And, surely, a sick man's offering to Wah-Taw, who once cured men through their faith in his power, cannot be too unacceptable to us who for centuries have had much the same belief.

But the inclusiveness of Chinese religious impulse is unquestioned. There was even a Joss House in Chinatown, in my youth, to the "Good Spirit Who Was Invisible"—the good spirit that could not be represented by an image. This was a shrine to the "unknown god" who transcended all others—the god who received the souls of all good Chinamen "whose dust was mingled, after death, with the sacred soil of China." A bit too exclusive to be universal, perhaps —a god receiving only his "chosen people" in the Abraham-and-Isaac-and-Jacob manner. But a distinct advance over the dirty-white Shon-Ton.

The Joss Houses being thus without dogma or creed had no mass or congregational worship. One went to the Joss House on only personal errands, so to speak. Your eldest son was sick; things were not going well with you in your business; you had need of advice about a financial venture. You entered and bought candles and incense from the priest in charge. Then you came into the presence of the divinity, clasped your hands and made a low bow. Next you lit your candles and incense, and kneeling on the mat before the god you called him by name three times.

It was now the moment to discover whether or not the god was in a receptive mood to hear your petition. You took two semi-oval pieces of wood, bowed to the god again and tossed them into air. If both pieces of wood fell in the same position, it was a sign that the god was not disposed to listen. If one fell with the oval side down and the other with

294

the flat side down, it was a good sign—the god's ear was inclined toward you.

Having determined this, one next took a bamboo cylinder filled with sticks, shaking them before the god until one fell to the floor. These were called sticks of fate. They were numbered and the priest, by consulting his book, gave you the answer to your petition.

Offerings of paper money were purchased from the priest and prayers could be bought for a consideration. These were burned in little furnaces near the shrines. In some Joss Houses, it was said, one could buy prayers written by the priests that could be placed before the god in a little contraption like a music box which wound and unwound the prayer over any given period of time. This was akin to the prayer wheels of the Tibetan Lamas. . . . Whenever, in the old days, Chinese returned to their native land, they used to buy prayers for a safe journey and release them as the ship pulled out. It was fascinating to watch these floods of red paper darting in the stiff Western breeze like flocks of scarlet swallows before they fell upon the waves and were devoured by them.

But if there were prayers for the benign gods there were likewise curses for devils. One bought these curses from the priest written in red ink upon yellow strips of paper. These were burned in a porcelain container and stirred into a cup of water. Then the priest, filling his mouth with the water and ashes, stamped about with a trident in one hand, spouting out the water and calling on the devils to begone.

The decorations in the Joss Houses were a curious mixture of beauty and tawdriness. Magnificent embroidered banners; golden silk flags; brass spears in symbolic design; walls of marble; furniture of ebony inlaid with mother-of-pearl; costly carvings splashed with gold-leaf; bronze incense bowls hundreds of years old mingled with paper decorations, battered kitchen chairs and saw-dust floors. In every Joss House was a bell to rouse gods, sleeping or inattentive.

Many of the lovely embroideries that draped the walls were thanks offerings from grateful worshipers. There was one such in a temple on Clay street, the gift of Doctor Lai Po Tai. This was a very handsome piece of silk, heavily fringed, and decorated with the figures of four Chinese characters, Shing, Shang, Mo and Keung—"gods whose holy age is perpetual." Doctor Lai Po Tai was an herb-doctor with a large Occidental practice. The good doctor went into a gas-filled room with a lighted match in the cool of one summer evening with explosive results. Needless to say that his herbs did not affect a cure. He fell into the hands of one of the leading white physicians of the town. When he got well he remembered these "gods whose holy age is perpetual" hoping, doubtless, that he might obtain a modicum of their everlasting life in the process.

Peacock feathers, symbols of wisdom, were always used extensively in Joss House decoration. Likewise, five-toed dragon embroideries of the protecting deity of the Emperor. He had scales like any self-respecting dragon but instead of ears he sported two horns through which he could hear. It is rather difficult to get an explanation of just what the dragon represents to the Chinese. Its origin like the origin of all dragons, is too legendary, too far back in human consciousness. Our Western dragons are usually symbols of destructive forces. Oftener than not they are the guardians of hapless creatures or of treasures withheld from mankind, until released by valor. The five-toed dragon, as we have seen, once guarded the sacred person of the Emperor, the Son of Heaven. What his occupation is now one can only conjecture, unless he has transferred his attention to

The Drama and the Joss House

the Emperor of Manchukuo. But the dragon, in general, is the guardian of the rains. He can release or withhold them at will. His importance to an agricultural people like the Chinese can be readily understood. In short, there is nothing particularly sinister about a Chinese dragon. He has power but it seems ranged on the side of good, rather than evil.

I went back early one evening, before any irreverent trippers were abroad to climb up four flights to the Joss House that had been barred to me in my daytime peregrinations.

All Joss Houses hold forth on the topmost floor of any building which harbors them in order to be as near Heaven as possible. This has something of the idea of our aspiring church steeples behind it.

The interior charmed and delighted me. Whatever else religious expression in Chinatown has lost it has gained on the side of taste and beauty. Gone were the tawdry paper garlands, the battered kitchen chairs, the saw-dust floors. In spite of the gilt and barbaric color this Temple to Tin How, the Goddess of Heaven, had a certain chaste beauty. The goddess, who also rules the Seven Seas, is the same goddess who sat before the original altar raised to her in the gold rush days. The printed history of this Joss House fixes her advent in California as the year 1844, when a temple was raised to her by one, Day Ju, a Chinese pioneer. But this sounds suspiciously like exaggeration. If Day Ju was in San Francisco in 1844, he must have been the only worshiper. Eighteen *fifty* four sounds more reasonable.

Sharing honors with Tin How is the smooth-shaven Man-Dii, God of Literature and the bearded Moi-Dii, God of the Military. Then there is Yan-Tan, the God of Justice. He rules over a supreme court that deals summarily with devils.

To the left of Tin How are the twelve goddesses of

motherhood. Ni-Lung they are called. Each one of these goddesses is the guardian angel of children born in the particular month over which she rules.

Ranged on either side of the main altar are eight wands or spears. One sees these in most Joss Houses. They are symbolic of eight holy people—seven men and one woman—who devised a plan to ward off devils by the simple expedient of being good. Their plan failing, they became, or were turned into, fairies and given wands, as a more practical method of dealing with evil spirits.

There is a singularly beautiful carved arch through which one glimpses the main altar. It is intricately carved into a scene depicting the life of Confucius. Before the door of the old philosopher's house are two dragons, symbols of his power. The altar contains some fine pewter pieces set with enamel and precious stones. The incense jars are crowned with Buddha lions.

This Joss House is a very typical example of the intricate pattern of religious beliefs which the Chinese have woven into coherence. The fairy wands on either side of the altar are relics of Taoism, the golden arch has the stamp of Confucianism, the incense jars with their lions are Buddhistic. The procession of gods and goddesses which sit in their dim recesses are undoubtedly most of them from a remote and pagan past.

Some of these gods and goddesses are pure abstractions rendered into visual terms. Others may be worthy characters of a by-gone day raised to a sort of sainthood by the legends of their holy exploits.

Choi-Sun, the Goddess of Finance, who has a shrine here, must be an abstraction. She rules the household and conserves money. She is the personification of the prudent wife, so esteemed in China. If one burns a punk stick to her, one does no more than reverence the perfect help mate.

The Drama and the Joss House

We are told that the chief virtue in prayer is that it fixes our minds on an ideal. To reverence Choi-Sun is, therefore, not idolatry, it is merely giving the idea of prudence its just due.

There is also a font of holy water in this Joss House to Tin How with an inscription admonishing visitors as they dip their fingers into its sacred depths to "cleanse mind, heart and body before worshiping." The drum and gong to wake the gods is in evidence as well as a fireplace in which prayers are burned. But, one has a feeling that a younger generation evokes them only on rare occasions, if at all.

In the ante-room are strips of red paper lining the walls giving the names of contributors to the fund for keeping up the Joss House. But even these have too correct and formal an air. One suspects that like so many contributors to the upkeep of old churches the donors send an annual check and let their interest halt there.

The Joss House of Tin How with all its beauty gives one the impression of a drawing room seldom used. It is too correct, too meticulously kept. Nothing seems out of place and there are no evidences of the minor confusions that use brings to drawing rooms and temples, alike. The gods in it seem to have reached a tranquil old age. They are like old people that the family keeps its petty discords from, or call upon only for some major problem.

Chapter XVI

IN CONCLUSION

ON the floor below the Temple of Tin How are the lodge rooms of the Sue Sing Association. The furnishings are Chinese throughout except for a grandfather's clock which ticks away amid teakwood chairs and an extraordinary conference table with a mirror top. A very benign god with flowing whiskers has an altar erected to him at the end of the room, before which offerings of mandarin oranges in green platters, give out an augury of good luck. This is the God of Rank and High Position. One evokes him—or the idea, if you wish—in order to succeed, to push one's way upward in the social scale.

The central tribunal of the Six Companies is on Stockton street. This is chromatically a striking building with a vermilion roof, a light blue-tiled façade and notes of red and yellow in window casings, balcony and balustrades. The

300

In Conclusion

top floor houses a primary school for acquainting children with the culture of China. This is open from six o'clock in the evening until eight, so that it will in nowise interfere with the public school instruction during the day.

The tribunal room of the Six Companies is dignified and lovely except for the intrusion of a roll-top desk or two strangely at odds with the main furnishings of teakwood and ebony inlaid with marble. On the walls are the pictures of the Christian Sun Yat Sen, General Tsai, and Wong Hing, the first speaker of the Chinese House of Representatives. The west wall is screened by colored glass, done in sapphire blue and ruby red squares, surrounding charming pictures, in glass, of birds nesting among the peach blossoms of spring.

The night I visited these quarters one of the younger officials was tracing calligraphs on a piece of rice paper. He was dipping his bamboo brush in ink made from the dried contents of a California cuttlefish, mixed with water. He offered to render my name in this wise, but long and vehement were the discussions between him and his companion before the feat was accomplished. My middle name "Caldwell" seemed the hardest to achieve. While the "drawing" of my name was in progress notes from a band from the school upstairs floated down to us. They were vociferously grinding out the "Washington Post March," "Boola Boola" and "The Music Goes Round and Round." This acceptance by the modern generation of our music is interesting and sometimes droll. It is a shock to come upon a Chinese boot-black with his kit on his back performing "Old Black Joe" or "Yes, We Have No Bananas" on a harmonica, between shines. The harmonica seems to be a favorite musical instrument with young China—at the Washington Irving School there is a harmonica band made up of twenty Chinese-American boys.

San Francisco's Chinatown

There is also another school for the dissemination of Chinese culture on Stockton street. This is The Central Chinese High School. It likewise is open at night and is, as its name implies, for more advanced students. . . . Stockton street is in many ways a street of transition. For many years, it was the western frontier of Chinatown which of late years has been extended to Powell street.

Here are old chair-mending factories and washhouses and lantern-making studios. But there are likewise "beauty shoppes," and sport emporiums where one can buy tennis rackets, baseballs and golf sticks. There are even cleaning and pressing establishments for clothes. But the Chinese evidently believe in making cleanliness unanimous. For the same man who presses your trousers, will take your parcel of laundry and provide a tub bath for you if that is your desire.

Likewise on Stockton street is the headquarters of the Kuo Ming Tang—the Chinese National Party. It is a strangely bleak place, without a trace of mellow Chinese atmosphere. Here is an illustration of how discontent can sweep away symbols of an old order. The furnishings are in the best Grand Rapids manner—stiff, weathered-oak chairs upholstered in leather, domestic rugs, only one of which has a Chinese design incorporated into it. One of the table lamps has as its base a vase of Chinese origin. But this surely must have crept in by mistake, so determined apparently were the founders to divest their movement of even visual links with the past.

It is a typical small-town American lodge room, really, with one exception—it has a curious note of grimness which is hard to define. Perhaps this grimness is supplied by the enlarged photographs of leaders and martyrs to the cause of a New China which are placed with impeccable precision,

In Conclusion

in uncompromising oak frames, to form a frieze about the room. Many of these patriots were photographed with their hands encased in curious Oriental handcuffs attached to an iron rod wound around the prisoner's neck. They seemed to have been taken as the victims were being led out to execution. One or two were photographed, lying dead after a massacre. These pictures bring home much more forcibly the crisis through which China is passing than cable dispatches in the newspapers.

There is the inevitable raised seat for the head of the organization, behind which is a picture of Sun Yat Sen, the first President of the Republic of China. This is likewise an enlarged photograph. Underneath the picture is a framed tablet in Chinese script. I thought it the by-laws of the Kuo Ming Tang, at first. But when I asked the secretary he replied that it was the will of Sun Yat Sen. The following translation shows it to be a sort of declaration of principles, an admonition to his people to stand firm in their new political faith.

For forty years I have devoted myself to the cause of the people's revolution with but one aim in view—the elevation of China to a position of freedom and equality among the nations. My experiences during these forty years have fully convinced me that to attain this goal we must bring about a thorough awakening of our own people and ally ourselves in a common struggle with those peoples of the world who treat us on an equal basis so that they may cooperate with us in our struggles.

The work of the Revolution is not yet over. All my comrades must continue to exert their efforts according to my "Programme of National Reconstruction," "Outline of Reconstruction," the "Three Principles of the People," and the "Manifesto" issued by the First National Congress of our Party, and strive on earnestly for the consummation of the end we have in view. Above all, our recent declarations in favour of the convocation of a People's Convention and the abolition of unequal treaties should be carried into effect with the least possible delay. This is my heartfelt charge to you.

(Signed) SUN WEN

February 20, 1925.

The only decorations are garlands of red, white and blue, contrived out of cheap cloth, which drape certain photographs, and hang in festoons between pillars supporting the ceiling. Is it an association of ideas with the tri-color of France that gives this ugly, austere room the suggestion of being a tribunal? It is hard to say. But the fact remains that one leaves the place with a sense of having touched hands with revolution, rapine and murder. It gives one also a sense of greater convulsions to follow. In the end, China will find herself, but the road will be long and hard.

Yet, the serene philosophy of the Chinese will temper the wind. A friend of mine, not so long since, was commiserating with a high-class Chinese on the inroads which Japan was making on Chinese territory. "It is of no moment," blandly replied the Chinaman. "In a couple of hundred years, it will be as if nothing had happened."

Waverly place, once a street of gambling clubs, is now given over to tong rooms. Family associations seem to predominate here. One interesting society with a building facing this street is the Wo Ping Woey Peace Association which has been organized for adjustment of difficulties between tongs. This is a sort of clearing house for problems that used to be settled by blackmail and at the pistol point.

The Tom family has by far the most attractive building. It is of clinker brick with window casings painted a rich purple. But the huge black and gold sign overlooking the balcony and proclaiming the tong's name and intention is the most striking note in the whole scheme. Such signs were

CHINESE SCHOOL, SACRAMENTO STREET

In Conclusion

once a decided feature of old Chinatown. I used to wonder in my youth if these signs would lose their charm and be prosaic and ugly as our own signs if one grew to know the language. I thought perhaps that their concealment added beauty and mystery. But in Paris, for instance, I discovered that ignorance of French did not serve to make the signs attractive. I realized that form entered into Chinese lettering, a term which, by the way, I one day learned was a misnomer. Chinese characters are something more than mere lettering—they are word pictures done with a beauty of line that makes them partake of both the literary and pictorial arts.

The present day signs have this beauty of line. But, so far as I can ascertain, they express little of the poetical content which used to supplement, or rather, amplify the announcement that a certain firm did business within or explained the nature of the business conducted.

The old restaurant signs were the most seductive. The announcement that "Manchu and Chinese, animal and vegetable food by the meal; with wine, diversion and entertainment," did not perhaps reach a highwater mark of poetry. But to hang out a sign calling one's eating establishment a "Fragrant Almond Chamber," or a "Chamber of the Odors of Different Lands," or "A Garden of the Golden Valley," or "A Balcony of Joy and Delight" was a very different matter.

Then there were the aphorisms which gave point to occupation and enterprise. There used to be a sign over an old pawn shop door that read: "Let each have his due." A very pleasant reflection until one remembers what a pawn dealer's interpretation of such a maxim was apt to be. But the sign before the door of a lottery stated the less ambiguous truth that "To be Lucky is to be Happy."

There were other pleasant and poetic reassurances in the

sign language to the customers and friends of industry, capable of broader application. Almost any business might declare itself as a business of "Ten Thousand Profits," or a concern of "Extensive Peace and Affluence," or a partnership of "Faith and Understanding."

The chemist shops were "Temples of Heavenly Harmonies," or "The Thousand Harmonies," or again "Producers of Harmony Everlasting," according to their inclination. All of them exceedingly apt when one considers the relation between harmony and good health that is so stressed by mental healers, past and present.

The signs over the doorways of homes paralleled the home-sweet-home mottoes that our grandmothers used to embroider for the edification of the household. "Domestic Happiness is Domestic Bliss." "Peace and Happiness Dwell Here." "Discord Bringeth Strife." All the virtues of family life were emblazoned for visitors to ponder. . . . Often there were charming dedication ceremonies when these signs were hung into place. A priest from the Joss House came and blessed the carved and gilded platitude.

Once in my youth, I passed through Chinatown and noticed a crowd gathered about a pile of evicted furnishings. They were carrying away chairs, saucepans, oil lamps, pewter spoons, water-pipes, tea-pots. A ravishing sign lay half-buried under the litter. Nobody seemed interested so I dipped into the mess and drew it forth. Its legend was in raised characters of gold upon an emerald-green background. Surrounding this was a carved framework featuring bamboo shoots that harbored red-breasted birds in their cool-green depth. Since pillage was the order of the moment, I carried the sign home. It swung before my doorway on a bracket, such as must have been originally designed for it, until fire consumed it one fateful April morning in 1906. Curiously enough I never learned its meaning. To my

In Conclusion

questions, most Chinamen gave vague replies. Had it been a sign before the door of a home, a tong, a restaurant, or a house of questionable delights? I never knew. . . . I wished I had saved it. Unhappily the day of this particular brand of loveliness in Chinatown has passed.

As I have said, the modern Chinese signs are practical matters but there is still beauty of line in them. They merit attention, first because the art of Chinese calligraphy is over two thousand years old, and, secondly, because this art is said to have provided "the esthetic basis for Chinese art." Every stroke of the calligraphist's brush has its origin in the "rhythm of nature," according to Lin Yutang, in his informing book on Chinese life, *My Country and My People*. He further states that:

Chinese calligraphy has explored every possible style of rhythm and form, and it has done so by deriving its artistic inspiration from nature, especially from plants and animals—the branches of the plum flower, a dried vine with hanging leaves, the springing body of the leopard, the massive paws of the tiger, the swift legs of the deer, the sinewy strength of the horse, the bushiness of the bear, the slimness of the stork, or the ruggedness of the pine branch. There is not one type of rhythm in nature which has not been copied in Chinese writing and formed directly or indirectly the inspiration for a particular "style."

If a Chinese scholar sees a certain beauty in a dry vine with its careless grace and elastic strength, the tip of the end curling upward and a few leaves still hanging on it haphazardly and yet most appropriately, he tried to incorporate that into his writing. If another scholar sees a pine tree that twists its trunk and bends its branches downward instead of upward, which shows a wonderful tenacity and force, he also tried to incorporate that into his style of writing. We have therefore the "dry-vine" style and the "pine-branch" style of writing. . . .

Thus Wang-Hsich (321–379), China's "prince of calligraphists," spoke about the art of calligraphy in terms of the imagery of nature: "Every horizontal stroke is like a mass of clouds in battle forma-

307

tion, every hook like a bent bow of the greatest strength, every dot like a falling rock from a high peak, every turning of the stroke like a brass hook, every drawn-out line like a dry vine of great old age, and every swift and free stroke like a runner on his start."

Of course the carved word, so to speak, cannot have the freedom and grace of the word traced by a swift moving brush but there is still the underlying principle of an inspiration from nature in any Chinese ideograph, however achieved. These ideographs, moreover, as their name implies have a pictorial content apart from their form. They suggest a word picture to him who understands.

To master the written language of China is a tremendous feat of memory. The laborer can do with a knowledge of some three hundred ideographs, the more leisurely class ten times that many, and the scholar ten times as many, again, or thirty thousand. There are fifty-five thousand in all! A man's position in Chinese society is said to be gauged by the extent of his knowledge of the written language. Even the spoken word is no mean accomplishment. The language consists of three hundred and thirty monosyllables, each of which, in turn, has four distinct sounds that convey a different idea.

No wonder commenters declare that "Chinese society stands on a literary base."

It would be easy to enumerate the features that have passed in Chinatown. One of the chief glories is the brilliant costuming. But, if one thinks it over soberly, the quarter blossomed out in festival clothing only upon occasion. For the rest of the time, it was as drably clothed as the remainder of the town. Highbinders with wide stiff-brimmed black hats and equally black garments were more picturesque than their white brethren but scarcely more colorful. The keepers of the food stalls, the vegetable

In Conclusion

hucksters, the laundrymen, the agricultural workers did better with their sky-blue denim outfits. The merchants, sometimes, wore lovely plum-colored coats of quilted silk, and, occasionally, a bound-foot woman lit up the quarter with a rich gown of pale lavender or light blue silk that formed a background for embroideries done with silken threads of every hue. . . . At the New Year a sudden metamorphosis took place. Camphor chests were opened and their silken treasures ravished. It was as if ten thousand cocoons had opened to release a swarm of butterflies.

It is of these festival seasons that the old San Franciscan thinks about when he visualizes Chinatown swarming with beauty. He forgets the intervening periods when a work-a-day world met its problems in work-a-day clothes that had more ease and grace than the clothes of the Occident but scarcely more vividness. But an annual taste of fairy-land was something. If the younger generation would grant us a glimpse of the old beauty once a year it would refresh eyes starving for color. Who knows, perhaps when the old order grows a little more remote the youngsters may find it diverting to revive its memories on occasion, very much as their white brethren do, with the lotus-eating days of California. There is scarcely a town with a Spanish name that does not once in awhile have a fiesta. Then the mantillas and wide combs and full skirts walk the streets again and the males develop side-burns and wrap red sashes tightly about their waists and put on sombreros or hats with red and yellow tassels dangling from the brim.

But however one may lament the passing of color in costume, one must concede that the women, at least, do very well by their adopted dress. If you ride downtown on the Powell street cable car you will have to admit that the flapper with Chinese blood in her veins dresses in far better taste and with greater *chic* than most of her white sisters.

309

San Francisco's Chinatown

She has an eye for line, and proper color accent. Moreover, sixty centuries of civilization have given her a certain fragile grace that fits perfectly the styles of today, modeled for slenderness. Her boy friend, who snuggles up to her in the most approved Caucasian manner, is not so happy in the foreign clothes. They are too stiff and formal. Clinging silk trousers would become his rather feminine structure better. But some of the more athletic types, the product of beefsteak, potatoes and basket ball—look fairly acceptable in bright sweaters and corduroy pants.

The cries of Chinatown are stilled, too. The soup vendor no longer calls his wares nor does the baker peddle cakes in the streets. But, one silent feature of the old life is left —the waiter from the restaurant who balances a tray with a full course meal on his head. Sometimes he holds one hand lightly on the tray's rim but oftener than not he releases all protection and ambles nonchalantly along, rolling a cigarette, the tray swaying rhythmically in time with his moving body but seemingly as safe as if it were clamped down on his head. The dishes of covered pewter are filled with hot soup, Pekin duck, noodles, rice—any delicacy that the *carte du jour* provides. One telephones at any hour of the day or night and the tray service is set in operation. Many Chinese families who are too busy with outside work to devote the proper attention to domestic science eat at least one meal a day served in this fashion. One sees these waiters, especially at eleven or twelve o'clock at night, trotting along with their savory burdens. There are scores of Chinamen whose work is not done until midnight, and it is then that suppers at home are in most demand.

There are still enough of the old conservative shops in Chinatown to minister to one's search for beauty. Every so often, their windows are strewn with a particular line of goods that tells a subtle story of the gradual mechanization

310

In Conclusion

of China. Recently the shops have been full of discarded Chinese irons, showing that irons of the electric variety must be making their way in the old country. Unless you read the label you would never guess that these exquisite objects were once put to a utilitarian purpose. They are made of copper and brass, beautifully chased, built to hold little charcoal fires. The handles are of carved ivory. The more elaborate ones have these handles studded with crude coral and turquoise ornaments. Tourists buy them up and use them for capacious ash-trays. This is another instance of how the Chinese bring art into their every-day life. There is scarcely another people who would conceive of making such a lowly instrument an object of beauty.

The architecture of the new Chinatown is definitely more national than the old. When the quarter started to build up again after the earthquake and fire it looked as if the city was to have another colorless section of cream-colored brick. The Telephone Company halted this drab tendency by putting up an exchange that looked like a miniature temple. Tong quarters, bazaars, food shops followed suit. The result has an outward appearance of the Orient, even if one suspects an emptiness under the shell. The neon light has added charm to the nocturnal aspects of the streets. With the passing of candle-lit lanterns, the restaurant balconies and other dim recesses grew garish with the white light of electric bulbs. But the neon lights gave the Chinese color to play with. The result is a triumph. Cherry-blossom pinks, ultramarine blues, deep shades of orange, chrome yellows, apple greens interweave and blend together with a success that makes the red and blue neon lights of the American quarters seem unimaginative and pallid.

Even when Chinamen deal in the charmless materials of a utilitarian age, their sense of design prevails. There is a wholesale firm on Grant avenue that carries a line of laundry supplies for the trade. The man who dresses the window can make the most stunning displays of bone buttons, safety-pins, bluing balls, packages of starch, clothespins. To state such a thing sounds ridiculous. Unless one has watched this window as I have every week for years, one cannot conceive the imagination and ingenuity that can go into such a performance. Since a Chinese laundryman obviously does not consult an attractive window display before putting in his order for supplies, it is obvious that the window dresser merely is indulging his fancy, expressing a creative urge.

Sometimes in a side street, a small shop-keeper instead of giving over his window to an adequate display of his goods, will decide to build up a fanciful landscape. I have one in mind fashioned out of slag. It is a mountain scene, with winding roads and villages and temples and forests. Miniature porcelain figures give point and life to the scene. It sets in a pool of water flashing with golden fish. The average Occidental, fashioning such a thing, would produce something grotesque, on a level with the things that confectioners sometimes do in an idle hour. But this is something more than a stunt. It is a labor of love and a thing of perfect proportion and beauty.

Then there are the windows of the dealers in tea. Here the appeal to a sense of beauty is through the poetry of words rather than an arrangement of materials. Mounds of tea on little paper doilies have not the possibilities that even safety-pins and bluing have for an infinite variety of design. Here are some of the names of the teas exhibited: *Morning Dew, White Cloud, Butterfly's Eyebrow, Second Pearl, Chrysanthemum Tea*, and, of course, the inevitable *Jasmine*. The Chrysanthemum Tea is apparently mixed with the dried petals of the yellow chrysanthemum.

But it is the little shops I like best—where one can run

into anything from a jade ring to a paper kite. . . . The kites are grotesque and lovely—fashioned into forms that suggest hawks and owls and butterflies. When March comes the narrow confines of Portsmouth square quiver with flying kites. And, in city-wide contests for kite-flying, it is always the Chinese boys who walk away with the prizes.

The street peddlers are now few and far between. Sometimes one comes upon an old gentleman who sells hard-boiled eggs or sea-snails as his fancy dictates. And there is another equally venerable huckster who makes a specialty of wild animals. A racoon, a skunk, a wildcat may be his stock for the day. But try to find out why the Chinese dip down into their pocket-books to purchase them. Certainly one does not use skunks and wildcats or even racoons for pets. It is said that the fat from a wildcat if eaten will make a man strong. If I were not above punning, there are obvious remarks that could be applied to the virtues of a skunk along these same lines. Of course, racoon is good eating just for its own sake, but I doubt if the Chinese have a taste for such fare. The truth probably is that this side-walk merchant deals in wonder-workers. He is a sort of a free-lance chemist and his wares revive failing powers.

On the whole it seems to me that the bazaars are as colorful as ever when the heads are bona fide Chinamen. But, of course, many of them today are Chinese in name only. The Japanese firms are the worst masqueraders, and there is an occasional Jew in the Chinatown trade. The Japanese install soda fountains in their shops in lieu of tea-rooms and fill the shelves with junk. When an old firm fails or goes out of business and a shop is vacated along the street of the bazaars it is almost a foregone conclusion that it will be succeeded by a Japanese concern. The younger generation seems indifferent to the rôle of shop-keeper and there is another subtle point involved. It is an old Chinese custom for any man who has developed a business in a special location to expect some goodwill money from anyone who succeeds him. It does not matter for what reason he is giving up the old situation—whether he is bankrupt, gone out of business, or merely moved. Failing to get this "cumshaw" he establishes a subtle boycott that ends in the rout of his successor.

The native-born Chinese will not subscribe to this polite extortion. He knows better than to buck it so he ends by letting his prospective venture die. The Japanese are at no pains to give the demands of a former occupant any consideration whatever. A Chinaman cannot touch him in family or personal relations and, since his business is conducted for white trade, a Chinese boycott is equally unavailing.

Quite recently the charge has been made that this boycott of vacant premises has developed into a scheme to force the price of property in Chinatown down so that it can fall into the hands of the Chinese, themselves, for a song. If we can believe the daily press, this new racket is one of the last surviving gasps of the tribute-raising organizations that once dictated the policies of Chinatown. Pressure is brought not only against white landlords but against the American born Chinese landowner, too. There is a tremendous under-the-surface conflict between the old and the new. The Chinese-American scorns the tongs. The Chinese Chamber of Commerce, composed of new blood, will not suffer any one of their members to belong to a tong. More and more, the youth are becoming individualists, resenting the interference of organizations in their private affairs. The invisible force that is operating to boycott property is called "the podii."

Tom Irwin, writing of the podii in the San Francisco *Chronicle,* gives a thumb-nail outline of the practice thus:

In Conclusion

As originally planned, the podii "guaranteed" an evicted tenant against unscrupulous practices, permitted him to place an indemnity on vacated property. Such property could not be rented until the indemnity was satisfied. Should any Chinese rent it, he would inevitably go broke. Not so much as a dried herring could he sell to a fellow countryman.

To make this silent boycott even more effective, the Chinese banded together in numerous societies and to the councils of these groups went all rental grievances. It took little time for the unscrupulous to see unlimited fields for exploration.

Complete secrecy surrounded all.

Thus in the eyes of Chinatown the podii was embraced as a tenant's extra-legal lien upon property—sanction by "custom and convenience."

Upon the landlord always fell the necessity of clearing not only the title in the eyes of the law, but in satisfying the claims of previous tenants.

Inevitably other forms of extortion were built up so that the podii in some cases included not only the claims of the former tenants but all the claims of the tenant's creditors.

Thus came the picture of the butcher, the baker and the candlestick maker, all shrilling for their bills to be paid before the podii could be lifted.

The system spread still further. At last, thieveries within firms, losses in gambling, costs of lottery operations, the price of slave girls and even small charities were added to the already incredible sizes of podiis, sometimes almost as great as the value of the affected property.

As the system grows, the income from rentals continues to decline, the value of properties continues to dwindle, the percentage of Chinese ownership continues to increase.

How do you find a podii is on your property?

After your tenant has moved out, you advertise for another. He asks if there has been trouble. Assured there has been none, he agrees to rent, but must first "advertise his intention." The next day the Chinese returns to tell you a podii is on your store. He has "advertised" and has reaped overnight a flock of podii signs that tell him to see anywhere from one to a dozen individuals and societies.

315

San Francisco's Chinatown

All Chinatown knows it at once. There is "trouble" at that place and no tenant will have it at the regular price.

Any variations from the old traditions that occur in Chinatown are given headlines in the daily press. Here is the story of a young bride of eighteen who fled to China to escape the forty-eight-year-old bridegroom, picked out by her father. Here is a notice of a Chinese woman suing for divorce. Better, still, here is a daughter of her father asking to be named heir to his estate, in defiance of the age-old custom that a man's property belongs to the clan and must be absorbed into the general family treasury, to be administered by the elder. . . . Is it significant that most of these revolts against custom are being staged by women?

Even the old misdemeanors are fewer and farther between. There are slave-girl cases in the courts, now, only occasionally. And when they do come to light, they are not the product of *organized* crime. One of the latest cases involved a presumably respectable merchant who had maintained a hardware store on Grant avenue for twenty-five years. He and his wife were charged with importing a "sing-song" girl from Hong Kong and selling her to a procuress for forty-five hundred dollars. But the racket has grown more hazardous and difficult. It is not unusual, now, for slave-girl importations to come in by way of the Atlantic seaboard. . . . Not so long ago the wife of one of the secretaries connected with the Chinese Consulate was deported for being concerned with an opium-smuggling plot. Which proves nothing except that law-breaking in Chinatown has become an individual matter. In other words, the gangster tongs have more or less faded out of the picture.

During the past two or three years there have been threats occasionally of the outbreak of old-fashioned tong wars but they have not come off. In 1935 there was a con-

In Conclusion

troversy between the Hop Sing Tong and the Four Families. The Chief of Police, fearing trouble, ordered a blockade of Chinatown, just as the New Year festivities were under way to the great indignation of the quarter. . . . In the end, the matter was adjusted by the Chinese Peace Society, an organization with headquarters in Waverly place. The head of the Peace Society was not the traditional old man of affairs nearing the allotted three-score and ten, but a youngster of thirty-six, with the hybrid name of Churchill Chiu. The tong war did not materialize. How much of this was due to the offices of Churchill Chiu and how much to the fact that assassins for hire are things of the past in Chinatown would be hard to determine. Both factors, doubtless, entered into the peaceful settlement.

Mr. Churchill Chiu is not wholly a product of American education, as he came into this country as a student some ten years ago to take a degree at the University of California. But one reason that his influence is felt perhaps is because the seed of his new philosophy falls upon soil made responsive to new traditions by a young population that has been educated entirely in America.

How many pupils of Chinese forebears are attending school at present is hard to determine since the Board of Education seems to find it inexpedient to keep a record of this detail. But there are several hundred in the Chinese Grammar School on Washington street and the Annex across the way. Several hundred more find a place in other schools near the district that are not strictly for pupils of Chinese blood only, for the Chinese are spreading out, in little groups to the west and north. A move to segregate these children, also, met with such opposition recently in Chinese circles that the proposal was dropped.

A Mr. Kenneth L. Fung of the Chinese-American Citizens' Alliance made this protest to the Superintendent of Schools:

San Francisco's Chinatown

Segregation does not make for good American citizenship; our children, born here, should be given American training comparable with that of other American students and should not be subjected to a humiliation which would only breed discontent.

This protest is interesting on two counts—the hybrid name of the protester as in the case of Mr. Chiu, and the fact that he was able to gain his point. These "Christian" names are more and more in vogue in Chinatown. Whether they are Christian in fact or merely a matter of conformance doubtless varies in individual cases.

But there is no question about the triumph of routing the forces of segregation. The Chinese have battled long and patiently for equality. The history of educational facilities— or if you prefer, the lack of them—in Chinatown, is a record of indifference, opposition and ridicule.

The first school of any kind was organized by a Mr. Moulton in 1853. Some wealthy Chinese aided and abetted by interested Americans provided the sinews of war for this venture. The pupils' ages ranged from fifteen to forty years.

Later, in 1857, we find the Chinese petitioning the Board of Education to permit Chinese to attend a night school which then operated. The Board of Education refused the request on the grounds that "while the idea seemed most desirable," the Chinese had better remain away as they would be subject to insult by "rude boys."

In 1867 there appeared a long account in the *Alta California* of a school that was being run at night by one William M. Dye. Mr. Dye, if we can trust the report, was so interested in helping the Chinese that he gave his time gratis every evening between the hours of seven and nine toward their education in "the idiom of the English language as well as brief oral instruction in the elements of geography, grammar, and arithmetic." Mr. Dye is described as "a gentleman

In Conclusion

long connected with the Chinese mercantile interests in San Francisco" and the site of his school "the basement of the Missionary Chapel, corner of Stockton and Sacramento streets." This venture of Mr. Dye's apparently was built upon the ruins of an attempt in the same direction sponsored by the Board of Education. A newspaper account reads as follows:

> The Chinese school was established about five years ago, under the direction of the Board of Education. It continued operation up to February last, when some difficulty occurred in reference to its management, and it was closed. No steps were taken to reopen it, and at the expiration of three months, Mr. Dye volunteered his services as teacher, and obtained the use of the basement of the Chinese Chapel for the purpose.

The article continues:

> The school has since gone on without public aid of any kind. On the first of May, when Mr. Dye took charge, seventy-nine boys were received. The room not being capacious enough to accommodate anything like that number, and as the crowd rendered it almost impossible to conduct the business of teaching, it was determined, as a matter of necessity, to reduce the number entitled to admission to forty. Cards were prepared and issued to boys selected for tuition. The only rules established were as follows: A scholar absent three consecutive times without good excuse, to forfeit his ticket and privileges therein contained. An expelled scholar may, with consent of the teacher, be restored to his former position by registering his name with the teacher, and when a vacancy occurs be reinstated in the order of his application.
>
> The attendance of scholars would very soon double in number if only sufficient provision were made for their accommodation. It is desirable that the Chinese growing up in this city should be taught a better style of English than that spoken in the mercantile houses on Sacramento and Dupont streets, so as to prevent mistakes, that must often happen in consequence of the inability of Americans to under-

stand correctly what is said by Chinese. More than this, they pay their full share of the school tax, and in accordance with the provisions of the statute, petitioned the Board of Education some months since to reopen the school. No action was taken by that body; and, later still, another petition was forwarded to the Board, signed by a large number of leading merchants and clergymen of the city, praying that the request be granted. For one reason or another, nothing has been done in the matter, though it is well known that if school accommodation was appropriated in proportion to the amount of school tax paid, the Chinese would have abundant facilities to educate their children. It is a mistake to suppose that they do not desire to take advantage of our school system. The fact that forty boys are applicants at present for admission into Mr. Dye's school, and who are excluded for want of accommodation, is conclusive on that point. It is to be hoped that the Board of Education will give attention to this subject, if for no other reason than that of inculcating ideas of Christianity and civilization among Chinese at that time of life when impressions take deepest root in the mind.

As with any movement directed in the interest of the Chinese, the old idea of "inculcating ideas of Christianity" seems to be the main rallying cry. The rights of the Chinese are secondary. But in this instance, the City Government seemed as indifferent to the "moral" advancement of their wards as to their rights as taxpayers. Not until 1887, some years after Chinese Exclusion was in operation, did the Board of Education establish a school for Chinese children. This was at 807 Stockton street, under the direction of Miss Rose Thayer, with an initial enrollment of ninety-two students.

Aside from the undenominational attempts, so to speak, to assist the Chinese toward a better understanding of the language and culture of America, the only course open to them was to attend classes in operation at the various Christian missions. The American public scornfully accused the Chinese of hypocrisy whenever figures were quoted to prove

GARDEN OF THE CHINESE Y.M.C.A.
ON CLAY STREET

that a high attendance at these schools demonstrated that Christianity was forging ahead. But, if so, the American public was party to it. Without other facilities for obtaining an education, one scarcely can blame the Chinese for assuming a virtue which they had not in order to advance their knowledge.

There was one move, however, looking toward the education of Chinese children that did not get beyond the stage of agitation. In 1885, two years before the Board of Education gave belated sanction to civic action, a group of citizens in the land of the free and the home of the brave, advanced an extraordinary plan. Finding that statistics at that time recorded seven hundred and twenty-two children in Chinatown, they seriously proposed that these children should be torn from their parents and given a "proper" education. This idea allied with others equally destructive of the rights of individuals guaranteed by the Constitution of the United States, gave them the hope that they could drive the Chinese "from our midst to Eastern states by enforcing drastic laws!" [The exclamation point is mine.]

However much the Chinese pretended Christianity in times past from ulterior motives, the day of such necessity is over. We may be fairly sure that the Christian convert today is sincere, except in an occasional case where someone under expectation of becoming involved in the courts for participation in a crime, has assumed the rôle of Christian in the hope of the moral support of the church with which he has affiliated.

There are eight Chinese Christian churches operating in Chinatown—Congregational, Methodist, Baptist, Presbyterian, Episcopal, Independent Baptist, Cumberland Presbyterian, and Roman Catholic. Any Christian with non-sectarian leanings, will wonder why the *Independent* Baptist and the *Cumberland* Presbyterian. But no matter, they are there. The communicants vary from a dozen or so to well over a thousand. With returns missing from some of the precincts one may assume that the actual professing Christians are something over two thousand. Not a great ratio in relation to Chinese population of thirty thousand but a sound bit of leaven, in any event. The different denominations seemed to have developed specialties and stick to them. The Presbyterians, for instance, go in for an occasional slave rescue and the care of delinquent girls; the Methodists look after the Chinese orphans and greet the immigrants at the Immigration Station on Angel Island and assist them in solving their problems; the Roman Catholics make a point of their Recreation Center, which boasts a gymnasium and theatre.

The Baptists have a boys' home; the Episcopalians a day school for youngsters and a night school for adults.

Nearly all the sects maintain kindergartens and many of them have what they call "nationalistic schools" where the children come in the evening to learn about old Chinese culture. Social service is, of course, an open field for all of them.

When one asks Father Johnson of the Catholic Mission what his church is doing along the lines of slave-girl rescue he replies with a smile: "We leave that to Miss Cameron at the Presbyterian Mission." One of the reasons is, doubtless, that in these days there are not enough slave-girls to go around. The other is that Miss Cameron has long been the acknowledged peer of slave-girl rescuers.

Miss Cameron—or Donaldina Cameron to be specific—has been rescuing slave-girls for upward of forty years. When you read about her exploits, especially the earlier ones; of her battles with gun-men infuriated at being robbed of their prey; of excursions into foul dens; of midnight trips to river towns on the trail of an abducted girl, you expect to meet a sort of glorified policewoman, with a six-shooter concealed somewhere up her sleeve. What you find is a cultivated

In Conclusion

woman of gentle voice and even gentler manner, who might be the head of a fashionable girls' school on the upper East side of New York. One feels sure that she never used any weapon to fight her way out of a tight place more deadly than a silk parasol—or at worst an umbrella.

Her force lies where it is always most effective in a calm determination to right what she considers a foul wrong. Donaldina Cameron's face is the face of a gentlewoman, as I have intimated, but there are lines of decision carved on it and a mouth and chin of resolve and resolution. Even a highbinder would know better than to try Miss Cameron's patience too profoundly. No rescue problem has ever been too hazardous for her to draw back from and at any hour of the day or night, she has been on call these forty years, to rout the forces of iniquity. Word comes to her even at this late date, through a mysterious grape-vine system that sends its tendrils down into the underworld, of the game which she has hunted all of her life—restrained and exploited women. Once she is given a clue, a scent, she is off at full speed to run it down. She never gives up, and, while it would be an exaggeration to say that she always succeeds, her failures have been so few that they are the exception and not the rule. . . . The police department often calls upon her to help them with a tough assignment. They welcome her coöperation and they give her theirs for the asking. No greater tribute could be paid her zeal or efficiency.

How far afield her labors take her may be judged from one of her latest achievements. In 1935 a slave-girl, hearing of the mission, fled from her imprisonment to it. This was one of the girls imported by the eminently respectable hardware merchant and his wife, previously mentioned in this narrative. The hardware business seems to have been a smoke screen for concealing the real activity of the pair. Their plan was to have a confederate who posed as father for the girls.

San Francisco's Chinatown

He was, naturally, a resident of this country and made trips to China and back with his charges.

It transpired that two other girls beside the one who fled to the mission had been brought into the United States. Acting on the slenderest of clues Miss Cameron traced one girl to the town of Salinas about a hundred miles south of San Francisco and the other girl to New York City. Both were rescued and the three are now at the mission awaiting deportation.

It is possible for a father who is a resident of the United States to bring in his children. This law is responsible for what few slave-girls slip past the vigilant immigration officers, as it opens the way to fraudulent entries. Until 1926, wives of bona fide residents of the United States were permitted to come in. But this provision led to so much imposture that it was revoked. In defense of the native born Chinese, the authorities say that they are rarely ever involved in these delinquencies. . . . The keeper of an infamous dive in Chinatown not so long since, facing deportation, called to her rescue a venerable old gentleman, over eighty, who swore he was her father. In the face of his declaration there was nothing to do but let her remain. But all these activities are narrowing more and more, in the face of a generation born to a different code of ethics plus an incorruptible set of immigration officials, and an efficient Chinatown police squad.

The Catholic Mission reports about a thousand converts —four hundred of whom are adults and six hundred children. They also run a parochial school where nuns teach the children. The attendance here is four hundred, half this number are non-Catholics, lured to the school by the efficient teaching of the sisters. The tuition is free.

Father Johnson hopes some day to have the chapel bear evidences of Chinese influence in the decorative scheme. At present, it is merely an expression of the Occident. The Sta-

In Conclusion

tions of the Cross are still in the best terra cotta manner reminiscent of Italian churches. Whenever the Chinese translate the Christian legend into their own artistic idiom one will be sure that it has reached beneath the surface.

There is nothing so futile as prophecy. What will happen to the Chinese in America is tied up with too many "ifs" and "buts" and "ands" to hazard anything more than a guess. But, in the nature of things, it would seem that the relative handful of people of Oriental blood on the Pacific Coast will slowly disintegrate. Whether they will be absorbed or drift away, depends a great deal upon how events in China shape themselves in the next few years.

I asked a young Chinese of American birth, not long ago, whether he considered himself American or Chinese. His answer was, "I have no choice." And I knew before he elaborated on this rather cryptic reply that he felt he could never enter fully into the privileges of American citizenship. . . . "I have a right to vote," he explained, "but it is an empty gesture." His ambition was to some day establish a business in China with an American connection. His allegiance was divided but one could see the wistful regret that he felt at being held at arms' length, so to speak, by the civilization into which he had been born.

A prominent business man of Chinatown confirmed this youth's dilemma. He pointed out that every year over a thousand young people graduated from Junior High Schools equipped for white collar jobs with the percentage for achieving one so slight as to be almost negligible. Except for an occasional post in a bank, insurance office or mercantile house that was connected in some way with Chinese trade, these avenues of activity were closed to them. In spite of a lip-service affection which all San Franciscans indulge in when they speak of the Chinese, they will not open their working ranks to receive them.

San Francisco's Chinatown

In the Hawaiian Islands things are different. There the
Chinese takes his place in mercantile life as readily as
any other race. Old San Franciscans, of course, deplore the
ambitions of the younger generation of Chinese to escape
domestic service—even the class who could by no stretch of
imagination afford to hire a servant. These folks have
daughters growing up who would rather work in a five-and-
ten store for fifteen dollars a week than go out to service at
any price. But they are impatient with the progeny of an
alien race for aspiring to the same false standard which
American snobbery has created. Not that I hold any brief for
domestic service. There is no tyranny like the tyranny of the
home. Except in the establishments of the very rich, the average servant is still a drudge subject to call as long as he is
under the roof of his employer. His uprisings and downsit-
tings are watched by every member of the family, and even
his days off are given grudgingly. But all this might be en-
dured if the servant had any social equality. A girl might
eventually live down the fact that she was once a shop girl
but that she was a cook or maid—*never!* In fact, since Prin-
cesses of the Blood Royal and Junior League girls have become salesladies and cloak models the status of a shop girl
has been on the "up and up." Once Grand Duchesses and
members of the "younger set" go out to service, we shall
have another story. Even the Chinese youngsters might then
be diverted from their pallid white collar aspirations.

When we remember that the Chinese have sprung from a
civilization that exalts the man who works with his hands—
the tiller of the soil, the manufacturer of necessities—above
the trader and every form of mercantile parasite, it seems
sad that our influence has been in the other direction. The
younger generation's scorn of frying ham-and-eggs in the
morning for a grouchy captain of finance, or carrying up a
tray to his equally grouchy daughter who has been out until

326

In Conclusion

four in the morning on some night-club "binge," I heartily sympathize with. But, there are other activities beside the activities behind a bronze wicket in a mercantile house. Even here, one cannot blame young Chinese. They are infected with the American scorn of the man who works with his hands. This scorn is felt even by the man, himself, who makes his living by the sweat of his brow. There is scarcely an artisan who is not proud to have his son "rise" to the rank of bank teller or insurance agent.

It is too bad that these young people are not ambitious to till the soil. The Chinese are geniuses when it comes to making two blades of corn grow where there was only one. But here, again, there is the American influence. The ideal of every American youth born on a farm is to escape it. . . . Some day, perhaps, the farmer may be exalted to a point where the President of the United States, like the old Emperor of China, will plough a furrow every year as an example of the honor in which the man who fills our white-collared bellies is held. But, until then, we must see our adopted sons contaminated by the American ideal to escape sweat-of-the-brow toil.

There is one Chinese characteristic which plainly shows how deep-seated the original culture is. Go into any foreign quarter in the land and you will find the children speaking English together in all their pleasures and pursuits. In fact, they are lamentably ashamed of the tongue of their emigrant forebears. Not so the Chinese. It is rare to find them conversing in anything but a Chinese dialect. Playing marbles, spinning tops, on their way to the American school, their chatter will be in the language of their fathers. Verily, there is nothing more indicative of race consciousness than a language.

One has a feeling that with a reasonable amount of security in China, many American-born Chinese will decide to

San Francisco's Chinatown

cast their lot with the people of their blood. Here, no matter how much they adopt our traditions, they can never hope to enter fully into a birthright. One fancies, too, that, in spite of many outward conformances to our ideals, the inner spirit still burns with the flame of centuries of culture peculiarly their own. It may flare up on occasion with a light new and strange, as a steady fire does when a handful of driftwood is thrown upon its sedate coals. But, in the end, it will be very much as it was except for a tiny tongue of fire here and there whose hue proclaims a remnant left of a fuel foreign to it.

BIBLIOGRAPHY

A California Tramp, T. S. Kenderdine (Press of Globe Printing House, Philadelphia, n.d.)

A Checkered Life, Colonel John A. Joyce (S. P. Rounds, Jr., Chicago, 1883)

A Flight in Spring, Reverend J. Harris Knowles (privately printed, New York, 1898)

A Ramble Through the United States, Alfred Gurney, M.A. (published lecture, n.p., n.d.)

A Short History of California, Rockwell D. Hunt and Nellie Van di Grift Sanchez (Thomas V. Crowell Company, New York, 1929)

A Vacation Excursion, John B. Clark (Manchester, N. H., 1884)

Across the Continent, Samuel Bowles (Hurd and Houghton, 1866)

Across the Continent, R. H. Redsecker (Harrisburg Printing and Binding House, Lebanon, Pa., 1879)

Across the Rocky Mountains, Lanson Boyer (E. Wells-Sackett and Bro., New York, 1878)

An Answer to the Common Objections to Chinese Testimony (Chinese Mission House, San Francisco, 1857)

Annals of San Francisco, Frank Soule, M. D. Gihon and James Nesbit (D. Appleton and Company, New York, 1855)

Between the Gates, Benj. F. Taylor (S. C. Griggs and Company, Chicago, 1878)

Between Two Oceans, Iza Duffus Hardy (Hurst and Blackett, London, 1884)

Beyond the Mississippi, Albert D. Richardson (Bliss and Company, New York, 1867)

California, Charles Nordhoff (Harper and Brothers, New York, 1873)

California, Marshall P. Wilder (Wright and Potter, Boston, 1871)

California and the West, L. Vernon Briggs (Wright and Potter Printing Co., Boston, n.d.)

California Historical Society Quarterly, files.

California Illustrated Magazine, files

Bibliography

California Magazine, files

California Recollections, Reverend James Wood (Joseph Winterburn and Co., San Francisco, 1878)

Chinese Immigration, S. Wells Williams, L.L.D. (Charles Scribner's Sons, New York, 1879)

Cold Facts About California, Owen O. Hope (The Star Publishing Company, Boston, n.d.)

Conditions of the Chinese Quarters in San Francisco (Municipal Report, 1884–85)

Doxey's Guide: San Francisco and the Pleasure Resorts of California (William Doxey, San Francisco, 1897)

Five Years Within the Golden Gate, Isabella Saxon (J. P. Lippincott and Co., Philadelphia, 1868)

From New England to the Pacific, J. A. S. in Hartford *Evening Post* (Case, Lockwood and Brainard Co., Hartford, 1884)

From Ocean to Ocean, Reverend Andrew Shiland, D.D. (American Tract Society, New York, 1892)

From Wisconsin to California, Honorable George Gary (Atwood and Rublee, Madison, Wis., 1869)

History of California, Zoeth Skinner Eldridge (The Century History Company, 1915)

How You Should Go West, Guide Book of American Express Company (C. D. Relyea, Chicago, 1873)

Hutching's California Magazine, files

Illustrated London News, files

Jolting of Travel, Virginia Seymour (Gilliss Brothers, New York, 1877)

Leland Stanford, Geo. T. Clark (Stanford University Press, 1931)

Letters from California, D. L. Phillips (Illinois State Journal Company, Springfield, Ill., 1877)

Letters from the Pacific Slope, Harvey Rue (D. Appleton and Company, New York, 1870)

Letters to Lebanon Courier, Zitella (Lebanon *Courier,* 1886)

Los Angeles *Times,* files

Must the Chinese Go? Mrs. S. L. Baldwin (Rand, Avery and Company, Boston, 1886)

My Country and My People, Lin Yutang (John Day Company, New York, 1935)

Northern California, Oregon and the Sandwich Islands, Charles Nordhoff (Harper and Brothers, New York, 1874)

Bibliography

Old Chinatown, Arnold Genthe and Will Irwin (Mitchell Kennerly, New York, 1913)

Our American Tour, Wm. and W. F. Robertson (W. Burness, Edinburgh, 1871)

Over Land and Sea, Arthur G. Guillemard (Tinsley Brothers, London, 1875)

Overland Monthly, files

Rambles Overland, Almor Gunnison (Universalist Publishing House, Boston, 1884)

Round the Globe, Sullivan Holman M'Collester (Universalist Publishing House, Boston, 1890)

Round the World, Wm. Perry Fogg (privately printed, Cleveland, 1872)

Sacramento *Bee,* files

Sacramento *Herald,* files

San Francisco *Alta California,* files

San Francisco *Argonaut,* files

San Francisco *Bulletin,* files

San Francisco *Chronicle,* files

San Francisco *Examiner,* files

San Francisco *Herald,* files

Sixty Years in California, William Heath Davis (A. J. Leary, San Francisco, 1889)

Ten Years in Nevada or Life on the Pacific Coast, Mrs. M. M. Mathews (Baker, Jones Co., Buffalo, 1880)

The Chinese-American Question, John Swinton (American News Company, New York, 1870)

The Chinese at Home and Abroad, Willard B. Farwell (A. L. Bancroft and Co., 1885)

The Chinese in California, B. S. Brooks, pamphlet

The Chinese Problem, L. T. Townsend, D.D. (Lee and Shepard, Boston, 1876)

The Closing of the Golden Gate, Reverend J. H. Laughlin (Board of Foreign Missions of the Presbyterian Church)

The Gun, Rod and Saddle, Reverend Isaac Mast, A.M. (M. E. Book and Publishing House, Philadelphia, 1875)

The House of Exile, Nora Waln (Little, Brown and Company, Boston, 1935)

The Invalidity of the "Queue Ordinance" (J. L. Rice and Co., San Francisco, 1879)

Bibliography

The Last Days of the Republic, P. W. Dooner (Alta California Publishing House, San Francisco, 1880)

The Monitor, Wm. Hoofman (Carleton, New York, 1863)

The New West, Charles Loring Brace (G. P. Putnam and Son, New York, 1869)

The Pacific Coast Scenic Tour, Henry T. Finck (Charles Scribner's Sons, New York, 1891)

The Pioneers of '49, Nicholas Ball (Lee and Shepard, Boston, 1891)

The Round Trip, John Codman (G. P. Putnam's Sons, New York, 1882)

The Sunset Land, Reverend John Todd, D.D. (Lee and Shepard, Boston, 1870)

Through Cities and Prairie Lands, Lady Duffus Hardy (Chapman and Hall, Ltd., London, 1881)

Through Dust and Foam, R. & G. D. Hook (Columbian Book Company, Hartford, 1876)

Through Storyland to Sunset Seas, H. S. Kneedler (The A. H. Pugh Printing Co., Cincinnati, 1898)

To San Francisco and Back, A London Parson (Society for Promoting Christian Knowledge, London)

To the Pacific and Back, Mrs. J. A. I. Washburn (Sunshine Publishing Co., 1887)

Travels in the South and Tour of California, Henry McElwin, bound pamphlets (1882)

Travels West, William Minturn (Samuel Tinsley, London, 1877)

Western Wanderings, J. W. Boddam-Whetham (Richard Bentley and Son, London, 1874)

Westward by Rail, W. F. Rae (D. Appleton and Company, New York, 1871)

Why Work Is Scarce, Wages Low, and Labor Restless, Henry George, pamphlet (San Francisco, 1878)

INDEX

Index

Index

335

Index

(1)